The Autobiography of a Yankee Mariner

The Autobiography
OF A *Yankee Mariner*

*Christopher Prince and the
American Revolution*

EDITED BY

Michael J. Crawford

BRASSEY'S, INC.

WASHINGTON, D.C.

LIBRARY OF CONGRESS CATALOGING-IN-PUBLICATION DATA

Prince, Christopher, 1751-1832.
The autobiography of a Yankee mariner : Christopher Prince and the American Revolution / edited by Michael J. Crawford.—1st ed.
p. cm.
ISBN 1-57488-440-9 (hardback : alk. paper)
1. Prince, Christopher, 1751-1832. 2. Sailors—United States—Biography. 3. United States. Navy—Biography. 4. United States—History—Revolution, 1775-1783—Personal narratives. 5. United States—History—Revolution, 1775-1783—Naval operations. 6. Seafaring life—United States—History—18th century. I. Crawford, Michael J. II. Title.
E207.P77 P75 2002
973.3′5′092—dc21

2002002717

Design and composition by Melissa Ehn at
Wilsted & Taylor Publishing Services

Printed in the United States of America on acid-free paper that meets the American National Standards Institute Z39-48 Standard.

Brassey's, Inc.
22841 Quicksilver Drive
Dulles, Virginia 20166

First Edition

10   9   8   7   6   5   4   3   2   1

To Elva and Evan

CONTENTS

Contents

MAPS & ILLUSTRATIONS

PREFACE

Christopher Prince's story has all the dramatic elements of a nautical adventure: danger, hairbreadth escapes, sea chases, villains, heroes, romance and romantic rivalry, character development, gain and loss, familial conflicts, moral dilemmas, and sin and redemption. My first reading of the manuscript of Prince's autobiography persuaded me that it was worthy of a wide audience, and I immediately decided that I wanted to prepare it for publication. What attracted me was more than that Prince had witnessed and played a part in some of the chief military and naval actions of the War of Independence. The autobiography affords new insights on the great events and personages of the Revolution, but more interesting, the work reveals the effect of the war on an ordinary American. Prince writes about how he felt, about the reasons behind the difficult choices he made, and about the effects of his involvement in the Revolutionary War on the rest of his life. Furthermore, Prince, an accomplished seafarer, writes with the authentic sound of the sea, more authentic than that of any nautical novel. Finally, Prince's tale unites two of my chief interests, the naval history and the religious history of early America.

James Lee, curator of the Naval Historical Foundation's historical collections, recognized the significance of Christopher Prince's autobiography, typed a preliminary transcription, and brought the manuscript to my attention. I hope that Jim deems seeing the work finally in print payment of the debt of gratitude I owe him.

The extraordinary resources for the study of the naval history of the American Revolution gathered together to support the *Naval Documents of the American Revolution* publication project in the Early History Branch of the Naval Historical Center, my place of employment, facilitated enormously the research required to verify and annotate Prince's account of his wartime adventures. I am thankful to all who over the years have worked on that ongoing monumental project. To my colleagues in the branch, I convey my appreciation for constant encouragement and moral support.

I am also thankful for the assistance of the librarians of the Navy Library in the Washington Navy Yard, the Library of Congress, Washington, D.C., and the Historical Society of Wisconsin, in Madison, where I did additional research.

Christopher McKee, Samuel R. and Marie-Louise Professor and Librarian of the College at Grinnell College in Iowa, introduced me to literature on the historical interpretation of autobiography. His studies of naval personnel during the age of sail guided my understanding of the significance of Christopher Prince's seagoing career. Even more than for his scholarship, I am grateful for his friendship. Footnotes indicate my debts to other scholars.

To my wife, Elva, I owe the discovery of a physical description of Christopher Prince. For this and the innumerable ways she has helped me along the way, she has my thanks.

Michael J. Crawford

EDITOR'S INTRODUCTION

In 1806, when retired sea captain Christopher Prince (1751–1832) sat down at a table, sharpened his quill pen, and began to write his life's story, he wanted simply to leave his family a record of his experiences. The facts that he had no children of his own and that the manuscript came down through the generations in the family of his youngest brother suggest that he wrote in response to the questions of nephews and nieces about what he had done during the War of Independence. In the course of delineating his life, Prince told what it was like to grow up in a seaport town in colonial Massachusetts, why a boy would choose a seafaring life, of the hardships of fishing on the Grand Banks, and of the education of a merchant seaman. His adventures and exploits during the war, on board both British and American ships, as a naval enlisted man, as an officer of privateers, and as a master of merchantmen, constitute the core of the autobiography. He recounts his narrow escapes from death and capture, his travails as a prisoner, and his financial gains and losses as a result of the war, as well as the romantic story of his courtship and marriage. He concludes with an account of his religious conversion and its transforming effect on his life as a merchant sea captain after American independence had been secured.

Christopher Prince's story, like any true-life adventure, tells us how people who came before us lived their lives and what was important to them. The immediacy resulting from the storyteller's telling his own story makes the tale all the more compelling. First-person accounts of ordinary people bring history alive for us because they enable us to identify with people of earlier ages and to imagine ourselves living their lives.

In his autobiography, Prince accomplished more than a delineation of his own life. He added to our knowledge, on the one hand, of the great events and major actors of the American Revolution, and, on the other, to our understanding of the social effects of the Revolution: what it meant to the people, particularly sailors, whose names seldom get into history textbooks.

Although never a key player, Prince had the fortune to witness several important episodes. He was in Boston, Massachusetts, for the implementation of the Coercive Acts in 1774 and for the commencement of hostilities in 1775. Later in 1775 he found himself an unwilling collaborator on board a Royal Navy vessel in the St. Lawrence River, witnessed Ethan Allen's treatment as a prisoner, and was present at the capitulation of Montreal and the siege of Quebec. Prince's description of a joint Indian and British attack on American positions outside Montreal is one of only two known extant accounts. Because Prince observed the action from a closer vantage point than the writer of the other eyewitness account, a French Canadian resident of Montreal, he provides hitherto unknown details and a more cogent explanation of the operation. Through Prince we learn for the first time the intimate particulars of the perfidy of General Richard Prescott of the British Army after his signing of the articles of capitulation.

Having arrived in New York City in 1776, Prince assisted the Patriots in the placing of submerged navigational obstructions in the Hudson River. Here Prince's narrative again both supplements and is confirmed by other accounts. His recounting of the defection to the British of the carpenter responsible for sinking the obstructions may help explain why the British warships had so little difficulty avoiding them. Prince narrowly escaped capture during the American retreat from New York after the Battle of Long Island.

Journeying to New London, he joined the crew of the Connecticut Navy ship *Oliver Cromwell.* In all the literature, there is nothing like Prince's narrative for the intimate particulars of how American naval enlisted personnel spent their time on shore or on board while their vessel was in port fitting out. His account will be of great value to those interested in the construction and fittings of Revolutionary ships of war. His unparalleled common seaman's view of the workings of a state navy reveals much about the motivations of recruits, relations between officers and men, the importance of the reputation of commanding officers, and how the Americans groped their way toward needed expertise in naval administration.

Leaving the Connecticut Navy on a change of commanders, Prince spent most of the remainder of the war as an officer on board New England privateers, a career that involved numerous dramatic adventures, including being captured several times and meeting the future king of England. Throughout, the narrative provides uncommon views into the social world and personal life of American sailors.

The narrative is a tale of spiritual as well as naval warfare. It provides an explanation of Prince's deep and abiding interest in the spiritual welfare of seafarers and insight into the origins of the antebellum seamen's reform movement. Although he descended from several of the early Pilgrim families and was raised by pious parents, Prince gave up praying when he began to swear like a sailor. His lack of faith tormented his conscience at such times as when he spent a winter with a Catholic French Canadian family that worshipped on their knees several times daily. After the war, returning to his home in New London following a trading voyage, he attended a revival meeting, felt conviction of sin, and dedicated himself to a life of striving for holiness. With his wife (Lucy Colfax Prince, 1755–1816), he joined the Congregational Church. Thereafter, as a merchant captain, he read Scripture, offered prayers twice daily, and allowed no swearing on board ship. Severe rheumatism forced Prince to give up oceangoing in the mid 1790s—his obituary says 1797, but after a visit to him in December 1793, his brother Hezekiah described Christopher as "a retired (1793) shipmaster."[1]

After retirement Christopher Prince retained his love for the sea and his interest in the religion of seamen. Indeed, Christopher Prince has been known to social historians of the early nineteenth-century maritime community as an ancient mariner taking an active role in the seaman's religious movement in New York City in the second two decades of that century. Before the discovery of his autobiography, all that historians of that movement knew about Prince's earlier life was what was written of him in his not wholly accurate obituary in the *Sailor's Magazine*, which offered only a brief but tantalizing hint of Prince's intriguing past.[2]

---

[1] Hezekiah Prince, *Remarks of My Life: Pr Me Hezekiah Prince, 1786–1792* (Thomaston, Maine: Thomaston Historical Society, 1979), 27.

[2] Joshua Leavitt, "Death of Captain Prince," *Sailor's Magazine, and Naval Journal* 4 (1832): 253. See appendix 1 below.

MARITIME NEW ENGLAND
IN CHRISTOPHER PRINCE'S TIME

Christopher Prince was one of the fewer than one in ten New Englanders who followed maritime pursuits during the colonial period. As such, he partook in a distinctive subculture. Yet, it was through those maritime pursuits—fishing and whaling, coastal shipping, deep sea commerce, shipbuilding and ship chandlery, wharfage, and like ancillary maritime businesses—that New England's economy prospered. The majority of New Englanders, the tillers of the soil, needed overseas markets for their produce and looked to imports to improve their standard of living. The major New England industries of timber harvesting, rum distilling, and sugar refining depended on the exporting and importing of raw and processed products. New England's market economy rested on the commercial connection with the West Indian sugar islands. Based in coastal towns, merchants supplied the sugar plantations with the products of New England's farming, fishing, and lumber industries, as well as flour from colonies further south that their ships collected through coastal trade. Their ships returned from the Caribbean with raw products to be distilled into rum and refined into sugar. New England ships also crossed the Atlantic, carrying fish to Spain and Portugal, and returning with salt, or returning via England with British manufactures; others carried rum to the coast of Africa, returning via the Caribbean with slaves to work on the sugar plantations.[3]

It was in New England's cod fishery, long considered by government policymakers as the "nursery of seamen," that Christopher Prince grasped the rudiments of seamanship. As a merchant seaman, he mastered the arts of navigation and learned the geog-

---

[3]Robert G. Albion, William A. Baker, and Benjamin W. Labaree, *New England and the Sea* (Middletown, Conn.: Wesleyan University Press, 1972), 21–44.

raphy of the waters between Canada and the Caribbean. He had been too young to have been one of the New England privateersmen who cruised against the enemy during the French and Indian War, but during the War of Independence, he participated in that New England tradition of preying on enemy commerce in wartime.

New England's maritime economy produced great wealth for some merchant families, while it gave employment to thousands of fisherman and common ship's hands. Most of the fishermen and sailors and their families never rose much above a level of subsistence and many slipped into poverty. Yet, a significant number of seafarers in the late colonial period and the era of the early American republic, particularly those who enjoyed the advantages of good family connections, rose, like Christopher Prince, into the ranks of ship masters who made comfortable livings.[4]

American seamen played a prominent role in America's dispute with Great Britain that led to the Revolutionary War. Seamen participated in disproportionate numbers in the mob actions that opposed British laws seen in America as tyrannical taxation without representation—the Stamp Act, the Townshend Duties, the tax on tea. Seamen helped enforce the boycotts on trade with Britain adopted by intercolonial agreement in an attempt to persuade Parliament to repeal the obnoxious laws. And, as in the case of the Boston Massacre, seamen were promi-

[4]For the economics of seafaring labor in colonial New England, see Ruth Wallis Herndon, "The Domestic Cost of Seafaring: Town Leaders and Seamen's Families in Eighteenth-Century Rhode Island," in *Iron Men, Wooden Women: Gender and Seafaring in the Atlantic World, 1700–1920,* ed. Margaret S. Creighton and Lisa Norling (Baltimore, Md.: Johns Hopkins University Press, 1996), 55–69; and Daniel Vickers, *Farmers and Fishermen: Two Centuries of Work in Essex County, Massachusetts, 1630–1850* (Chapel Hill, N.C.: University of North Carolina, 1994).

nent in confrontations with the British forces sent to American seaports to uphold British rule. American seamen had witnessed or personally experienced British tyranny in the form of impressment into the Royal Navy and had had practice in mob action, in the form of anti-impressment riots. They nursed the additional resentment against British rule that British trade regulations aggravated their difficulties in finding employment on commercial voyages. American seamen came to view British garrison soldiers as rivals for work on shore, because the Redcoats frequently supplemented their wages by working during their off hours on the wharves and in the rope walks. The seamen's hatred of the British, historians suggest, was a source of their American patriotism and explains why, during the War of Independence, they were willing to endure harsh imprisonment when captured in American vessels rather than agree to serve in ships of the Royal Navy.[5]

Christopher Prince's ardent American patriotism appears clearly in his narrative, but there is no evidence that it had its roots in the experience of British tyranny or hatred of the British. Prince makes no mention of impressment; he appears to have had no involvement in the Stamp Act incident and other anti-British riots in Boston. He seems to have been fully employed during the years before the war; even when the British closed down the port of Boston in 1774, Prince found work ferrying supplies in Massachusetts Bay for the British. Rather than coming to hate the British, he developed an admiration for the Royal Navy and a friend-

---

[5] Jesse Lemisch, *Jack Tar vs. John Bull: The Role of New York's Seamen in Precipitating the Revolution* (New York: Garland Publishing, 1997); Jesse Lemisch, "Jack Tar in the Streets: Merchant Seamen in the Politics of Revolutionary America," *William and Mary Quarterly,* 3d ser., 25 (1968): 371–407; Jesse Lemisch, "Listening to the 'Inarticulate': William Widger's Dream and the Loyalties of American Revolutionary Seamen in British Prisons," *Journal of Social History* 3 (Fall 1969): 1–29. For the relationship between American seamen's patriotism and their hatred of impressment, see George Athan Billias, *General John Glover and His Marblehead Mariners* (New York: Henry Holt, 1960), 29–30, 54–55.

ship with several of its officers. When Prince fell into the hands of the British at the beginning of the war, he was willing to compromise to an extent to avoid imprisonment, but identifying himself as an American, he drew the line at bearing arms against his countrymen. Historical motivation is a complex matter and generalizations dissolve in the particularities of individual lives.

THE MANUSCRIPT

The autobiography of Christopher Prince, a manuscript previously unknown to historians, is one of the extremely rare participants' accounts that treat seafaring in the period of the American Revolution. The most thorough inventory of its kind, *Fighters for Independence*, edited by J. Todd White and Charles H. Lesser, lists approximately 530 diaries, journals, memoirs, and autobiographies of Americans who fought as either soldiers or sailors during the War of Independence.[6] Of those 530 autobiographical sources, only twenty-nine were by men who served on board American warships—either government vessels or privateers—as officers, seamen, marines, or surgeons. The majority of these autobiographical writings by men who served at sea during the war are short, bare chronologies. Only a dozen or so are full autobiographical narratives like Prince's.

The manuscript of Christopher Prince's autobiography comes to us in the form of a transcription entitled "A Brief Sketch of my Life," written in what appears to be a late nineteenth- or early twentieth-century hand on lined sheets of paper, of a heavy grade, 8 x 10 inches, numbered 1 through 226. Captain Edward S. Kellogg, USN (Retired) donated the transcription to the Naval Historical Foundation in 1943. A member of the foundation and

[6]J. Todd White and Charles H. Lesser, eds. *Fighters for Independence: A Guide to Sources of Biographical Information on Soldiers and Sailors of the American Revolution* (Chicago: University of Chicago Press, 1977).

frequent donor to the institution's collection of manuscripts, Captain Kellogg was the foundation's honorary curator. Captain Kellogg was the son of Edward N. Kellogg, who was the son of Sarah Prince Kellogg, who was the daughter of Hezekiah Prince, who was Christopher's youngest brother. Hezekiah (1771–1840) became a leading citizen of Thomaston, Maine, representing the town in the General Court, serving a term in the Maine Senate (1831), and being employed as the United States Revenue Inspector from 1812 until his death.[7] Christopher and his wife had no children, and it is reasonable to conclude that the original autobiographical writing was handed down through Christopher's brother's line and was at some point transcribed by a family member. The fate of the original manuscript is unknown. In 1947 the foundation announced plans to publish a limited edition of Prince's autobiography sometime in the future.[8] Those plans never came to fruition, and in 1998 the foundation transferred ownership of the transcription to the Library of Congress. It is now housed in the Naval Historical Foundation Collection in the Manuscript Division of the Library of Congress.

The account appears to be candidly truthful. Prince does not neglect the less-patriotic interludes of his career, such as his assisting the Royal Navy during the closing of the port of Boston, or his acting as master on board British vessels of war in the St. Lawrence River. Yet he was aware that his motives could be open to question and, during his service with the Connecticut Navy, took pains to conceal his former service with the British. In one in-

---

[7]Louise M. Prince, *Outstanding Members of the Prince Family, 1660–1950's* (Bangor, Maine.: Louise M. Prince, 1975), 117, 128; *A Gathering of Descendants of Hezekiah and Isabella Prince of Thomaston, Maine, Spencer, Mass.,* 20 to 30 August 1891 (n.p., n.d.); accession files of the Naval Historical Foundation, Washington, D.C.

[8]*The Naval Historical Foundation 1947* (Washington, D.C.: Naval Historical Foundation, n.d.), 11.

stance where one might suspect Prince of whitewashing his behavior, in recounting his charity to Ethan Allen while Allen was
his prisoner, Allen himself indirectly confirmed Prince's kind-
nesses.

Although Prince's autobiography is undoubtedly authentic,[9]
it is not altogether accurate. A work of memory, it suffers the errors to which memory is prone. Psychologists who study "autobiographical memory" conclude that certain factors influence
the accuracy of a person's recall of the content of an event. Memory degrades with time, but the rate of degradation slows down
dramatically after a while. People retain the essential aspects, or
the gist, of an event longer than they retain incidental details.
They remember more accurately events in which they actively
took part than those they merely witnessed. They recall better
events relating directly to themselves than those relating to others. The higher the level of mental involvement and the more
intense the emotions aroused the better remembered the event.
Researchers into autobiographical memory have also found that
certain factors influence the accuracy of a person's recall of the
timing of an event. Long after an event, people tend to date it
more recently than it actually took place. And people date more
accurately events that relate directly to themselves than those
that relate to others.[10]

Prince's autobiography fulfills most of these psychological ex-
pectations. Recalling deeds thirty years past, Prince gets dates and

[9]So many of the minute details of the narrative can be verified through
rather obscure sources that any reasonable judge would be convinced that no
one but Christopher Prince could have been the author. Besides, it is difficult to
imagine any gain one could have sought from falsifying such a narrative.

[10]Charles P. Thompson, et al., *Autobiographical Memory: Remembering What
and Remembering When* (Mahwah, N.J.: Lawrence Erlbaum Associates, 1996),
204–16.

names wrong, he telescopes events into shorter spans of time than they actually took, and he mistakes the order in which things happened. His mistakes in recounting the dramatic events in Boston between 1770 and 1775, leading up to the outbreak of war, contrast starkly with the vivid and precise account of those same events by a fellow resident of Boston of the time, George Robert Twelves Hewes, who dictated his memories a quarter century later than Prince inscribed his. The difference in accuracy reflects the difference in circumstances between the two autobiographers. Hewes, a shoemaker, directly witnessed or took part in the events, including the storming of the home of Customs informer Ebenezer Richardson, the Boston Massacre, and the Boston Tea Party.[11] Prince, in contrast, spent most of those years on ocean voyages and appears to have been disengaged from Massachusetts politics. He provides a confused account of the one mob action he claims to have witnessed. Yet he had vivid and accurate recall of those events that affected him most closely, such as his graphic hallucinations while he had smallpox, the amount of his prize money for particular voyages, the sums he invested in Continental loan certificates, and the date of his marriage. He recalled the names of the ships in which he served and the captains that commanded them, but often misremembered the names of ships and their captains that sailed in company.

Despite its occasional factual errors, Prince's memoir is valuable for what it reveals about the meaning of the American Revolution to participants who lived into the nineteenth century. From the point of view of the larger context of what the Revolution meant to Prince, the individual discrepancies are unimpor-

---

[11]Alfred F. Young, "George Robert Twelves Hewes (1742–1820): A Boston Shoemaker and the Memory of the American Revolution," *William and Mary Quarterly*, 3d ser., 38 (1981): 561–623.

tant. Similarly, the individual factual imprecisions do not detract from the value of the autobiography as a source of information about the lives of New England seamen at the end of the eighteenth century.

LITERARY MODELS

As a literary work, Prince's autobiography shares characteristics of three genres: the war story, the captivity narrative, and the spiritual autobiography.

To leave a record for family members was the original impetus for a number of Revolutionary War memoirs that eventually appeared in print.[12] It is unlikely that Prince had in mind a larger audience than his own relatives. He composed his memoir well before a postrevolutionary generation in the 1820s began romanticizing the War of Independence and, viewing Revolutionary War veterans as a disappearing asset, eagerly sought them out as guests or speakers at Independence Day celebrations.[13]

There is no indication that Prince intended his work for publication. Before 1806, when Prince wrote his autobiography, a mere handful of memoirs of Revolutionary War veterans had been published.[14] By then only two naval memoirs of the Revolution had seen print, the *Narrative of the Life and Captivity of John Blatchford...a Prisoner of War in the Late American Revolution,* (New London, 1788); and *An Historical Sketch to the End of the Revo-*

---

[12]Richard M. Dorson, *America Rebels: Narratives of the Patriots* (New York: Pantheon, 1953), 3–4.

[13]Michael Kamman, *A Season of Youth: The American Revolution and the Historical Imagination* (Alfred A. Knopf: New York, 1978), 26–27, 44.

[14]Among the more notable of these were: William Heath, *Memoirs of Major-General Heath; Containing Anecdotes, Details of Skirmishes, Battles, and Other Military Events during the American War* (Boston: [n.p.] 1798), 388 pp.; and William Moultrie, *Memoirs of the American Revolution, So Far as It Related to the States of North and South Carolina, and Georgia* (New York: [n.p.] 1802), 2 vols.

lutionary War of the Life of Silas Talbot (New York, 1803). Prince could have been aware of the former work, since he lived in New London at the time of its publication. It is doubtful that Prince would have read Nathaniel Fanning's memoir, *Fanning's Narrative: Being the Memoirs of Nathaniel Fanning, an Officer of the Revolutionary Navy, 1778–1783,* published in 1806, the same year Prince wrote his, for it had an extremely small circulation when first published.[15] The few passages in Prince's work that are similar to ones found in Blatchford's and Fanning's are more likely a product of coincidence than of influence.

As a war story—"What did you do during the war, Uncle Christopher?"—Prince's memoir has many moments of exciting drama. Given the nature of his war experiences, with several moves from one theater of action to another, the narrative is somewhat episodic. Yet each major episode—the Canadian sojourn, sinking obstructions in the Hudson River, service in the Connecticut Navy, privateering adventures, escape from the Outer Banks, and others—possesses its own coherence.

In recounting his part in the War of Independence, Prince does his share of bragging. His bragging, however, has little to do with military accomplishments and much to do with his superior seamanship. Prince portrays himself as a thorough seaman, knowledgeable of not only ship handling but also navigation and geography. Indeed, while he was master of the British brig *Gaspee* in the St. Lawrence River, pride in his skill induced him to handle the brig properly instead of taking the opportunity to render the vessel into the hands of the Americans:

> All I could decide upon was, that the Commander in Chief put more confidence in me than any other man under his

[15] John S. Barnes, ed., *Fanning's Narrative: Being the Memoirs of Nathaniel Fanning, an Officer of the Revolutionary Navy, 1778–1783* (New York: Naval History Society, 1912), "Editor's Preface," xii–xv.

charge, or he would not have given the *Gaspie* the preference out of twenty one vessels, to perform the duties he required in his own safety, and the protection of everything under his care which was of great importance.

Prince was so much a seaman that he was awkward on shore—both socially and physically: He had to work hard to learn how to behave in polite society; and, inexperienced as an equestrian, he could ride only the gentlest of horses. By ridiculing himself on shore, Prince emphasizes his identity as a seafarer.

A number of the autobiographical writings of seamen of the Revolution are principally narratives of the writers' experiences as prisoners. By the time of the Revolution, the Indian captivity narrative had been established as a popular genre. Prisoner of war captivity narratives mirrored these in emphasizing the cruel atrocities of the captors and the captives' attempts to escape.[16] Prince's narrative differs in its lack of atrocity stories, for Prince's experiences in captivity were relatively mild, either because of his willingness to cooperate with the enemy, as in Canada; because of his family connections, as in England; or because of early release, as on the coasts of North Carolina and New Jersey. Yet the narrative does contain one dramatic, hair-raising escape—from ruffians on the Virginia-North Carolina border.

The elements of spiritual autobiography give Prince's memoir its unity and coherence, and the internal conflict between piety and worldliness keeps the narrative interesting. Prince's account of his religious experience is much less introspective than are conversion narratives and other spiritual autobiographies written in the New England Puritan tradition before the American Revolution.[17] Instead of emphasizing internal emotional states,

[16]Dorson, *America Rebels*, 6–10.

[17]Michael J. Crawford, ed., "The Spiritual Travels of Nathan Cole," *William and Mary Quarterly*, 3d ser., 33 (1976): 89–126, is a notable example.

Prince focuses on objective behavior: praying versus swearing, reading the Bible versus carousing. The pragmatic emphases on moral reform and active choice give the work the character much more of the Evangelicalism of the nineteenth century than that of the eighteenth.[18]

EDITORIAL METHOD

The text of Christopher Prince's autobiography runs some sixty thousand words, unbroken by chapter divisions, and with very few paragraph breaks. To provide signals to the reader of the narrative's structure, the editor has divided the work into chapters, provided chapter headings, and introduced additional paragraphing. Names of ships have been set in italics. The second in paired redundant words, such as "the the," has been eliminated; crossed out words have not been reproduced, since these were presumably the original transcriber's copying errors and not Christopher Prince's words; and interlineations have been placed in the text where the original transcriber indicated. Except for place names, spelling has been modernized. Wherever doing so does not alter the meaning, punctuation has been modernized, chiefly to eliminate run-on sentences. Words and passages within square brackets are insertions of the editor to clarify the text. Aside from these modifications, the text presented here is word for word as found in the manuscript. All footnotes are those of the editor. Editorial comments and observations on the text introduce and conclude several chapters.

---

[18]On New England conversion narratives and spiritual autobiographies, see Patricia Caldwell, *The Puritan Conversion Narrative: The Beginnings of American Expression* (Cambridge, U.K.: Cambridge University Press, 1983), and John Owen King, *The Iron of Melancholy: Structures of Spiritual Conversion in America from the Puritan Conscience to Victorian Neurosis* (Middletown, Conn.: Wesleyan University Press, 1983).

A Brief Sketch of my Life

CHAPTER ONE

A Sailor's Education

1751–1773

HISTORICAL CONTEXT

Writing his life's story for the benefit of family members, Christopher Prince chose to begin with the arrival of the Mayflower *and the establishment of the family in America. His account of the* Mayflower, *evidently based on oral tradition, comes close to modern, scholarly reconstructions of the events.*

Christopher lived a youth typical of that of other boys of a colonial New England seacoast town. Holding education in high esteem, not the least because the ability to read the Bible was instrumental in the religious judgment and informed conscience Protestants were expected to exercise, as early as 1647 Massachusetts's legislature required every town of fifty households or more to maintain a school teacher to teach reading and writing. Larger towns were to support Latin grammar schools. Through his twelfth year Christopher attended a local Kingston, Massachusetts, school taught by a schoolmaster. Christopher's parents brought him up in the Congregational Church, where he was bap-

tized 15 June 1755,[1] *and taught him his prayers, his Bible lessons, and orthodox Protestant doctrine. This training had a deep influence on him in his youth, an influence that would reassert its power later in his life.*

As he entered adolescence, Christopher encountered a rivalry that reached back to the beginnings of Puritanism between the values of Reformed religion and those of English folk culture. Serious piety and social enjoyments contended for the attention of many New England youths, and the contest may have been a major source of the psychological tension that energized many religious conversion experiences and religious revivals in colonial America.[2]

Given his family background, it is not surprising that Christopher chose a seafaring profession. His father had followed the sea until 1760, when, at the age of thirty-four, he devoted himself to farming and carpentry. Two of his father's brothers were merchant captains, and Christopher was named after one of these uncles. Sharing a belief common in the eighteenth century and held by leading New England preachers, that a seafarer's life was conducive to sin and vice,[3] *Christopher's father sought to discourage him from his choice by insisting that his introduction to life at sea be not on board a merchantman, but on board a fishing vessel.*

[1] *Vital Records of Kingston Massachusetts to the Year 1850* (Boston: New England Historic Genealogical Society, 1911), 116.

[2] Philip J. Greven, Jr., "Youth, Maturity, and Religious Conversion: A Note on the Ages of Converts in Andover, Massachusetts, 1711–1749," *Essex Institute Historical Collections* 108 (1972): 119–34; David D. Hall, *Worlds of Wonder, Days of Judgment: Popular Religious Belief in Early New England* (New York: Alfred A. Knopf, 1989), 10; N. Ray Hiner, "Adolescence in Eighteenth-Century America," *History of Childhood Quarterly* 3 (1975): 253–80; Gerald F. Moran, "Conditions of Religious Conversion in the First Society of Norwich, Connecticut, 1718–1744," *Journal of Social History* 5 (1972): 331–43; Gerald F. Moran, "The Puritan Saint," Ph.D. dissertation, Rutgers University, 1974; Roger Thompson, "Adolescent Culture in Colonial Massachusetts," *Journal of Family History* 9 (1984): 127–44; William F. Willingham, "Religious Conversion in the Second Society of Windham, Connecticut," *Societas* 6 (1976): 109–19.

[3] Cotton Mather, *The Religious Marriner* (Boston, 1700) and *The Sailor's Companion and Counsellour* (Boston, 1709).

Although Marblehead and Gloucester were New England's lead-
ing fishing ports on the eve of the American Revolution, Plymouth
was one of a score of other towns also involved in dispatching vessels
to the cod fisheries off Newfoundland. Altogether, about five hundred
vessels, employing some five thousand men, went out from New
England each year. The fishing fleet consisted mostly of sloops and
schooners of fifty tons or more, with crews of seven or eight. Rather
than working for wages, each man received a share of the proceeds,
based on the proportion of the catch for which he was responsible. If
young Christopher could not pull in fish, he would not make money.[4]
The father expected that the harsh working conditions in a fishing
schooner would alter the son's aspirations.

When his father realized that Christopher would not be dissuaded
from a seafaring life, he apprenticed him to his brother, Christopher's
uncle, Job Prince, a wealthy merchant and shipowner of Boston. By
the time he was sixteen years old, Christopher was an able seaman.
When he was nineteen, Uncle Job set him to studying navigation and
then employed him as a master's mate. After his twenty-first birthday,
having completed his apprenticeship, Christopher returned home and
settled accounts with his father.

I n reading the Scriptures, as well as Historical publications, I
have every reason to believe there was, without a few excep-
tions, a family record kept from the early ages of time, and many
centuries after our Savior was on earth by almost every family,

[4]Robert G. Albion, William A. Baker, and Benjamin W. Labaree, *New England and the Sea* (Middletown, Conn.: Wesleyan University Press, 1972), 27–29.

to let their descendants know their place of nativity, and from whom they had descended, and many of the occurrences of life, and not so well provided with pen, ink, and paper, as we are now.

But now in America, and throughout the world, there are but few that gives any more than a verbal communication, which brings on among many of the descendants dispute and contention, which produces discord until it is entirely obliterated. There are many to my certain knowledge who are unacquainted with the birth of their Grandfathers and the place of their nativity.

I will first state my Father's side. He descended from one of three brothers[5] who fled from persecution on account of their religious principles among the first who landed in Plymouth in Massachusetts. The conflict, the hunger and poverty they endured is too well known by nearly all who have been born in the United States[6] for me to mention here, although it has often been related to me by my Father, and many others who were older than he was.

One of the three brothers above mentioned was the second Governor of that Province, but not the one from which I descended. I was told that all who bore the name of Prince were born in France, but there were but three who bore that name which first landed in America.

There are some particulars relating to the first landing of my fore-fathers in Plymouth. While crossing the Atlantic, not knowing whither they were going, and more than they were bound to

[5]The first of the three "brothers" to whom Christopher Prince refers here is his great great grandfather, Ruling Elder John Prince, who emigrated to America in 1633; the second may be Thomas Prence (spelled with an "e"), who arrived at Plymouth Colony in 1621, was governor in 1634, 1638, and 1658–72, and called Ruling Elder John Prince cousin; the third "brother's" identification remains a mystery.

[6]In place of "United States," the manuscript has "UNS."

America, after being out many days encountering many dangers, they discovered land which had always been called Cape Cod on account of catching fish by that name. As there was no place they could anchor in safety, they ran until they came to the cape which was then and now is called the Race point, on account of the rapidity of the current which makes round it both flood and ebb, which enters into a very large bay called Barnstable Bay.[7] Under the west part of the point, there is a curious hook which forms an excellent harbor from an easterly and northerly wind. But they soon see by going on shore that there were no inhabitants, water, or provision. They were sure that the land must proceed from some continent. The weather became clear, and they discovered high land S.W. from where they lay. After some deliberation, they concluded to send the boat across the bay, and see if there was any safe harbor for the ship to lay and get water. Two of my ancestors went in the boat with many others. They set out early in the morning so as to cross the Bay before it became dark, but they did not arrive until the night set in and took from them the sight of the land. They still continued on until they discovered land on the right hand and on the left. The sea began to smooth and soon became without any motion, which gave them a sufficient evidence they were in a safe harbor. I must make some remarks now on this wonderful display of the goodness of God in their protection—for there is not another place they could have entered in safety, within 20 miles each side of them, and they must all have perished, for the wind and sea would have prevented them from going on shore in safety. They continued their entrance until about ten o'clock, and they grounded and no land in sight. A man by the name of Clark got out of the boat and soon got where there was no water, and returned and told them they

---

[7]*Barnstable Bay:* Southern Cape Cod Bay.

were on an island, and it was low water, for there was nothing but eel grass there, which must be covered at high water. They then called it Clark's island, and remains so till this day. I have been many times on that island. After the tide rose they continued on until they saw a beach, and soon saw lights on shore a long distance off. They came to the end of the beach and made for the lights which they saw, and before daylight they struck on a rock which they found was large and not covered at high water, where they remained until daylight. They then saw a number of Indians who flocked down to the shore. They still remained on the rock which was about 30 feet from the shore. After they had made all the discovery they could, they returned to the ship, and she was carried into that harbor which was called Plymouth, and that rock on which they landed has been broken into a million pieces and distributed in many parts of America and Europe.[8] I could fill many pages of what transpired after the ship got into port, and what took place between them and the Indians, but they have been long recorded.

My Grandfather Prince married a woman by the name of Abigail Kimball, by whom he had six sons and one daughter. My father was the second son; his name was Kimball and was born in May 1726. He married Deborah Fuller, by whom he had six sons and three daughters, among which I was the first born. My mother descended from a family who came here in the first ship. My Grandfather Fuller married Deborah Ring, by whom he had

---

[8]The tradition that the Pilgrims came on shore at Plymouth Rock dates from a statement made by a ninety-five-year-old church elder in 1741. Local veneration of the rock began in earnest during the era of the Revolution, and by the early nineteenth century, pieces of the rock were being taken as souvenirs. William Bradford, *Of Plymouth Plantation 1620–1647*, ed. by Samuel Eliot Morison (New York: Alfred A. Knopf, 1952), 59–72; Kate Caffrey, *The Mayflower* (New York: Stein and Day, 1974), 111–28; Francis Russell, "The Pilgrims and the Rock," *American Heritage* 13, no. 6 (October 1962): 48–55.

seven sons and three daughters. My mother was born in December 1729.[9] These families all continued in piety until the present generation, always remarkably strict in the observance of the Sabbath, family worship, and closet devotions. The House of God was always strictly attended. All my relations lived for the first hundred years in Kingston, adjoining to Plymouth. Plymouth, Kingston, and Duxbury are all surrounding a delightful bay which receives its water from the ocean between the Gurnet, a narrow beach which runs north about six miles, which forms a beautiful harbor; and on the south of the inlet is a high land called Barnstable Height, which runs in a south direction up to the head of the Bay about twenty miles: which form a part of the main land on which Plymouth is situated. The ground that Plymouth is built upon is barren and unfruitful, but about one mile west it is very fertile, and thus it continues to Kingston and Duxbury, which surrounds the Bay which is not less than ten miles across from east to west, and north to south. At high water it looks like the ocean unless the weather is clear, and at low water there is nothing seen but eel grass when we stand on shore. Tide ebbs and flows from 15 to 17 feet, which will permit vessels of 500 tons to enter and go to Plymouth and Kingston, but not so much water to Duxbury. Many valuable vessels are built at Kingston and Duxbury because they have good timber which has always been their principal employment. Where I was born is one of the most beautiful places I ever saw, a little distance from the landing. On the top of the house as far as my eyes could reach, no high

[9]Kimball Prince and Deborah Fuller wed on 2 November 1749. Their children were: Christopher (b. 11 July 1751), Kimball (b. 20 July 1753), Sarah (b. 15 January 1756), Ruth (b. 7 May 1758), Deborah (b. 13 July 1760), Noah (b. 18 January 1763), Job (b. 22 March 1765), John (b. 23 February 1768), and Hezekiah (b. 7 February 1771). *Vital Records of Kingston*, 116–17, 226; Louise M. Prince, *Outstanding Members of the Prince Family, 1660–1950's* (Bangor, Maine: Louise M. Prince, 1975), 119–23.

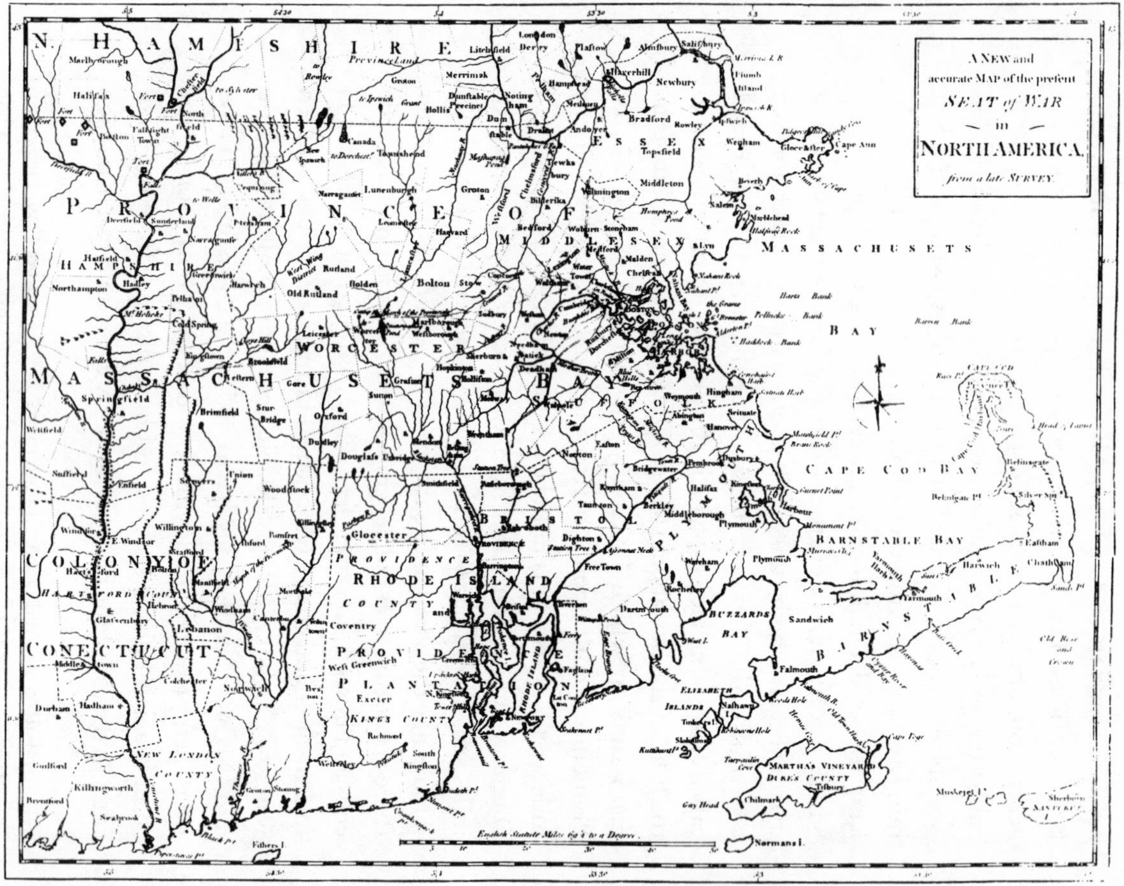

FIGURE 1. Southeastern New England

ground nor woods to obstruct the sight. I could see ponds, rivers, beautiful farms, houses, barns, orchards containing all kinds of fruit trees; the whole country was under cultivation. The road was so straight I could stand at my Father's door and see half a mile each way.

In this delightful spot did my eyes open upon this world in the year 1751—under the direction and instruction of pious parents who brought me up under the nurture and admonition of the Lord, who joined the church of Christ before they were married. There was no other professors of Religion than the Congregational Presbyterians, which was brought there by our forefathers, who fled away from their native land to save their lives. There was but very few in all that country over twenty years old, but what had joined the church when I was a boy, and many children from the examples and piety of their parents were truly pious at the age of six years. O that I could say as much in favor of piety now of the young and rising generation, and of the inhabitants in general in the place of my nativity.

About a quarter of a mile from my Father's house, almost due north, was the place where my Grandfather Prince lived, and where my Father was born, on a small eminence which overlooked all the farm and many miles adjacent. Two rivers were between the two buildings filled with trout and other small fish.

My Grandfather Prince died before I was born, and my Grandmother had married a man by the name of Evertson, by whom she had four sons and one daughter. My Grandfather Evertson died in the year 1756, and my Grandmother in the year 1769.[10] My Grandfather Fuller lived about one mile south of my Father. His situation was not as pleasant as many places in that vi-

[10]Grandmother Abigail Kimball Prince married Ephraim Everson on 15 March 1732. Ephraim died 7 July 1757, and Abigail on 6 September 1780. *Vital Records of Kingston*, 216, 344–45.

cinity. My Grandmother Fuller died in the year 1760, and my Grandfather Fuller in the year 1789.

My father served as an apprentice at the carpenter trade. After his time expired, he followed the sea, which he continued until the year 1760, and then altered his situation and went into the farming business, in addition to his carpenter trade, and spent the remainder of his days with his family.

As soon as I was old enough to walk I was sent to school to a man by the name of Ricketts, who was a very pious man and always opened his school with prayer, and closed it in the same duties. I went to his school until I was about twelve years old, but many weeks and days during that time I could not go, as it was some distance, and other hindrances.

The Christian religion took possession of my heart when I was about eight years of age. The closet devotions, morning and evening, was my constant employment which made serious impressions on my mind. The Bible was the only book I read. Although I had never committed any known sins, yet I thought I was one of the greatest of sinners, and my views of salvation through a Redeemer were as correct as can be enjoyed by any who are professors in riper years. After I was eleven years of age, I was permitted to go to husking corn among our neighbors in the fall of the year. It was a custom among all the farmers to gather their corn and lay it in a row which would seat one hundred people. In some farms that produced much, but some less; and after the corn was husked all went into the house and there treated with milk punch, and dancing, for there was always girls assembled there for that purpose. These meetings did not do me any good; it rather reduced my pious feelings. But it did not make much odds until I was in my 13th year. My Father then took me from school and set me to work on his farm. I had not been there long in the spring of the year before I began to feel impatient. For some time I did not know what to do, whether to go to sea or learn a trade. I at last formed a resolution to go to sea. My mother was unwilling for me to go. My Father consented without any opposition, upon the following condition, I must have a master at sea or on shore, and might have my choice. If on shore, he would be my guardian. Let what would befall me, he would be my friend, until I was 21 years old, and all my earning must go into his hands, and then he would do me justice. But I must go a fishing on the banks first, although I was young and small, too much so to catch fish and lift them out of the water on deck, which my father knew I was unable to do, and of which I was entirely ignorant of, as I was never outside of the Gurnet, which forms one side of the entrance of the bay. At that time I did not know my father's motives in sending me a fishing, but they will be related hereafter. He went himself and got a place on board of a vessel, Captain Cushman, with whom he gave instruction how to proceed with me, and committed me to his care.

In May 1764, I departed from my parents and place of nativity on the trackless ocean, which was the second time I ever left my Father's house. The first time was when I was in my twelfth year. I was sent for to Boston by my Uncle Christopher Prince, who my parents named me after when I was dedicated unto the Lord by baptism. My Uncle C Prince was a long time a sea captain in the European trade, and when I was born it was reported that he was wrecked at sea on a passage home and all on board were lost, and by that report I obtained his name. Soon after I was baptized he arrived safe at Boston, where he lived and had a family. As he had never seen me as I lived forty miles from Boston, as I have said, he sent for me. My Father sent me there; he received me as one of his sons. Although I was decently clothed, he took me to a tailors who took a measure on me for a coat, vest, and breeches, which he made of superfine blue broadcloth. He had two shirts made for me ruffled in the bosom and hands. He then took me to a shoe-maker and got me a pair of shoes, and then got me a pair of silver buckles, and two pair of stockings. He then took me to a hatter and got me a hat. I was then dressed, and there was not one of his sons that had such a suite of clothes as I had—they could not be better. When I arrived home, my parents were astonished, and all my brothers and sisters. On Sunday when I went to church my school mates flocked round me. Some treated me with respect, and some with ridicule. I do believe that in seeing my uncle Christopher who had always followed the sea from a boy until I saw him, and had been many years a commander, and had made considerable property, and very respectable in his character, was the means of inducing me to go to sea and step into his place and follow his example. As he was a going to quit the seafaring life after going one voyage more, prevented me from going with him.

I will now relate some particulars on my first trip out on the fishing banks. Soon after we left the Gurnet where a light-house was erected, we saw the race point of Cape Cod, which brought to my mind what had been related to me by my Father and others, the situation our forefathers was in, who first discovered that track of land which I named in the second page.[11]

Soon after we passed the point, I became so seasick I could not go off of the deck, and I should not struggled any if they hove me overboard! I continued in this situation for three days. I then began to move and eat. When we got down on the bank I was perfectly well. We soon began to fish, and I found it a great amusement; and for some days I was very lucky, and one of my shipmates on each side of me, often took my fish on board, which I was not able to do when they were large and heavy which was often the case while on the banks, and when I had two fish, one on

[11]P. 7, above.

each hook. I soon began to neglect my morning and evening prayers which I had strictly attended to for five years; and some of the crew were often using profane words which I was not in a habit of hearing, which at first hurt my feelings, but I was determined never to be guilty of. On our first trip we entered into several harbors on the Nova Scotia shore for wood and water, where we got hurtle berries, strawberries, juniper berries, all of which were innumerable. In about ten weeks we returned to Kingston loaded with fish. By that time my inclination to follow the sea had increased. My parents were glad to see me, although I had not one clean garment to wear. Many questions were asked me by Mother and many others about my voyage and intention of going out again, but my Father said but little to me on the subject. We soon sailed again, not for the banks, but for mackerel in Boston Bay where we remained about three weeks, and returned into port with many barrels of mackerel. We then fit out for our fall trip on the banks; but as there were many severe gales we had to go into harbors very often, in different parts of Nova Scotia. Notwithstanding, we got a cargo of fish. Late in the fall we returned to Kingston. During the winter while I was at home, I did not enjoy the family devotions offered up by my Father as I did before I left home. I was away somewhere almost every evening. One night I came home and after I entered the house I heard my Father at prayer, which brought on my mind some serious reflections. I listened to what he said while I stood in the entry until he had finished, and then went up stairs with a broken heart which continued for many days, which made some of my former feelings return.

In the Spring of 1765, my Father asked me if I was a going a fishing again that season. I told him I was. He told me to go and get a vessel, which I did. Captain Stutson, an experienced seaman, was the commander, and a large schooner which sailed very early; and during the season she went into many harbors, and through the Gulf of Cancer, into the bayshalore, and the island of St. John's, and round Cape Briton, which gave me much instruction of that coast.[12]

It is painful to reflect upon what I did during the season that has past, in respect to my never-dying soul. God had begun to withdraw his grace from my heart for many months past; but this season has sealed my condemnation in the world to come. All my religion was gone. I parted with it with less reluctance than a child would with a toy. Little did I know that going a fishing voyage is the most trying of any employment for an ambitious mind than any that can be named on the face of the earth. Previous to my being offended at this trying employment so as to murmur at it, I often heard oaths uttered from many lips on board which always hurt my feelings. When we come across a school of fish, every one is anxious to get as many as any of his shipmates. At one time we came among a large quantity of fish, and they were hauling of them in almost every one but myself, without any intermission, and I could not get one. If I felt a bite, it was only to rob my hooks of their bait, and sometimes I would hook one and get it near to the top of the water and then it would break off. After experiencing many of these trials, which I bore for some time with christian patience, I at last gave way and for the first time in all my life I uttered a profane word. As soon as it had proceeded out of my lips, it filled my heart with anguish. I could not refrain from weeping aloud. All on board heard and saw me crying, and supposed it was because I had not caught but few fish, when they all had caught many. For many days I wept in private for what I had said. But not long after that I was several times placed in the

[12] *Cancer:* Canso, Nova Scotia; *Bay of Shalore* or *Bayshalore:* Chaleur Bay or Baie de Chaleur, inlet of western Gulf of St. Lawrence, extending between northern New Brunswick and the Gaspé Peninsula; *island of St. John's:* Isle St. John, renamed Prince Edward Island in 1798; *Cape Briton:* Cape Breton Island.

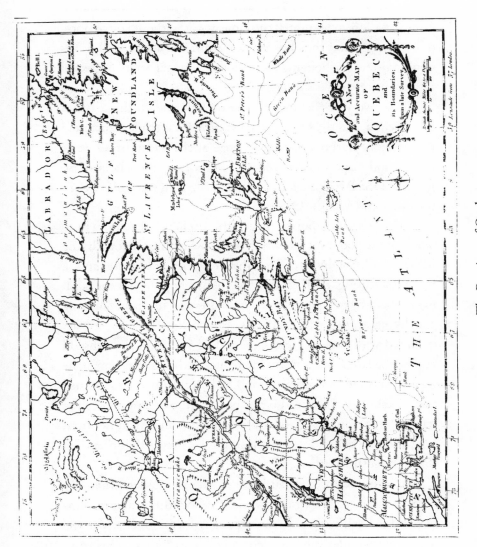

FIGURE 2. The Province of Quebec

same situation and repeated the same words without any remorse of conscience; and thus I continued again and again until it was done without a thought I had done wrong. I soon neglected prayer entirely and reading the Bible.

These two years fishing on Quero Bank, and on the coasts of Nova Scotia, and the Bay of St. Lawrence, I was made acquainted with twenty harbors between Jaboge at the westward of Seale Island, and Cape Cancer, and two harbors in the island of St. John's, in the Bay of St. Lawrence, and through the Gulf of Cancer, out of the Atlantic Ocean.[13]

After I returned home in the fall, my Father then began to question me about my intention of following the sea for a living the remainder of my days. I told him my request was to go to sea, but not a fishing. He then told me he had hopes from the commencement by my going a fishing would wean me from pursuing and living such a wicked life as seamen lived, for he was acquainted with both sea and land and he was in hopes I should choose the latter; but if it was my request to become a seaman, he would send me to Boston to my Uncle Job Prince, who owned many vessels, and I would never be destitute of employ. As the winter had set in, I did not go immediately, and I had not been long at home before I was taken sick with a fever that prevailed throughout the country.

My fever increased, until I was in a dangerous situation. My life was despaired of for many weeks. In about three months I was restored to health and took my departure for Boston early in the Spring of 1766. I delivered my letter, which my father wrote to my Uncle Job. After he read it, he asked me many questions about my

---

[13]*Quero Bank:* Banquereau Bank, easternmost of the Nova Scotia Banks, located WNW of Sable Island; *Jaboge:* Chebogue Harbor, near Yarmouth, Nova Scotia; *Seale Island:* Seal Island, Nova Scotia; *Cape Cancer:* Cape Canso, cape at northeast end of Nova Scotia mainland, at south entrance of Chedabucto Bay.

views and desires, which I answered very imperfect. He then told me to make his house my home, and he would do that for me which he considered would be to my advantage. He had a long time been a commander of vessels out of Boston, and had obtained much property, and lived in as high style as any man in Boston. He had five sons and three daughters. His oldest son was gone to sea and supposed to be lost on account of his long absence, which proved to be the case, which was confirmed soon after I arrived there.[14] My Uncle Christopher had left off from going to sea, and was gone down to the north part of Nova Scotia, which forms a part of the Bay of Fundy, to purchase a place where he lived the remainder of his days.

All my Father's brothers had been seafaring men and ship masters, and stood high in the estimation of merchants, as able commanders of vessels, all of which obtained much property. I was anxious to obtain that knowledge which would qualify me to be a commander of a ship, although I was an inexperienced lad. I was unacquainted with almost every kind of business, although I had been two years a fishing I knew but very little of seaman's duty, and was no seaman. I was well acquainted with reading, writing, and arithmetic, and yet I felt unhappy by seeing boys not older than I was in Boston, who was a doing business of many kind as though they were twenty years of age. My Aunt Prince was very kind to me, and all my cousins. I did not remain there but a little while. My uncle had a vessel a going to one of the West India Islands. I soon went on board to work, but I could not do my duty as a seaman, and they treated me as I deserved, although I

---

[14]Job Prince (1723–1790), wealthy shipmaster, married Elizabeth Allen (1725–1785), great granddaughter of Rev. James Allen, pastor of the First Church in Boston, in December 1745. They lived with their large family on Chamber Street, between North and South Allen Streets, in Boston. Louise M. Prince, *Prince Family,* 226.

could hand, reef, knot, splice, and steer. Yet I did not expect sea-
mens' wages, which was five dollars, and three barrels privilege
as an adventure. But many seamen were not able to put in one
barrel, and myself for one, and I knew I should not have but four
dollars per month, which would not be more than I wanted for
clothes. I did not know what to do. I felt unhappy! My uncle
asked me, "what I was going to carry as a venture." I told him my
Father had not given me one shilling, and I could not get any. He
then said, "you shall not go without an adventure," and he gave
me a good one. Our voyage was long but profitable. I sold my adventure at a great profit. My father wrote me on my return to
clothe myself by my wages and not to send him any of the money
if I wanted it. I then clothed myself well. After that voyage I had
full wages and purchased my own adventure, which I always considered as my own property after I had paid my Uncle for what he
had advanced me. At the close of the year 1767 I was a complete
seaman, and I was treated as such, but I was small of my age when
I was sixteen years old. By that time I was qualified to go as a seaman to any part of the world, and got to be a thoughtless wicked
creature. After roving about from one clime to another until the
year 1770, and was still in my nineteenth year, my uncle requested
me to learn the art of navigation, which I did, and was put in one
of his vessels as mate, and when I returned, one of his daughters
was married to a man by the name of Higgins who lived in the island of St. John's, in the Bay of Shalore.[15] Being acquainted with
that coast, I went there as mate and pilot, and loaded the vessel
with fish and went to one of the West India Islands, where we
made an excellent voyage. When I returned to Boston, I went to

[15]David Higgins, Esquire, and Elizabeth Prince wed 3 June 1773. *A Volume of
Records Relating to the Early History of Boston, Containing Boston Marriages from
1752 to 1809*, Volume 30 of Boston Record Commissioners' Reports (Boston: Mu-
nicipal Printing Office, 1903), 65.

see my parents, and carried my father considerable money, for I then had considerable money, for I then had ten dollars per month; and I had nearly one hundred dollars which I had got by my adventures, for I was allowed two hogshead privilege after I was Mate.

In the year 1772, when I was twenty-one years of age, I arrived late in the fall from a long voyage. I considered it my duty to go and settle all my accounts with my Father, and be in future my own guardian, and possess all my hard earnings at sea. When I arrived at my Father's house, I was received with great affection. After I had given my father all the money I had to give him for my wages, I told him I could not stay but a day or two as the vessel was loading and would go to sea very soon, and as I was mate of the vessel, I must immediately return.

I then told my Father, "here I am, and a going to begin the world anew for myself, I hope you will give me something to assist me in my ardent labors."

"Yes my son, you shall not be destitute of something. When do you go?"

"Tomorrow morning!"

"Very well my son, you shall not go empty away."

I thought he would give me fifty dollars. In the morning I was a going, and bid my parents, brothers, and sisters good bye. My Father followed me to the door, and handed me an English Crown.[16]

"There my son is more than I had when I was 21 years of age, and if you are industrious and prudent, you will soon have sufficient, which will always increase by industry. Much money often leads young men into vice, which destroys their Constitution and character, and leads them on to eternal ruin."

---

[16] *Crown:* A silver coin worth five shillings.

All he said on that subject was nonsense to me. I was in such a passion I was a going to throw the crown down and go off without saying a word, but fear of offending my Father prevented me from doing it. I never informed my father of the money I made by my adventures, which was considerable, and I had many dollars then, although I had spent many in riotous living. I never left my father with such feelings as I did at that time. Many unfavorable reflections crossed my mind. Soon after I left him, I fell in company with 3 or 4 of my old schoolmates, and told them where I was a going that day, and wanted them to go with me to a tavern, and I would treat them with anything they were a mind to drink. They made some objection on account of its being so early in the day, but I prevailed on them to go. After we got there, I took out the crown my Father gave me and told them how it came into my hands, and I was determined to spend every penny of it before I left the house, which I did. It soon came on to snow and I had forty miles to walk; and before I arrived at Boston, which was at eight o'clock in the evening, the snow was a foot deep. I had laid out considerable of my own money for clothes, for my Uncle Job's daughters wanted to make shirts for me, which they would do without any expense, and more, they would give me a trimming of cambric[17] for bosom and hand ruffles for the purpose of appearing at all times like their brothers, which I accepted as a present, and they made for me, two and a half dozen of shirts, and all my expense was nothing more than the linen; and in addition to them they made me a number of stocks, which I always wore when I was on shore in the place of a handkerchief around my neck.[18]

[17] *Cambric:* A fine thin white linen fabric.
[18] *Stock:* A wide band or scarf worn about the neck commonly by men during the eighteenth century and often wrapped twice around and tied in front with a knot.

OBSERVATIONS AND COMMENTS

*Investigating the lives of early American seafarers, some historians
conclude that there were few seamen older than thirty-five years,
because the cruel usage of the sea either ended their lives prematurely
or so injured their health that they finished out their years ashore, broken men.*[19] *In Christopher Prince's narrative, we find nothing of the
oppressed seamen who populate the pages of labor histories. The narrative is no sermon against habits of improvidence ashore that produced
the poverty that forced men into dangerous and arduous service at sea.
Nor is it a diatribe against the landlords and crimps who encouraged
the rounds of indebtedness that, in turn, compelled sailors repeatedly
to sign up for another voyage.*

*Rather, how and why Christopher Prince chose the seafaring life
and rose from seaman to mate closely follow the pattern described by
Samuel Eliot Morison in his* Maritime History of Massachusetts.

*Morison judged that "The Bay State ... never had a native deep-sea
proletariat. Her fleet was manned by successive waves of adventure-
seeking boys, and officered by such of them as determined to make the
sea their calling.... If [a boy] enjoyed his first voyage and made good,
he was soon given an officer's berth.... If quickly cured of his wander-
lust, he went back to the farm, and was replaced by another boy." According to Morison, we find few older seamen on the rolls of sailing
merchant ships, because if young men did not soon rise to officer status,
they returned to the land to farm.*[20]

[19]Jesse Lemisch, "Jack Tar in the Streets: Merchant Seamen in the Politics of Revolutionary America," *William and Mary Quarterly*, 3d ser., 25 (1968): 371–407; Gary B. Nash, *The Urban Crucible: Social Change, Political Consciousness, and the Origins of the American Revolution* (Cambridge, Mass.: Harvard University Press, 1979), 16, 64; Marcus Rediker, *Between the Devil and the Deep Blue Sea: Merchant Seamen, Pirates, and the Anglo-American Maritime World, 1700–1750* (Cambridge, U.K.: Cambridge University Press, 1987).

[20]Samuel Eliot Morison, *The Maritime History of Massachusetts, 1783–1860* (Boston and New York: Houghton Mifflin, 1921), 106.

Christopher Prince's early career followed the pattern perceived by Morison as typical. Although Christopher benefited from elite family connections, the pattern of his early career seems indeed to have been true for a substantial portion of New England's seafaring community at the end of the eighteenth century. The labor force of international commerce certainly included "runaway slaves, thieves, murderers, fugitives and floaters,"[21] but it was not until after the War of 1812 that increasingly harsh working conditions drove New England's "superb, ambitious, 'good-family' young seamen" away from the merchant marine.[22]

[21]Lemisch, "Jack Tar in the Streets," 377, note.

[22]Elmo Paul Hohman, *History of American Merchant Seamen* (Hamden, Conn.: Shoe String Press, 1956), 7. "In the years between the Revolution and the War of 1812, seafaring was a well-regarded profession that attracted respectable men both before the mast and onto the quarterdeck." K. Jack Bauer, *A Maritime History of the United States: The Role of America's Seas and Waterways* (Columbia, S.C.: University of South Carolina Press, 1988), 58–59.

CHAPTER TWO

A Yankee in
King George's Navy
The Canadian Campaign
1774–July 1776

HISTORICAL CONTEXT

While Christopher was learning his trade and maturing into a young man, the events that led to the American Revolution were unfolding. Boston was a focal point of the tax revolt that led to the breach between the British colonies in America and their mother country, beginning in 1765 with resistance to the stamp tax imposed by Parliament. Although Christopher Prince lived in Boston, the resistance movement had little influence on his life until a year or two after he had completed his apprenticeship.

Prince reports that in the spring of 1775 he witnessed a riot between Bostonians and British soldiers in King Street. On the evening of 20 January 1775, the town watch and several redcoated officers accosted each other, an altercation ensued, and a number on both sides received blade wounds.[1] This could very well have been the episode that Prince

---

[1]John Barker, *The British in Boston: The Diary of Lt. John Barker* (Cambridge, Mass.: Harvard University Press, 1924; reprint ed., New York: New York Times and Arno Press, 1969), 21–22.

witnessed, but in recalling it, he confused it with two better-known incidents that occurred nearly five years earlier. The first of these was the shooting of Christian Seider (or Snider). On 23 February 1770 a number of Boston youths accosted customs informer Ebenezer Richardson, pelted him with stones and snowballs, and then broke all the windows of the house where he fled for refuge. Richardson fired a musket loaded with bird shot in an attempt to disperse the mob, fatally wounding a small boy. The second incident is known to history as the Boston Massacre. On 5 March 1770 another gang of youths cornered a British sentry guarding the customhouse in King Street and started throwing snowballs and chunks of ice. A corporal's guard attempted to rescue the sentry. When the episode ended, five civilians were dead and six wounded.

The aftermath of two events drew Christopher Prince into the middle of the Revolutionary struggle. The first of these events was the closing of the port of Boston in June of 1774. By closing the port, the British government sought to coerce the town of Boston into paying for the East India Company tea dumped into Boston Harbor during the Boston Tea Party, an act of defiance against the Parliamentary tax on tea.² While they kept the port closed, British authorities took Prince into their employ, providing him an opportunity to become acquainted with officers of the Royal Navy.

The second event was the firing of "the shot heard around the world," on 19 April 1775. After the battles of Lexington and Concord on that date, a number of wealthy loyalist Massachusetts families residing outside Boston, which the British Army occupied, decided to flee from harassment by patriots. One of these was the family of John Vassall (1738–97) of Cambridge, Massachusetts. Vassall's wife, Eliza-

---

²The text of the Boston Port Act arrived in Boston on 10 May 1774 and was published in the newspapers on 12 May. After 1 June the harbor was closed to incoming vessels; outgoing vessels had until 14 June to complete their lading and depart.

beth, was sister of the staunchly loyalist lieutenant governor of Massachusetts, Thomas Oliver. Vassall left with his family for Halifax,
Nova Scotia, shortly after the outbreak of war and sailed from there to
England in May 1776. Christopher Prince served as the mate on board
the Polly, the schooner commissioned to transport the Vassall family
to Halifax.[3] When the Polly continued on to Quebec, Prince found
himself in a position from which he would witness close at hand the
drama of the American invasion of Canada.

On 9 June 1775 Governor of Quebec and Major General Guy Carleton declared martial law in response to the capture of Fort Ticonderoga
and Crown Point by an American force.[4] Those posts, at the southern end of Lake Champlain, guarded the traditional invasion route
between the Hudson and St. Lawrence Rivers. The Canadian authorities seized the Polly and employed it as a guard ship in the St. Lawrence River. On 6 August, Carleton placed the Polly, along with two
other schooners "taken up for the River Service," under the "care and
management" of Lt. William Hunter, commanding HM brig Gaspee.[5]

In September 1775 Ethan Allen, a leader of Vermont's "Green
Mountain Boys," concerted a plan with Col. John Brown of the Continental Army to capture Montreal. Brown, with his 200 men, was to
cross the river and land to the south, while Allen with his force of 110

[3]Hugh Edward Egerton, ed., *The Royal Commission on the Losses and Services
of American Loyalists 1783–1785: Being the Notes of Mr. Daniel Parker Coke, M.P.,
One of the Commissioners during that Period* (1915; reprint ed., New York: Burt
Franklin, 1971), 230–31; Clifford K. Shipton, *Biographical Sketches of Those Who
Attended Harvard College in the Class of 1756–1760*, Volume 14 of *Sibley's Harvard
Graduates* (Boston: Massachusetts Historical Society, 1968): 230–32.

[4]On 20 May 1775, Governor and Maj. Gen. Guy Carleton (1724–1808)
learned that on 10 May an American force captured the British garrisons at Fort
Ticonderoga and Crown Point. Adam Shortt and Arthur G. Doughty, eds., *Canadian Archives: Documents Relating to the Constitutional History of Canada 1759–
1791*, 2d and rev. ed., Pt. II (Ottawa, 1918), 663–66.

[5]William Bell Clark, William James Morgan, et al., eds., *Naval Documents of
the American Revolution*, 10 vols. to date (Washington, D.C.: Naval Historical
Center, 1964–), 1: 1076–77.

crossed to the north of the town in the night. Each party was to give three loud huzzas as a signal to the other that it had landed and was ready for the assault. By the early morning of the 25th, as appointed, Allen's men had crossed the river, but there was no sign of Brown's force, which for an unknown reason had not crossed over. Allen's crossing had taken several trips because of a shortage of boats. Before Allen could devise an escape, the British garrison detected his presence and overwhelmed and captured his force. Allen was taken prisoner and sent on board HM brig Gaspee, where Christopher Prince met him.[6]

The British fort at St. Johns, on the Richelieu River, had been under attack by forces of Brigadier General Richard Montgomery of the Continental Army since September. The British post at Chambly, north of St. Johns, fell on 18 October, and on 30 October Carleton sent a mixed force of Canadians, Royal Fusiliers, and Indians to relieve the siege of St. Johns. A detachment of New Yorkers and Green Mountain Boys that Montgomery had posted at Longueuil, on the bank opposite Montreal, halted them. In the exhaustively researched study, Our Struggle for the Fourteenth Colony, Justin H. Smith observed that "we have no contemporary report of this affair from one who was present."[7] With one exception, American and British sources report the engagement in very general terms. Thus, Prince's eyewitness account, unknown to Smith, makes a valuable addition to our knowledge of this battle.

Having secured St. Johns, Montgomery's men moved on to Montreal. Montgomery also sent a body of soldiers under Col. James Easton to Sorel at the mouth of the Richelieu River to block the British troops' escape route. Unable to contest possession of Montreal with his

[6]Ethan Allen, *A Narrative of Colonel Ethan Allen's Captivity, from the Time of His Being Taken by the British, near Montreal, on the 25th Day of September, in the Year 1775, to the Time of His Exchange, on the 6th Day of May, 1778,* 1st ed. (Philadelphia: Bell, 1779), 10–11. See appendix 2.

[7]Justin H. Smith, *Our Struggle for the Fourteenth Colony: Canada and the American Revolution,* 2 vols. (New York: G. P. Putnam's Sons, 1907) 1: 453, n. 27.

150 regulars and handful of militia, Carleton sailed away with his forces and military supplies aboard three armed ships and eight transports. Contrary winds prevented them from passing American shore batteries at Sorel, where they were forced to surrender. Carleton, however, left the Gaspee *in disguise and escaped to Quebec.*

Released by the British, Prince now encamped with the American forces laying siege to Quebec. In November, Benedict Arnold arrived at the outskirts of Quebec with a force of some six hundred Continentals after a trek through 350 miles of wilderness that began a month and a half earlier on the Maine coast. On New Year's Eve, under cover of a blizzard, Montgomery led his reinforced command in a unsuccessful assault on Quebec, during which he lost his life. In May 1776, the ice in the St. Lawrence broke up, allowing British warships, convoying reinforcements, to reach Quebec and break the siege.[8] The American army, decimated by smallpox, retreated precipitously down Lake Champlain and the Hudson River.[9]

In 1774 I arrived from a long voyage, and found in Boston many British ships of war, and troops on shore. My uncle then gave me the command of a vessel which was partly loaded for one of the West India Islands. I soon got her ready for sea. I dined every

[8]On 6 May 1776, HMS *Isis,* HM frigate *Surprise,* and HM sloop *Martin* arrived at Quebec, convoying considerable reinforcements of British and Hessian troops under Maj. Gen. John Burgoyne. In consequence, the American forces made a precipitous retreat, leaving behind large volumes of supplies. Robert McConnell Hatch, *Thrust for Canada: The American Attempt on Quebec in 1775–1776* (Boston: Houghton Mifflin, 1979), 183.

[9]The Americans began to retreat from Sorel on 13 June 1776, fell rapidly back through Chambly, St. Johns, and Ile aux Noix, arriving at Crown Point by early July.

FIGURE 3. Landing of British Troops at Boston, 1768. Christopher Prince became intimately acquainted with several Royal Navy officers stationed in Boston during the British occupation.

day at my Uncle's, and there was always some of the British Navy Officers dined with him, a number of which I became acquainted with. The day before I was to sail, the English laid an embargo on all the vessels in port and would not permit one to go out. My Uncle tried for several days with the Admiral[10] to let me go, and with the rest of the Captains, but with no effect. They soon told him that some of his vessels should not be idle, they would employ them, and pay him for them. They told him they wanted the vessel I was a going in immediately. I was ordered to unload her, which I did in a few days. While I was a doing that, I was asked by one of the Lieutenants of the ship *Asia* if I would take charge of her as one of the master's mates of that ship and receive the same wages they had, for that was the only way they could employ me.[11] I had often been on board the *Asia,* 74 guns, and several nights had slept on board, with an invitation from some of the officers who had dined at my Uncle Job's. I accepted the offer made me but did not sign any articles. They then gave me the charge of the vessel I had before, and put some men on board, and sent me to Newburyport. After I returned from there, they sent me to Salem, Cape Ann, and Marblehead. On my return from those ports, the winter set in so severe, the vessel was laid up, and I remained on board the ship. There I had an opportunity to examine into the duties of every officer from the highest to the lowest, which was all new to me. She had about six hundred men on board. Every morning all the under officers assembled on the quarter-deck and were taught by an experienced man the art of using the sword and cutlass, some with files,[12] and some with

[10]Vice Admiral Samuel Graves, commanding Royal Navy squadron, North America Station.

[11]The sixty-four-gun ship of the line HMS *Asia* arrived in Boston Harbor early in December 1774 and remained until early May 1775.

[12]*Foil:* A slender, blunt sword used in fencing.

swords. I was astonished at what I see in art and practice. The teacher would call on almost every one to come with either sword or cutlass and use all their exertion to run the sword into him or cut him with a cutlass, and there was not one that could touch him. He would often draw the swords out of their hands by his own, and throw them on deck, and disarm those who had the cutlasses. I practiced for a long time with files, but never dare to use a sword or cutlass. I examined much into the duties of the Purser and Stewards, Quarter Masters and Quarter Gunners, and every other officer's duty which I was unacquainted with, not that I had the least thought at that time we were a going to war with them, or any nation. I found that the Purser or Steward was as profitable an office as any on board. Upon the whole, I was never in a more useful school in all my life, which proved so to be after the war commenced.

There was a young man on board that ship, about my age (a son to the sailing-master of the ship), who had been a midshipman for many years. His name was Edward Thornberrough. No man could be more friendly to any one than he was to me. He never would leave me one day or hour, either on board or on shore, and I was as much attached to him as he was to me; and during the winter we were ashore much of our time.[13]

In the spring of 1775, after the weather had become mild and pleasant, I went on board of my vessel again and got her ready to comply with the orders I should receive. About this time many things transpired which put on a very unfavorable appearance.

[13]Edward Thornbrough (1754–1834) entered the Royal Navy before his seventh birthday and attained the rank of lieutenant in 1773, a year before his father was promoted commander. He took part in several operations of the American Revolution, including the Battle of Bunker Hill, and was posted captain before the end of the war. He attained flag rank in 1801, became full admiral in 1813, and was knighted in 1815. Sidney Lee, ed., *Dictionary of National Biography*, 63 vols. (1885–1900), 56: 287–89.

One was, a number of the citizens assembled in King street (now called State street) to take an inspector of the customs, who had violated a law of the place, and was protected by the British soldiers. A number who were there and were prevented from entering the house took up some of the paving stones and broke all the windows, and stove in the door. By that time about twelve soldiers came among us, as I was one of the number, and ordered us away. Myself with several others retreated at a small distance, but about fifty remained. The soldiers walked up to them with their bayonets and drove them away into another street, they then resisted them, and the soldiers then discharged their muskets, and killed eight of the men among them, which brought immediate confusion throughout the town. From that time no one was allowed to come into town, and none go out without permission, and every house was entered, and every weapon of war was taken from every individual. All this confusion kept increasing until nearly one half of the inhabitants got permission to go out of town. I began to have some unfavorable feelings and sentiments towards the proceedings of the English among us, and I communicated my feelings to a number of the Midshipmen and Master's mates on board the *Asia,* some of which agreed with me. I could not restrain my feelings from any one I was acquainted with on board. All went on well on my part until the 16th day of April, 1775,[14] which was an awful day! At one o'clock in the morning, a number of English troops went out of town to destroy the powder magazine at Concord, about eight miles from town. They got out unmolested, but they were seen by many of the inhabitants in the country, and had some suspicion what they were a going to do, as there about eight hundred English troops which were all well armed. About 70 of our countrymen surrounded the Magazine

[14]I.e., 19 April.

with a determination to protect it, and some ran to and fro and called the inhabitants to arms, but before they got together the English got to the magazine and destroyed it, and killed several of the men that were there. By the time the sun rose, I and two of my cousins had been out, and on our return we see General Gage[15] and a number of officers on Beacon Hill with spy-glasses, looking towards Cambridge. We went up on the hill, and saw with our eyes the English troops retreating on the north side of the bay, and there was a continual firing, but we could not see where it went from. By 8 o'clock in the morning there were as many as a thousand people on the hill, and nearly all had spy-glasses, and would often say, O how the soldiers drop. I often heard General Gage groan. By 12 o'clock they got about half way from Cambridge to Charlestown, and about sundown they got to Charlestown, in a melancholy situation. We soon heard that sixty five were killed, and many wounded. We were informed in a short time that fifty of our countrymen were killed and wounded. The next day we were informed that many of the inhabitants of Concord and Lexington who had lost some of their relations were determined to kill all the English they could find, and a number had come from Salem and Marblehead, which prevented any of the English troops to leave Boston, or any one who wore a uniform. There were several thousand on the following day that surrounded Boston on every side, which threw the city and all the English troops into confusion.

There was a gentleman out at Lexington, who had been a Governor at Jamaica, by the name of Varsell, who had come on to Boston on account of his ill-health, with his wife and daughter, about sixteen years old. He had to disguise himself to get into Boston, which he did on the 18th, the day after the battle of Lexington.

---

[15]Lieutenant General Thomas Gage, commander in chief of the British Army in North America and governor of Massachusetts.

FIGURE 4. Having sailed from Boston in April 1775, shortly after the Battles of Lexington and Concord, Christopher Prince arrived in Quebec unaware of the escalation of hostilities that led to the Battle of Bunker Hill on 17 June.

His wife and daughter followed him the same day. The British government got a schooner from my Uncle Job to carry Colonel Varsell to Halifax Nova Scotia, one which was bound to the Mediterranean previous to the embargo, commanded by a man whose name was Pepper, and owned a small part of her. After he had landed Colonel Varsell and his family at Halifax, he was permitted to go where he pleased, but not permitted to take out anything but ballast when he went from Boston. My Uncle complied with the offer and ordered Captain Pepper to go to Quebec, and take in a cargo there and go to Leghorn in the Mediterranean. But Pepper was unacquainted with the coasts and river which led to Quebec and dare not undertake it without a pilot. My uncle then requested me to go in her as mate and pilot, which I consented to do as I had been at Quebec, and well acquainted with every foot of the way.

As I wanted to leave Boston, I went immediately on board the schooner, for I disapproved of the proceedings of the English to us, but I little expected the contention was a going to continue. I took on board everything I had, and I was surprised in seeing Captain Pepper's family there, his wife and five children. His oldest son had been to sea with him. He was about sixteen years of age, his youngest about three years old.[16] Colonel Varsell wife and daughter was on board, and we sailed immediately, which was the 21st April, five days after the battle of Lexington. I was entirely unacquainted with Captain Pepper. I never had seen him before. Third day after we sailed we had a violent gale of wind at S.E., which commenced about nine P.M., which caused great alarm among our passengers. I heard Mrs. Varsell and others a

---

[16]On 25 April 1775, Vice Admiral Samuel Graves, R.N., signed a permission for Samuel Pepper, "Master of the Schr *Polly*," to carry out of Boston "his Wife and three Children with their bedding and other Necessaries." Clark and Morgan, eds., *Naval Documents of the American Revolution*, Vol. 1, 221.

screaming below but I did not know the cause of their distress, for none of us could leave the deck. Colonel Varsell came up the gangway and requested Captain Pepper to go below, which he did. He soon came on deck again. I thought the noise and distress below increased, soon after Captain Pepper came out of the cabin. Colonel Varsell came up again and asked me to go below. I saw he was much agitated and I went down.

As soon as I entered the cabin Mrs. Varsell said, "are we all a going to perish?"

I told her no.

"Why you differ from the Captain he says we are in a dangerous situation."

I told her the gale would cease at twelve o'clock, in less than an hour, and all would be well.

The Colonel then said, "I believe what you have said is true."

I went up on deck and not a groan or a scream was heard afterwards. At twelve o'clock the colonel asked me to go down below again, and when I went down I was asked whether the gale continued as it had done. I told them it did not, and all was silent, and in a few minutes it was calm, but a dreadful swell a running. That woman treated me after that in a very friendly manner so much so she made me blush, and the Colonel did the same. We soon arrived at Halifax. Captain Pepper was never on that coast before, and not one on board knew the land nor the harbor but myself. After we arrived, the Colonel treated me with wonderful friendship. He asked me what he should do for me, name anything and it shall be done. I told him nothing. He then said, "if it had not been for you my wife would have gone into fits in that gale we had, and she might have died, and she wants me to do something for you." He then gave me ten dollars, which I took with some reluctance, and he offered me more but I would not take it.

We sailed immediately for Quebec. After we arrived at Cancer harbor we entered it and went across the bay into the Cancer Gut[17] and Pepper insisted upon it that we were not safe. It is seven miles through the Gut. I told him I was surprised to hear a nautical man say what he did, for there was not a ship that crossed the ocean but what I could carry through there in safety. After we entered the bay of Shalore, he was still astonished, for the island of St. Johns was ahead of us, which kept us from the sight of the Gulf of St. Lawrence. But after we passed the island of St. Johns, we soon lost sight of land in every point of compass, and the first land we saw was Cape Gaspie, and entered the river St. Lawrence, which led us to Quebec, where we arrived in May. We came to anchor abreast of the city about ten A.M. and before we got our sails handed, a man came on board and asked us where we were from, and after we told him, he went forward and stamped a broad arrow[18] on the foremast and said, "this is now the King's vessel and you are all prisoners of war, for the Governor of this city has declared war against every one who has been born in America, and will treat them as enemies unless they become British subjects. For the Americans had taken Ticonderoga and Crown Point, and blood had been shed on both sides." The seamen were all ordered into the boat to be carried on shore and put into prison. Captain Pepper's oldest son was one of the seamen. The boat returned again, and he ordered his wife and all his children on shore.

Captain Pepper then said unto the man, "What am I to do? what are you a going to do with my wife and children?"

He said, "I will let you know directly."

After the boat was gone he said, "I am now a going to make you an offer which you may accept or refuse. Will you remain on

---

[17]*Cancer:* Canso, Nova Scotia
[18]The mark of a broad arrow indicated British crown property. The manuscript actually reads "stamped a broad R on the foremast."

board this vessel in the King's service, or will you be confined as a prisoner on shore, separated from your family?"

He said, "I do not know what to say. What are you a going to do with my mate?"

"I am a going to make him the same offer I have done to you."

"Do it now."

He then addressed me in the same language. I then told him. "If you do not send me out of the river St. Lawrence, I will remain on board in the same office I am now in, if you will give me the same wages, but I will not be considered as a British subject, but if I behave amiss you may put me in prison as a rebel."

He said, "I agree to your answer."

Captain Pepper said, "I will remain on board on the same conditions, if you will take care of my wife and children while I am absent from Quebec."

The officer then said, "This vessel is a going to be made a guard ship and placed in the river St. Lawrence, at the mouth of the river Sorrel, which leads to Chamberlé, which is within three miles of the Fort St. Johns, at the head of Lake Champlain;[19] but you cannot remain the commander of this vessel, unless you remain a British subject."

"I cannot consent to be a British subject, but I will perform my duty as a commander."

The officer said, "you shall remain on board."

Captain Pepper had some furniture on board which he sent ashore to his wife.

In three days we had sixteen brass six pounders on board, and port holes made for them fore and aft, breechings and tackles,

---

[19]*Sorel River:* The northern portion of the Richelieu River. *Chamberlé:* Chambly, ca. 10 miles north of St. Johns, on the Richelieu River. *St. Johns:* British fort located twenty miles southeast of Montreal near the head of navigation from Lake Champlain down the Richelieu River to the St. Lawrence.

sponges, wormers and rammers, powder and shot, yea everything complete for a ship of war. A large quantity of provisions of every kind was sent on board. A few seamen, or in the room of seamen, and a pilot. Captain Pepper nor myself were permitted to go on shore. In three days we were ordered up the river, which gave me a view of all the country on each side the river from Quebec, to river Sorrel within twenty five miles of Montreal. There we moored the vessel, the pilot left us, and not an officer on board but Captain Pepper and myself, and not more than eight men and they were no seamen. On the south side of the river where we lay there was a small town called Sorrel containing about fifty houses; on the north side there was an extensive swamp where no human being could live. We performed our duties without any contention or disturbance from any person. We had no real duty to do but to keep a regular watch on deck night and day. On the first day of July, an aged man came on board by the name of Friend,[20] and a young man by the name of Livingston, and brought with them a quantity of baggage. Mr. Friend then said to us, "we are informed what your duties are on board this vessel as nautical men. We have no knowledge of vessels for we are no seamen. You are to perform all your duties on board this vessel as seaman in moving her, and in keeping her in order either under sail or at anchor. You are to keep a regular watch on deck day and night, and suffer no one to come on board without my permission. You must not expect Mr. Livingston or me to do anything with the vessel. You are to provide her with wood and water.

[20]Friend was listed as master of the *Polly* when General Richard Montgomery's forces captured it on 20 November 1775. "Return of Ordnance and Ordnance Stores on board the different Vessels, November 20, 1775." Peter Force, *American Archives,* 4th ser., vol. 3 (Washington, 1840): 1693. But Pepper was listed as master in a "Return of Provisions . . . at Montreal," dated 27 November 1775. Washington, D.C., National Archives, *Papers of the Continental Congress,* item 58, page 407.

FIGURE 5. The American capture of St. John's, Quebec, was a prelude to the capture of Montreal, which Christopher Prince witnessed in the autumn of 1775.

On our part, we are to obey all the orders sent unto us respecting implements of war and provisions, which is to be conveyed to St. Johns. They will be received and discharged from this vessel and conveyed in boats to Chamberle."

I began this new life which was of much advantage to me. I devoted much of my time in reading histories of importance, some of them religious books. The new Captain was a very pious man; in consequence there was not a profane word uttered on board. In fact it had a wonderful effect on my feelings and behavior. Mr. Livingston was about my age. He was an excellent young man. He had a complete education and an amiable disposition. No two could be more attached to each other than we were. Mr. Friend treated me like a son. He was about 55 years old. Captain Pepper and I were always united in sentiments in everything. We had never one word of controversy from our first acquaintance. In fact I never spent any time in all my life with so much enjoyment as I did on board that vessel while we lay at the mouth of the river Sorrel. I went several times up to Fort Chamberlé, and at one time I went to Fort St. John's, where the English were building a frigate of thirty-two guns. We often heard there was a bloody war going on between the English and Americans.

About the first of September, General Carleton, the commanding officer in Canada, was a going to Fort St. Johns, and on his way he came on board of our vessel, and after he was there some time conversing with Mr. Friend below he came on deck with several other officers with him. He came up to me and asked me some questions about my feelings in respect to the war in my country where I was born. I said but very little to him on the subject. I told him I considered myself a prisoner, and I was very much obliged to him and all under his charge, and I never should forget it as long as I lived.

He smiled and said "I am willing to increase these feelings."

I said that was almost impossible.

"If you will accept the offer, I will now appoint you Sailing Master of the frigate we are now building for Lake Champlain which is as respectable an office almost as any in our navy."

"I am sir much obliged to you for granting me my first request, as I have said before I cannot consent to be a British subject."

He said but a few words more, and left the vessel. Captain Pepper asked me what General Carleton had been saying to me, and I told him.

"Why did you not accept the offer."

"Would you have done it?"

He went away without an answer.

Three or four days after that, General Prescott,[21] second in command, came on board and made me the same offer, and urged me to accept the offer he had made, and said many things which were very tempting, but I still declined. He then called Mr. Friend and said, "do not give Mr. Prince any peace until he accepts the offer I have made him, and act as a sailing master on board the frigate which will soon sail on Lake Champlain." Mr. Friend then said many things on the subject. "Although I am unwilling to part with you, I advise you to accept the offer. There must be a sailing master on board, and you see they have given you the preference." I then told them I could not consent to lift a finger against my country, and they themselves would never think favorable of me for doing it. No it would be to my condemnation. "And now, gentlemen, I tell you as I did General Carleton, I am much obliged to you for granting me my first request, as a prisoner without becoming a British subject, you have employed me as one, and I am willing to perform all the duties I ought to do,

---

[21]Brig. Gen. Richard Prescott (1725–83).

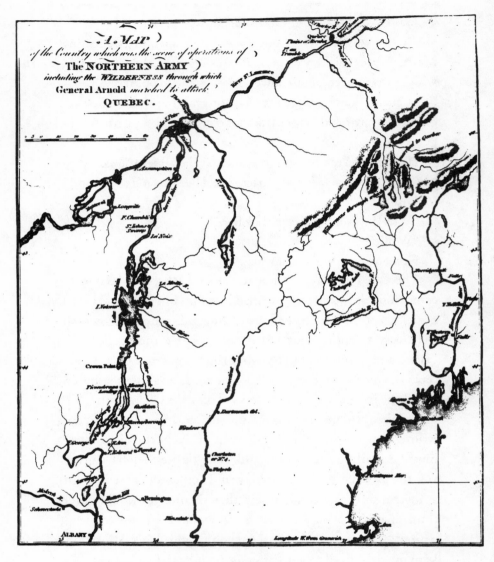

FIGURE 6. Northern Theater of Military Operations, 1775–1776

and I do amiss as I said before, send me to prison; and you have now laid me under greater obligations than I ever was before in offering me such an honorable office in the British navy. It is what I do not deserve if I was an Englishman born. But I do now believe if I was to accept your offer, you would call me a man of no confidence and unworthy of any notice of an Englishman or an American, and I hope you will permit me to enjoy my principles undisturbed." General Prescott then said, "you shall never go unnoticed." After that I was treated with much respect.

Captain Pepper saw them conversing with me and understood some things they said and became very unsociable. I asked him some questions why he was so cold and unfriendly.

He said, "it is no matter I do not do it for nothing, I have a cause and reason for what I do."

I then told him he was offended because they had made me an offer to such an honorable station, and it convinced me he had an envious disposition. "Why do you not say to me I approve of your conduct for not accepting the offer that was made you and not condemn me? It convinces me that you are angry because they did not make the same offer to you, and if they had, you would have accepted it."

"Do you believe so?"

"Yes, I do, or you would highly approve of what I have done."

He said, "I dispute what you say"; and I could never get him to be sociable after that.

In October we were ordered to Montreal, soon after we arrived there I was ordered on board the brig *Gaspie* of fourteen guns.[22] General Prescott was on board. He said, "all the officers are gone from this vessel on board the frigate on Lake Champlain, and I

---

[22]HM brig *Gaspee*, Lt. William Hunter. Put in command of the armed schooner *Royal Savage* at Fort St. John's, Hunter was taken prisoner when that place fell to the Americans in November.

wish you to take charge of this brig until the officers return." I went on board without any reluctance, and took all my things out of the schooner.

We had not been long at Montreal before we heard that General Montgomery had made his way though the wilderness and swamps along the north side of Lake Champlain into Canada, and taken up his stand with a large army between Fort Chambleé and Fort St. John's, which stopped all intercourse between those places and Montreal. This information threw Montreal into a state of confusion, for they had but few English troops there. We was soon informed that General Montgomery had taken Fort St. Johns and Chambleé and was on his way to the river St. Lawrence at Sorrel, and opposite to Montreal. We soon heard that they had taken possession of Sorrel, and built a strong fort, which was the place where we lay as a guard-ship. And on the same day a number of American troops were seen on the opposite side of the river to Montreal. This cut off all communication from Quebec. There we was confined to a small limited place, and no means of escape without much danger.

It altered my feelings to an unlimited degree. It was with difficulty I could refrain from exposing myself in what I said. On board the brig *Gaspie* where I was, there was but one officer and he was a Midshipman, and he and I differed but very little in our political principles. We often talked on the subject. There was a vessel, a tender, a schooner of sixteen guns, laying at Montreal in addition to the schooner I had been in. Those two schooners and the brig *Gaspie* was all the armed vessels at Montreal.

The Americans began to assemble in large numbers to all appearance opposite to Montreal, erecting batteries of safety and defence of any force that should come against them. There is an island between Montreal and the opposite shore which protected the shipping from the batteries. The first attack that was made in the vicinity of Montreal by the Americans was in the night by Ethan Allen. He crossed the river St. Lawrence with about eighty men, about two miles below Montreal unbeknown to anyone except the inhabitants where he landed. What his motive was in landing there with so few men was a wonder to me and others. He remained there until near daylight, and some of his men took the boats and recrossed the river, and left Colonel Allen with about thirty men exposed to the enemy, for they could not make their escape. About a mile from where they landed there was an encampment of Indians of about fifteen hundred men, women, and children, among which were about eight hundred warriors. We were afterwards informed that Allen landed there to destroy those Indians. If so, he ought to have brought with him more than eighty men. Early in the morning, as soon as daylight appeared, we heard the drums and fifes a going in the city, which was new to us. We soon saw the gates open, and about five hundred soldiers and militia came out and paraded a little distance from the walls of the city. We soon saw the Indian Warriors assemble about eight hundred, and they all soon commenced their march. None of us could tell what they were going for. I went aloft, and hundreds of others to see what they were gone for. They got about one mile from the city and surrounded several buildings, and discharged hundreds of muskets, and what that was for we could not imagine. Very soon all was silent, and we saw them returning.

As soon as they returned back to Montreal one man only was sent on board the brig *Gaspie,* which was Colonel Allen. And I received orders to have him put in irons on his hands and legs, and put down into the forecastle. I had a considerable conversation with him. He answered some of my questions freely and some he would not answer at all. When I asked him about his men, he said he believed they were all dead. Whether that was true or not I never knew. After he had been a few days on board, a boat came along side with orders to put him into that boat in irons, as he was a going to be sent to Quebec, and from there to England; all which I cheerfully did, for he was not allowed to eat anything on board but bread and water. Every day I carried him a part of my rations, and the Midshipman on board did the same; and that we were obliged to do in a private manner, for fear of being detected.

By this time everything began to put on a very gloomy appearance. Winter approaching, and almost impossible to pass the forts they had erected at Sorrel. The American army daily increasing, and we had news of the surrender of St. Johns to General Montgomery, and they could then bring all their force against Montreal.

The English were determined to drive the Americans from the opposite shore if possible. They had many flat bottomed boats built which would carry forty men each. One day the three armed vessels were ordered down below the island which protected us from the American batteries. The English had about fifteen hundred men, soldiers, militia, and indians. They all embarked in the boats about twelve P.M. We had moved the armed vessels down, but not a shot was fired to us. We could scarcely see a man move, all was still and silent. After the boats were manned with troops and hauled off from the shore, they had a grand appearance. There were nearly forty boats filled. General Prescott was in one as the commander. When they got in the eddy they were to inform every boat whether they must proceed or retreat, by two flags from the Commander's boat. One was to proceed if hoisted, the other to retreat if hoisted. This was understood by the commander of every boat.

There was a very heavy current running down the river at that time and in particular on the southern shore where the Americans were, not less than ten knots, for there is a heavy fall or rapid just above on that side the island, so much so it is not navigable for any vessel. But there is an eddy at the lower part of the island which will contain twenty or thirty vessels. That was the place where we lay and where the boats stopped.

Many of the Indians were in the boats with the English, but three of them had none but Indians in them. All the boats were rowed with oars, but the three Indian boats, and they were paddled. After they had passed the armed vessels a small distance in the eddy under the island, the Indian boats were ahead of the rest and very near the stream. The officers took their spy-glasses out and examined the batteries and shore. They continued in that situation for twenty minutes. Those who rowed had their faces all directed to the colors, but those who paddled had their backs towards the colors. Finally the retreating colors were hoisted on board General Prescott's boat. In an instant I heard a shouting on board the Indian boats and they sprung at their paddles and in one moment they were in the current, and before they could turn their boats they were carried down to a rock opposite the cove where the Americans were stationed. It was a high and a very steep rock on every side. They all sprung out of the boats, but the current was so strong they could not hold their boats, and they all drifted down on a point of land at the eastern part of the cove. The rest of the boats dare not go there to relieve and rescue them from death.

We soon saw the Americans come down and secure the boats. They then brought down a field piece on the point and fired among them and a number were killed and wounded, and rolled off the rock into the water and sunk in an instant or at any rate they disappeared from us. They continued firing until they took all off, which were in sight. The rest got round on the other side of the rock, where the shot could not reach them. They took another field piece on the opposite side of the cove, which drove them from their shelter, and seventy of them were soon driven from the rock and killed. They then hove out a signal, and soon they ceased from firing, and took some boats to the rock and took them all on shore. They immediately put them into the batteaus they went there in, and hoisted a flag of truce, and carried them all over to Montreal and landed them, and returned to the American side again without saying a word to anyone. Thus ended this expedition.

This act of humanity by the Americans to those savages is without example, who were their most bitter enemies falling into their hands, and not detained from their wives and children as prisoners one minute; and those who one hour before were rushing on them with savage ferocity to murder everyone who came within their reach. These proceedings of the Americans had a wonderful effect on the savage hearts. It softened them to an unknown degree; and it filled the hearts of all the English and Canadians with astonishment. I heard many English officers together with General Prescott say they never saw such humanity before, among any people on the face of the earth. It was nearly dark when they landed those savages at Montreal; it was while we were getting the armed vessels to their former station, and not a gun was fired on either side. We went there to protect the landing of the army which I have named. Although I was the commander of the vessel, I had nothing to do with the guns, if we had gone into action, that was known from the highest to the lowest, for all the officers were acquainted with my political sentiments. As General Montgomery had taken all on Lake Champlain, not one of the officers of the brig *Gaspie* could return. The two schooners had some naval officers on board, but none to spare, and the Midshipman I have before mentioned was the only officer on board the brig, and they have nothing to do with the vessel. He was about my age, and had married a Boston girl, which he had on board the brig. He was one of the most amiable young men I ever saw, in temper, and principles, and sentiments. He was a moral, and I may say a religious man, for he and his wife and myself lived in the ward room, where we eat, drank, and slept. I had every reason to believe he and his wife devoted some of their time in prayer to Almighty God. I never heard a profane word of any kind come from his lips. As I had refrained from swearing while in the presence of Mr. Friend on board the schooner, I still felt no inclination to do it. In fact my feelings would not permit me to do it. We had not more than fifteen men on board the brig besides the boatswain and one or two of his mates, the Gunner, Steward, Cook, and Quarter Gunners, and waiters. But a very little or no profane words among the whole, no intoxication. On board of them two vessels, I got more knowledge of my duty to God and man than I ever got in all my life. In truth, I was unacquainted with historical, geographical, and theological instruction. But on board the schooner and brig they had all those books, which I read near half my time. Mr. Friend was a friend to me. He was a wonderful instructor, and the Midshipman on board the brig did the same, but he did not take the same liberty with me on that account as Mr. Friend as we were so near of age, and he considered me to be his superior officer. Mr. Livingston was of great advantage to me, he had a liberal education, and as he and I were on a footing in point of office, we could say anything we wanted to each other. If I said anything amiss he would tell me of it, and in fact he rectified my conversation, which I often thanked him for.

As I had devoted about three months to this important instruction, I can say in safety, I was an altered man. During that time I was often filled with shame and confusion, and even then I was obliged to have a check on my thoughts, words, and actions.

November had now commenced. We knew that the winter would soon set in, and that was the reason the English attempted to drive the Americans from the opposite shore. They placed great confidence in the Indian warriors in defending and protecting Montreal against the Americans. But all of a sudden their hopes and confidence in them was taken away. In one hour after the Americans had landed them on the Montreal side, they assembled together, and all who were related to those who had been killed, painted themselves, which put on a hideous appearance, and began their usual ceremony of revenge, on some one of any nation or any color, if it was one of their own tribe. They built up a large fire, and all that were painted took hold of each others hands, and danced round that fire until nine o'clock at night. While they were dancing around the fire, all was silent for some time. The rest of the men, women, and children went away into their wigwams and not one was in sight. The brig was very near the shore and we could see every countenance as well as if we were among them. All of a sudden every light was out, and they began to make an awful noise and separated. The gates of the city were shut so that they could not enter there. We began to be alarmed on board of all the vessels present, which was twenty-one, eighteen besides the armed vessels. We thought it was our duty to protect them as well as ourselves. We got our guns all in order, and lit the matches, and not one left the deck during the night, for they had as many as one hundred and thirty bark canoes which they could launch and board a vessel in five minutes. It was so dark we could hear them, but not see them. Thus they continued roving round all night. At daylight we saw them going about frothing, foaming, and spurting in every direction. But they did not go down on the farms where Allen landed. If they had they would have soon found a victim. There were no inhabitants so near the city as to be much exposed to their vengeance. And not a man, woman, or child of their own nation came out of their tents all day, nor one of the gates of the city were opened. The walls and the roofs of houses were full of people. As soon as the sun had set, they all came down to the river and washed off all their paint. As soon as that was done the rest of the Indians, male and female, rushed out of their tents, and in an instant mixed together. Tranquility was restored all around them, and the gates of the city were opened, and their rations dealt out to every one, for they had not eaten anything all day. Early next morning they brought out to them their rations. After that, young and old, male and female, went up to the gate and returned with a blanket which was given to every one who could wear it. As soon as they returned to their tents, in ten minutes every one was taken down and brought to the river, and their canoes all launched down to the river, their tents, wives, and children put in. Many of the English officers came down and talked to them, but they paid but little attention to what they said. General Carleton and Prescott were walking on the southern ramparts to all appearance much agitated in seeing the Indians going away. They crossed the river and went over to the American side with a flag of truce flying in one of the canoes, and were all received. This movement weakened the English force very much.

There were eighteen vessels there from Quebec as coasters to take down produce to merchantmen laying there from England, some of them were loaded. Orders were sent on board of every vessel to unload immediately, and make preparations to receive provisions and implements of war. A schooner of sixteen guns (not the one I was in) was filled with powder, and all the others were receiving everything that was sent on board. All on a sudden we received orders to work night and day until the vessels were loaded. General Prescott was often on board the brig, and after we had received orders to use these exertions, he told us that General Carleton had received a letter from General Montgomery that he should take possession of Montreal on such a day, which he named, not exceeding four days from that time. About this time the wind came out at N.E., which made every British heart tremble, as it prevented us from making our escape in safety. The vessels were all loaded. Many things were left we could not receive. Guns, shot, and shells were thrown into the river, and many other things were destroyed. I cannot describe my feelings, I did not know what to say or do, for I knew if I applied for permission to go on shore, I should be denied, not on account of my being a prisoner, but because there was no one they could get to command the brig in my room. A more friendly man no one could have [been] than General Prescott was to me; and I had considerable money due to me which I was unwilling to lose. Upon the whole I thought I would wait and see the events of Divine Providence, which at that time put on a favorable appearance, as the wind was at N.E., which was in my favor, for I knew we could not pass the batteries at Sorrel without being sunk by the guns at that fort, unless the wind shifted.

The day arrived when General Montgomery was a coming to Montreal. Very early in the morning we saw them preparing their boats to cross the river. We all weighed our anchors, twenty one vessels, and commenced beating down the river. I had received on board about fifty English soldiers, and the only officers among them were one or two Serjeants. General Carleton and General Prescott came on board the brig *Gaspie*. They both went down into the cabin as soon as they got on board, where no one resided. There were two state rooms in the cabin, which gave them good accommodations. We passed some of the American boats which were crossing the river not more than a musket shot from us. We said nothing to them, nor they to us, and many of them landed at Montreal in our sight. About five miles from Montreal there was a place of anchorage where we all came to, where we lay two days waiting for a fair wind which was still blowing at N.E. Every signal for every movement was given from the brig *Gaspie*. On the third day we made sail again and went down within five miles of Sorrel, where we all came to anchor again. I was often sent for in the cabin, and conversed with from General Carleton, who treated me in a very friendly manner. He sometimes asked for my advice, and from him I received all my orders. There was a point of land projecting into the river westward of the river Sorrel which a very narrow channel between that and the north shore. Sorrel was so situated we could lay within a quarter of a mile of Sorrel batteries in safety. We lay at our second anchorage two days longer waiting for a shift of wind, which still continued at N.E., a part of the time very violent with heavy snow. On the third day at our last anchorage, the brig *Gaspie* and the schooner *Polly* (the one I was taken in) were ordered down and reconnoitre the fort at Sorrel, and see if it was possible for us to pass it in safety. I was ordered to double the point before the schooner. As soon as we doubled the point with our starboard tacks on board, they opened the fort upon us, which threw us in such confusion not a gun was fired from us. I wore the brig round on her heal in an instant without any orders from General Carleton who was standing in the gangway. He did not say a word to me, why do you do so. In ten minutes I doubled the point. The schooner did not expose herself. She wore round before she got to the point. Although we had several shot that struck us, we were all safe. We ran about a mile from the point and came to anchor, as it snowed so heavy, we could not see the land. About one o'clock P.M. it ceased snowing and cleared away and we found ourselves within half a mile of the southern shore, and to our surprise we saw a number of men on shore, but as it snowed a little, it prevented us from knowing what they were about. I could not leave the deck, for I was sure they were a going to fire into us. It cleared away so for a minute I saw the guns, and ran to the companion way to the cabin, and asked General Prescott if he would be so kind as to come up on deck. He came up and said to me, what do you want. He was then in the companion. I told him there was a number of people on shore and had field pieces and were a going to fire into us.

"Hut, hut, hut," he said and came up on deck. "Ho, ho, they are countrymen come there to see the vessel."

"Do you not see the guns?"

Before he answered me, we had a shot, which went through both bulwarks. He then said, "get the brig out of their reach," and went below. I ordered the men to weigh the anchor, and while they were doing it, the shot came on board in such a quantity all the soldiers left the deck. I then ordered the fore-topsail loosed. Three men got up into the foretop, and the grape shot and musket-balls came on board in such quantities they kept under the head of the foremast and I could not get one of them to go on the yard. Three more men said they would go up. One of them was about half way to the top and said he was wounded, and they all came down. I told them in the top to cut the gaskets, and come down, which they did. We then cut the cable and went off out of their reach, and anchored with the other vessels. We had not gone more than two miles from where we escaped before we saw a boat astern of us with a truce flag flying in her. As we were under easy sail, she overhauled us and was but a little distance from us when we came to anchor. We had hoisted our flag to show them who was the Commodore of the fleet. In a few minutes they came along side and asked permission to come on board. General Prescott being on deck told them to come.

The officer who came out of the boat said, "I want to see General Carleton."

Prescott, "I am the commanding officer."

American, "Are you General Carleton."

Prescott, "I am the only one to transact any business with friends or enemies."

He was still dissatisfied and wanted to go below. Prescott would not consent to that. "We can do all our business where we are."

American, "if you trifle with me it will operate much against you. I am an officer belonging to the American army, and I am authorized by the commander to come here and make proposals to you if you are the commander and chief, which are favorable to you and all under your charge, and if you are not, woe be to you and many others."

Prescott, "I am the commander who decides every event."

The conditions were given to Prescott on paper, and after he received it and read it, he said, "in one hour I will give you an answer."

My mind was crowded with reflections on what had passed through the day, and what was now before me. I was astonished when I retraced my feeling which I had when shot and balls were pouring into us, exposing every one on board to death, which did not enter my mind at the time. No, I did not think of death. The vessel was committed to my charge, which made me forget everything else but her safety, and yet it was in my power to give her into the hands of my countrymen, and rescue myself from the hands of my enemy. And that never entered my mind. All I could decide upon was that the Commander in Chief put more confidence in me than any other man under his charge, or he would not have given the *Gaspie* the preference out of twenty one vessels, to perform the duties he required in his own safety, and the protection of everything under his care which was of great importance. If I had been with my own countrymen and was a going

against an enemy, I should not have been more anxious to perform my duty than I had done through the day.

The American officer returned punctual at the time allowed.
As soon as he came on board, General Prescott said, "he could not
nor would not sign his proposals."

American, "What alteration do you want?"

The answer he gave him was in a low voice which was unknown to me.

The American turned from him and said, "I shall not alter the
proposals I have made," and got into his boat, and ordered her off.
After he had got about two rods from the brig, he ordered his men
to stop and said, "now, General I am going on shore, and I think it
my duty to tell you that before tomorrow, many of you will [be]
enfolded in the arms of death and you for one." And then ordered
his men to row away.

He had not got more than ten rods before General Prescott
called on him to come on board again. He returned and came on
board, with a different countenance he had before. General Prescott said something to him I did not understand. The American
gave his decided disapprobation and turned away to get into his
boat again and walked several times fore and aft the Quarter deck
and made for the boat. While he was getting in, General Prescott
called to him again and said, "I will sign the Articles of Capitulation," which he did, and they were signed by both. The American
then said, "Sir, at eight o'clock this evening I shall take charge of
all these vessels and everything on board, and I shall expect to
find them as I leave them," and got into his boat and left us.[23]

I cannot now describe my feelings, I was no longer a prisoner.
I was freed from confinement, of liberty of speech and sentiments. I could feel for the cause of freedom, but I dare not say

[23]Prescott capitulated on 19 November 1775.

a word in presence of my superiors, nor any British subject, although the articles of capitulation were signed in my presence, and my eyes beheld the trait. I was still on board of a British vessel and under the command of British subjects; and by the power of Omnipotence alone, I should be freed from thraldom and an insurmountable situation which I had long been in. Although I had not been laboring under that conflict, which often brings sorrow and grief into a prisoner's heart, yet I was absent from my friends, my country, and the cause of freedom. After the American officer left us and I was walking the deck, meditating on the wonderful events that had transpired since the sun arose, and was now setting, and what was to take place before it rose again, my mind was thrown into confusion in the sudden alteration of weather, and the proceedings of the officers on board. The Midshipman was sent for to go into the cabin. As soon as he came on deck, all the boats were ordered to be manned, and he with some of the other under officers went into them and left the vessel. By this time it was very dark, but the N.E. wind had ceased from blowing, and it was calm, which we had not seen for twelve days. In about half an hour, the boats returned. Where they had been and what for, I knew not, neither had I one desire to know. My mind would not have been so calm and undisturbed, if I had known they carried orders on board of vessels to heave overboard all the powder, and nearly all the provisions, and a number of other articles. One schooner had four hundred barrels of powder, and she was ordered to heave over three hundred and fifty of them, and all the rest of the vessels were to reduce their cargoes to no more than a sufficient ballast. That was soon related to me by the Midshipman who had disapproved of the proceedings after the articles of capitulation had been signed, that with many other things, kept my mind quite disturbed. At seven o'clock in the evening the wind came out from the N.W., in a perfect gale, and yet it did not drive one of the vessels from their anchors. I had to veer out about one hundred fathoms of cable, which is recorded in the 23d. page.[24] After the wind had shifted, General Prescott ordered the Midshipman to man the boat and go on board of every vessel, and tell them they are ordered by the General to make every preparation to get under way and follow the brig *Gaspie* down to Quebec. As soon as he had given the above orders to the Midshipman, he turned to me and said, "get the brig under way." As nearly one half of the seamen had gone in the boat, as the wind was so heavy she could not be rowed by less than six men, I then told him I had not men enough on board to weigh the anchor. He said, "take the soldiers." I told him I had no command over them. He turned round and seemed to disapprove what I had said, and looked angry, and ordered one of the Serjeants aft. I immediately ordered my men to the windlass, and asked some of the soldiers if they would take hold of the cable, which they did, and they began to heave.

While I was giving these orders, the serjeant came up on the quarter-deck and walked up to the General and said, "What is your will, Sir."

The General said, "Sir, you and your men assist in getting up the anchor."

The Serjeant said, "Sir, I have always obeyed your orders with pleasure, and I am now willing to do everything that is consistent to my situation, for you have told me, and all on board that we are prisoners of war, and you said many things to ameliorate our feelings. I am willing to die for my King and Country. I should die a shameful death if we fall into the hands of our enemies, if we should not succeed in making our escape. It is more than I can bear in giving my assistance in breaking the articles of capitula-

---

[24]Probably p. 56, where Prince had the cable cut.

tion which you have signed, and you have informed everyone in the fleet that you was under the necessity of making them all prisoners to the rebels."

At the close of his sentence, General Prescott drew his sword, and made a pass at him, and would have run it through his body, if the Brig at that moment had not make a violent plunge as the waves had risen to a great height. The Serjeant discovered his intention and sprung, but the General in making his stroke fell on his hands and knees and the point of his sword went an inch into the deck, and broke in three pieces. The General hurt himself considerably by the fall. As soon as he rose, he said, "put that rascal in irons."

As soon as he had given them orders about the Serjeant, I turned to the General and asked him what he was a going to do with the brig, and why he had ordered her to be got under way, and where he was a going.

He said, "you have heard me say where we are a going."

"Do you know that it is impossible to get under way without going on shore when it is so dark and such a gale?"

"She shall go down to Quebec, heave up the anchor."

I was then determined not to weigh the anchor, and went forward, and when she plunged into a sea and brought a heavy strain on the cable, I told them to slack, and three or four fathoms would fly out before they could stop it, although we had as many as twenty soldiers holding on the cable. This I continued until the whole shot of cable was out one hundred and twenty fathoms. General Prescott saw the situation in which we were placed, and said, "You are all rebels," and went into the cabin. The boat returned which was sent to order all the vessels to get under way, and told us there was not one which would move from where they was until daylight, for they should lose their vessels, and perhaps their lives. As soon as General Prescott received this information, he put on a more placid countenance, and in particular when he said anything to me. The hour had come when the Americans were to come and take charge of the vessels, but the wind was so violent I knew they could not come on board in their batteaus. My mind was crowded with doubt and perplexity, I could not leave the deck.

A few minutes after 8 o'clock, the boat was ordered alongside and manned. General Carleton came up and got into her and ordered her off, and she was soon out of sight. It came into my mind, he was a going to Quebec in that boat, and I was sure if he attempted to pass the fort at Sorrel they would all be killed. At that time it did not enter my mind there was a little Indian village at the mouth of a river that empties into the River St. Lawrence which forms a part of the island where Montreal is built upon. It contains but a few males and females, who cultivate the ground where they live and mix with no tribes or people. They had large bark canoes to fish in and go where they please. About twelve o'clock the boat returned to the brig without General Carleton.[25]

Soon after that General Prescott sent for me to go into the cabin and told me General Carleton was gone to Quebec, and an Indian canoe was a going to take him down to Three Rivers.[26] "Do you believe they will pass the fort at Sorrel in safety?" I then told him what my apprehension was if he was going past Sorrel in the boat he went from here in, that he would have been unsafe even with muffled oars, but now he could pass under the shade of the swamp, I had no doubt, in safety. He then said to me, "Sir, you are no longer my prisoner. Your conduct from time to time has

[25]Carleton made his escape in a whaleboat the night of 16 November 1775. Carleton to the Earl of Dartmouth, 20 November 1775, in K. G. Davies, ed., *Documents of the American Revolution 1770–1783* (Colonial Office Series), vol. 11, *Transcriptions 1775 July–December* (Dublin: Irish University Press, 1976), 185.

[26]*Three Rivers:* Trois-Rivières, on the northern bank of the St. Lawrence River and at the mouth of the St. Maurice River.

pleased General Carleton and me, much, and now if I can render you any service, I will do it cheerfully and with pleasure." I then told him I might meet with some difficulty in convincing the Americans I had been a prisoner, and if that should be the case, that he would say what was necessary which might be of great advantage to me. He promised to do it. He then told me the contents of the articles of capitulation, that all were to be sent to the Simsbury Mines,[27] and exchanged as soon as there was an offer made for the purpose. He then opened his trunk which contained many books of a valuable collection. "I will take out some French books which I set much store by, and you may have the remainder." I thanked him for his kind offer, and took about forty, which was not more than one third he offered me. The reason was I had no where to keep or put them. I then told him my apprehensions about Captain Pepper, how he had conducted himself towards me since I had the offer of a sailing master's berth on board the frigate on Lake Champlain, and since I had been as a Commander on board the brig, he would use all his endeavors to continue me as a prisoner. He told me, "not to give myself any uneasiness on that or anything else that would not secure my liberty." He then told me, "as I have no command over you, I wish you well, and may the Lord protect and prosper you wherever you are." "I thank you Sir, and wish you the same." As the wind continued to blow very heavy, the Americans could not get on board until nearly daylight, and then there was but three battalions of about forty men. The commander of the boat who came on board the brig soon became much exasperated and said to General Prescott, that he had brought himself into complete condemnation in destroying so much provisions and powder which he had thrown into the river, he saw floating on the water on his passage from the

---

[27]*Simsbury Mines:* Abandoned copper mines near Hartford, Connecticut, used as a prisoner of war camp.

Engraved for the Universal Magazine for A.Hinton at the King's Arms in Newgate Street.

A Perspective View of the City of QUEBEC, the Capital of Canada.

FIGURE 7. Christopher Prince spent the winter of 1775–1776 outside Quebec, among the Americans besieging the city.

shore on board the brig. "When the Colonel comes on board if he sees what I have, he will make you feel very unpleasant." Soon after daylight, many hundreds arrived, and when the boats returned many prisoners were carried a shore in them.

About twelve o'clock they came on board the Brig to take us into the boats. They ordered me in as one. I told them I had been a prisoner six months and had not been released for more than six hours, and you have restored me unto me my freedom.

"O, you have been named to us in particular, as an enemy to our country."

"Who had done that?"

"We had this order from Major Westervelt, who is at present the commander, and we must obey his orders."[28]

I then asked him if he would permit me to see Major Westervelt?

"I have no time to do that."

"Will you ask General Prescott some questions on this subject. Perhaps he will convince you that you are doing wrong in making me a prisoner as a British subject?"

He went down into the cabin, and in five minutes he came up and said, "you shall not be made a prisoner, I now appoint you as the commander of this vessel to take her down to Quebec." He then told me his name was Mott, and he was a Captain of a regiment in the American army.[29] "This information of your being an enemy to your country was given to Major Westervelt in my hearing, by a man whose name is Pepper. I am a going down to Quebec in this vessel and we shall have more conversation on this subject."

[28]Research indicates there was no Maj. Westervelt. Prince probably means Major General David Wooster, whom Montgomery put in charge at Montreal. Wooster left for Montreal the same day that Prince has his Maj. Westervelt depart, 5 May 1776, see below, p. 78.

[29]Edward Mott, Capt. 6th Connecticut Regiment.

Every person belonging to the fleet but Pepper and myself were sent on shore, but Pilots. In three days after the British surrendered, every vessel was filled with American troops, and we immediately sailed. We had many officers and men on board the brig. We had a remarkably quick passage to Quebec. We came to anchor three miles from Quebec where there was a cove we could enter, a complete place of safety against wind and ice. All the troops landed immediately. We stripped all the vessels and laid them up for the winter, as we knew it would set in very soon. The troops went down to Abrahams Plains about one mile from Quebec, a very high hill between the encampment and the city. I took all my things on shore and lodged in a house near the shipping. The snow was very deep which prevented me from going out much for ten days, and I did not like my lodgings as well as I wanted. On the tenth day the weather was pleasant, I went down to the encampment, Abraham's Plains, two miles. After I arrived I enquired for my friend Captain Mott. I was directed to the house and room where I found him and one of his Lieutenants. I had not been there more than ten minutes before Major Westervelt came into the room. It was the first time I ever was so near him. Captain Mott introduced me to him. In a few moments he said, "I am credibly informed you are an enemy to your country you was born in, and you must not live near the camp. You must go back to Montreal." I expostulated with him on his treatment to me without any just cause, for the man he had received that information from was as much a stranger to him as myself, and that he had been credulous in a great degree in believing everything he had said about me, and disbelieving everything that was said in my favor by General Prescott to Captain Mott, my only friend.

"Will you not believe what Captain Mott has said to you that General Prescott told him, that I had been a prisoner for six months, and that I preferred being a prisoner than to accept the office of Sailing Master in the British navy, which is as honorable a station as any man can be employed in? Does that prove I am an enemy to my country?"

"I believe Captain Pepper more than any one that was on board that fleet we took, and more, I would place as much confidence in him as any man in America."

"Very well, Sir, I see you remain incorrigible, and I cannot get you to relax in your opinion of me. I will not go to Montreal at my own expense. If I am a prisoner treat me as such, for you have gone too far already to answer for your abuse. Captain Pepper has got a family in Quebec, and I have no doubt his heart is there also, and I have no doubt but what he often sends letters into Quebec and gives them all the information they want about the situation you are in, and all the movements you are a going to make before they go into operation, and I am confident all his malice towards me proceeds from the offer that was made to me and not to him, for I know from what he said to me at the time, if he had the offer I had, he would have accepted it, and would now be one of your prisoners made on Lake Champlain. Nothing would have induced me to have given these sentiments towards that man to any individual on the face of the earth if I was not compelled as I now am to do it. I am an American born, and it is not you nor any man in the world can make me an enemy to my country. I now tell you Major to look out for I am now convinced Pepper is a suspicious character."

He then seemed to be cooled down, and said, "go to your quarters but I shall keep a look out for you."

On my return about a mile from the headquarters, I entered into a good looking farm house, where they could not one of them understand a word of English. I spoke all the French I could, which was sufficient to understand each other very well, and engaged my board there, at two dollars per week. His name was Badeau. It was a very amiable family. He and his wife must have been more than fifty years old. They had a son who lived with them, and his wife, but they had no children, and they were between twenty and thirty years old, and they had a daughter about seventeen years still unmarried. She was the handsomest girl I ever saw, but she was a cripple, having an inflammation in one of her legs. These five were all the family; a very large convenient house; they had a large stove nearly in the middle of the room which kept it very warm the coldest weather we had during the winter. There was much snow on the ground. He took a sleigh and went with me to my other quarters and took all my things to his own house, where I had a bed room, joining the room where the stove was, which was always kept warm, day and night, which made my situation as comfortable as it could possibly be.

Being thus situated, and nothing to do, I devoted my whole time in learning French. I was well assisted in books for this purpose which I received from General Prescott, among which was a French and English Grammar, the history of Telemachus, in French and English, all which made it impossible for me to have more useful books to aid me in learning the French language, and not a word of English spoke in the house. In 20 days after I entered that habitation, I understood every word that was spoken. I had some previous knowledge of that language, but it was very imperfect. And I was well provided with paper, pen, and ink, and another wonderful gift of Divine Providence cannot go unnoticed. I never was in such a pious family all the days of my life—although they were Roman Catholics. Three times a day kneeled down in various parts of the room to pray, and not a word was heard from one of their lips. It sometimes melted my heart, not that I approved of their religion, but I saw there was sincerity in every heart in the house but mine. The girl prayed four times a day. It often brought to my mind how I had been brought up, and

how I had bowed down at the mercy seat and could not live without prayer to God. The example and admonitions I had through
the summer had made serious impressions on my mind, which
prevented me from uttering but very few profane words—but no
inclination to pray. In seeing them pray every day without one
omission, it brought to my mind that I was not only obnoxious in
the sight of God, but even those with whom I lived. In fact, I often
saw that, from their countenances. Notwithstanding all these reflections and examples, never brought me on my knees while I
was there.

The winter had set in very severe, the river frozen over, and all
nature hushed into silence, except the wind which was often pen-
etrating every crevice. After I had been at Badeau's about a fortnight, I had an inclination to go to the headquarters and see my
friend Captain Mott. The day was pleasant. About ten o'clock I
set out on foot which was one mile. I soon came to the sentinels,
and told them where I was going, and who I wanted to see, and
they let me pass. I entered the house and went up stairs and found
Captain Mott in his room and several other officers. He sprung up
and took me by the hand, and said, "I am glad to see you, and I
hope Major Westervelt will not know you are here," and I had not
taken my seat more than a minute before he entered the room. As
soon as he shut the door he jumped up as much as two feet from
the floor five or six times, with his eyes fixed on me, and in such a
passion he could not speak. He stopped for nearly a minute, and
then came out with violent oaths, the first were, "you damn'd
rascal," which he repeated seven or eight times until he was out
of breath, and all this time he did not move his length from the
door, and then he jumped up again and struck his hands together,
and repeated the above words over again a number of times. He
finally was silent with his eyes still upon me.

I then said, "Major, have you done?"

"Done, no, I am thinking what I shall do with you."

I felt as composed and undisturbed, as if nothing had taken place, and said, "Major, I am very sorry in seeing one of my countrymen in such a passion. For several days I have felt very anxious for you and all my dear countrymen, in seeing bomb-shells bursting in the air over your heads."

"How can you see the shells where you are, at such a distance, and in that valley?"

"I do not live there."

"Where do you live now?"

"At Mr. Badeau's, about a mile from here, where I can see every shell that comes over the hill."

"You moved nearer the camp, O, you worst of all rascals, I will put you now under guard," and went to the door and opened it, and said to the waiter, "tell the Serjeant to come here."

I had a smile on my countenance and said, "Major, I wish you to tell me if any of my dear countrymen have been killed since you have come here?"

He did not answer me. I turned to Captain Mott and asked him the same question, and told him I felt so anxious for them I could not sleep, and for that reason I had come to see if they were alive and what was going on among them? Major Westervelt shut the door and said, "go to your lodgings, and stay there. If I hear or see you out of the house I will confine you, and you must have a pass or you cannot go there." He wrote one and gave it to me.

They told me there was but two or three killed and wounded, but they had sent the smallpox in some of the shells which had operated on a number of the soldiers. I returned home with a full determination not to leave the house to any distance unless I was permitted to do so. One day a brother of Mr. Badeau's came there, who had a family in the vicinity of Quebec near to the foot of the mountain. He had been in the Monastery preparing to be a Friar, but when General Wolfe took Quebec in the year 1759, all were dispersed from the Monastery, and after men have intercourse with females, they are not permitted to be Friars. He was a man of learning and piety, which was different from his brother and family, for they could not read nor write. As I was able to converse with him in French, in one of his visits to his brothers, he conversed seriously with me on the subject of religion, and said many serious things that made me listen with much attention to what he said.

I was unprepared to vindicate myself, why I did not give some evidence that I was a religious man. I told him I was brought up by pious parents who were Presbyterians, which religion differed from theirs in point of ceremonies and duties which we owed to God.

He said, "there is no denomination of Christians but what goes down on their knees before they go to bed, and when they get up in the morning, and render unto him a sacrifice of thanks, and plead for mercy, and you was never seen by any here to do it."

"How do you know but what I pray to God after I get into my bed?"

"Is God to be worshipped in such a way as that? Is that all the respect you owe to your Savior? O, for shame!"

I felt ashamed, and I did not know what to say. I candidly confessed I was a sinner, I was not so all my days, I had often prayed before I went to sea, but for many years I had been and still was a wicked creature, and I hoped God would forgive me. I then addressed every one in the room, "O, do forgive me! It gives me pleasure to see you pray. I wish I had a heart to do the same." I never saw such an alteration as there was in every countenance. They all smiled and some took me by the hand, and said, "my heart rejoices at what you have said, we do forgive you and we hope the Lord will forgive you all your sins." After that, the young woman would often come near me and kneel down and pray with her beads in her hands, and lift her eyes to Heaven, and remain there sometimes twenty minutes. I spent many days in learning her to read, and before I left there, she could read considerable. Mr. Badeau's brother became one of my best friends. Almost every day he would come there, although he lived more than a mile off. It was to teach me the French language, in the pronunciation and verbal expressions, which gave me all the instruction that any teacher could have done. The conjugation of verbs, singular and plural, past and to come, male and female, is full of conflict to any one learning the French language without a teacher. In that important information, he was the man who gave me all the knowledge I stood in need of. I lived in that house nearly five months, and before three months expired, I could speak the French language more grammatical than I could the English. My pronunciation was so correct many thought I was a Frenchman. Reading, writing, and translation were done with ease and correctness.

I must now go back and retrace some important occurrences that took place soon after I left Major Westervelt the last time. A day or two after I returned home I wrote a letter to my Father and sent it to Captain Mott, unsealed, by Mr. Badeau, who went to the Head Quarters very often to carry them some produce of his farm. I requested Captain Mott to read my letter, and if he had no objections to its contents, to seal it, and send it on the first opportunity. That letter was dated about the 12th of December 1775. Mr. Badeau often informed me of the prevalence of the smallpox in the American Army, which was spreading through the country, and told me of the arrival of Colonel Arnold from the province of Maine through the distant country to Quebec, with about four hundred men, who had all suffered much with fatigue and hunger. The house I lived in stood back from the road about six rods, with a pale fence from the road to the house. I often took a walk out with snow-shoes, which would not penetrate into the snow more than three inches. I only went to the barn, and a brook which never froze let the weather be ever so cold. About the 22d of December, I was returning one day, and saw a man passing the house under guard as a prisoner. I immediately recognized him to be Captain Pepper. I felt confused at the sight because he must have committed a crime. The next day I received a note from Major Westervelt, requesting me to go to Head Quarters for he wanted to see me. The day after, I went there. I felt confused in my mind from the time I received his letter until I arrived, for I could not imagine what he wanted of me. It was impossible to meet a man with more friendship than he showed to me. He took hold of my hand, and said, "I am glad to see you. Let everything that has passed between us go unnoticed and forgotten. I shall be glad to see you here as often as you can come. You shall always be welcome at my table." I told him I was much obliged to him for his friendship. It would never be forgotten by me. He then informed me what Captain Pepper had done. "I never was more deceived in any man in all my life. I had such confidence in him that I would have trusted anything which was connected with our present contest with England into his care. But he has been a traitor. He was detected in sending letters into Quebec, informing our enemy of the situation of our army, which are nearly all sick with the smallpox. He is now sent to Montreal as a traitor."[30] Thus

[30]Before discovery of Pepper's treachery, the Americans had offered him the command of a gondola. This, at least, is what Pepper's son, who apparently remained with Capt. Pepper when the rest of the family took up residence in Quebec at the time the British seized the *Polly,* reported upon defecting to the British on 10 April 1776. "A young man, named Pepper, came in this morning. . . . This young man's father was offered the command of a gondola." "Jour-

ended this interview, after telling him I believed Pepper had not deviated from his political sentiments.

On the 27th of December I went to Head Quarters again. I was informed they were a going to storm Quebec very soon. I told them I hoped they would have a storm below and aloft, which would keep them from the sight of their enemy. On the 31st of December, I was at the Head Quarters, and there I saw every exertion possible going on for the important result of the night. In the afternoon the weather thickened up, and put on appearance of a violent storm, and early in the evening it came on to blow and snow to a great degree. —O, the horrors of war! I saw many that day who were infolded in the arms of death before another rising sun, although the Heavens were covered with darkness. It brought joy into the heart of General Montgomery when he left his habitation with heroes on his right and left to guard him against those who wanted to take his soul from his body. He did not want to do that. All his desire was to hush their raving into silence. Although he was called a rebel, he was no Barbarian. He looked on the sorrows of his fellow creatures, with pity, looking to the captain of his salvation to put it in him to help them from plunging their bodies into an untimely grave stained with blood.

Before twelve o'clock that night, before the year 1775 ended in America, the soul of General Montgomery took its flight into the eternal world. While I was on my bed, asleep or awake, my mind was fixed on the important conflict which was then going on between my friends and foes. Early on the morning of the 1st day of January 1776, I went to the Head Quarters to hear the result of the preceding night: as soon as I entered the house I saw every face

---

nal of the most remarkable Occurrences in Quebec, from the 14th of November, 1775, to the 7th of May, 1776. By an Officer of the Garrison," *Remembrancer; or, Impartial Repository of Public Events. For the Year 1778* (London: J. Almon) 6 (1778): 26–27.

FIGURE 8. Christopher Prince reported the dismay in the American camp at the news of the death of Richard Montgomery during the New Year's Eve attack on Quebec.

covered with a gloom, and all I could do was to sympathize with them on this melancholy event. Many tears came from many eyes. General Montgomery is gone, he is gone, and some of our valuable officers are gone with him into the eternal world. They then related the capture of General Arnold and his men in the lower part of the city. There they were without any officer higher in station than a Colonel.[31]

Nothing of importance took place after that. I attended entirely in learning the French language, which I have already recorded.

I must not omit making some remarks of the kindness, attention, and friendship of the people I boarded with. About the middle of February, Lent commenced, and all their food was cabbage, soup, and fish, and not a mouthful of meat, butter, or hogs lard for forty days, and Sunday but seldom any food at all. But not so with me. Every day they cooked for me, either boiled or baked meat or fowls, and everything I wished to have. After the forty days expired, they altered their food, but they were much emaciated. And many other fast days followed which they strictly observed.

About the first of April, General Thomas arrived there and took command of the army. I saw him when he rode by my lodgings, and I recognized him at the first sight, for he and I were both born in the town of Kingston. He and my Father were near of age and remarkably friendly all their lives.[32] I went down to Head Quarters to see him, for I knew he would treat me as one of his

---

[31]Although most of his command was captured during the attempt to storm Quebec, and despite a serious leg wound, Benedict Arnold managed to escape. After Montgomery's death, Colonel Donald Campbell had the command of the American forces before Quebec.

[32]It was Maj. Gen. David Wooster who arrived at Quebec on 1 April. Maj. Gen. John Thomas (1724–76) arrived at Montreal in late April and at Quebec on 1 May. Thomas was born in Marshfield, Massachusetts, and practiced medicine in Green Harbor before moving to Kingston, which he made his home until his death.

sons; but his tedious journey had made him a little unwell, which confined him to his room, and I could not see him. I told Major Westervelt of my intimate acquaintance with General Thomas, and I knew he would rejoice to see me, for he always treated me with affection from a child, if I was to ask any favor of him, let it be what it may, and he would grant it.

"Is it possible that General Thomas is acquainted with you, and you with him?"

"It is so."

Major Westervelt then told me, "he was in hopes I would continue to remain among them, and take charge of the schooner *Polly,* I was taken in, and assist them in the conveyance of provisions and troops during the summer. I should be well paid for my labor, for they must have some vessels plying between there and Montreal."

I told him I would accept his offer.

He then told me, "that he wished I would take charge of the vessel then, and see that she was fitted up and go as soon as the ice left the river, to Montreal, and get a load of wheat and bring it down to Three Rivers where it would be ground into flour for the army."

I told him to get men and a pilot, and I would go immediately on board.

"They will call at your house tomorrow morning."

The following day I went on board, and set the people to work, and we soon had her complete. About the tenth or twelfth of April the ice began to break up and disappear.[33]

---

[33]Maj. Gen. Wooster mentioned Prince in a letter dated 26 April 1776, to Hector McNeill, at Point aux Trembles: "The Articles for the *Maria* with a Gunner were sent from this place yesterday. I have sent for Capn Goforth from Three Rivers, a very good man, to take charge of her—Prince, Pepper's Mate, I shall send after immediately." Clark and Morgan, eds., *Naval Documents of the American Revolution,* Vol. 4, 1259. At that time, a Capt. Tenyck was on his way to Point

Major Westervelt told me that he was a going to the State of New York to get a recruit to the army and wished to go up with me to Montreal. The day was fixed for my departure, and the same day we were informed there were three or four vessels in sight coming up to Quebec, and one had the appearance of a frigate.[34] Major Westervelt had a boat near the Head Quarters taking in his baggage to carry on board the schooner, but she was not ready, and he requested me to send my vessel off, and follow her with him in his boat. All that was done. I took leave of Mr. Badeau and family, and told them, I should not take but a few of my things from their house, as I did not want them then. I left my chest with all my books, one dozen and a half of shirts and cravats, my quadrant and charts, one pair of boots, and a great coat, which I have never seen since. About ten A.M., we took our departure in the boat. Several Captains and Lieutenants were in the boat with the Major, who was going with him to get more soldiers, as many had died with the smallpox, and many others could not perform their duties.[35] The weather was remarkably pleasant. As soon as we turned the point we did not see the schooner, for she had a fair wind which was much in our favor. We had a small sail in the boat, but all our dependence was on the oars, which could go against wind and freshet. That was the only reason why the Major took the boat, supposing he would get to Montreal long before the schooner. In the afternoon we heard a heavy firing at Quebec, believing that one of the vessels that was seen

aux Trembles in command of the *Polly*, with orders to take up suspected vessels and boats. James Lockwood to Hector McNeill, 25 April 1777, in *New England Historical and Genealogical Register* 30 (1876): 333.

[34]On 5 May, when Wooster was scheduled to leave for Montreal, the Americans heard that British warships were only a few miles below Quebec. Hatch, *Thrust for Canada*, 183.

[35]"At Quebec, Thomas found an army of only nineteen hundred, nearly half of them down with smallpox." Ibid., 182.

before we left there was a Frigate, and she was trying to kill some of the Americans. Night came on and we had not seen the schooner, and at daylight next morning she was not in sight. A little after twelve o'clock that day, we arrived at Three Rivers. The schooner had been there and stayed but a little while on account of her having a fair wind which would soon carry them up the river against a strong freshet, which always runs down that river in the spring of the year. We were much fatigued in the boat. We had to stay at Three Rivers until we got refreshed. And while we were there, an express came on informing us that several armed vessels had arrived at Quebec, and a large fleet of shipping in sight below. As soon as we felt refreshed, we took our departure for Montreal, where we arrived safe the following day. The schooner had arrived; she had a remarkable passage. We had not been there but a short time, before an express came that informed us a large force of English had arrived at Quebec, and had attempted to drive our army from their quarters. But they had not strength enough to overpower them, and they retreated slowly up the river and took all the sick soldiers with them, and every article they stood in need of. General Thomas was dangerously sick with the smallpox. As they expected a reinforcement to the British army, they continued their movement every day until they got to Three Rivers, where General Thomas died.[36]

I then began to reflect on my situation, that I could not return to Mr. Badeau's and get my clothes, books, and quadrant, which was a great loss to me, not less than one hundred dollars. As I had not been compensated for my labor and duty while a prisoner in the British service, I would apply to the agent in Montreal for that which was my due. He was a Deputy Paymaster permitted to remain there by General Montgomery to settle all accounts that

---

[36]Thomas died at Chambly on 2 June. Ibid., 210.

remained unpaid. I made out my account and carried it to him. He examined his books but did not find my name there, and told me he could not pay me any money unless I could prove my account. I then related to him all the particulars from the time I was made a prisoner, to the day of capitulation. He then told me if I would bring a certificate from any one that would justify him for paying me, he would do it. I then told him about Captain Pepper, and there was no one but him I could make any application to. "You get one from him, and I will pay you." I was almost sure I should not succeed in that, but I made the attempt. As he was not in close confinement I had easy access to him, but all in vain. When I entered his room, he did not treat me as one he ever saw before. After I stated to him my request, he treated it with contempt, and made many malicious expressions, and treated me as I was never treated before. I left him, and went to Major Westervelt's, and related to him all the particulars. He soon rose and said, "that man shall give you a certificate," and went with me to his house. As soon as he entered it he asked him why he had not granted my request? Pepper made but little or no reply to his questions, and he could not obtain a decisive answer. The Major then rose and said, "prepare yourself to go to the Simsbury Mines, in one hour" and went to the door and said, "come Prince, let us go."

Pepper then said, "Major if you will permit me to stay here, I will go with you to the Paymaster."

The Major then said, "comply with my request, and I will comply with yours."

We all went to the Paymaster's, and Pepper was very careful and particular in what he said, and I received my money which was about forty dollars.

Major Westervelt then told me he had heard some unfavorable news respecting our army, and orders had been given to build some Gun-boats at the head of Sorrell, in Chamberlé, and wished me to go and superintend them for the present, as I could not go in the schooner. I had a long conversation then with the Major, and told him many things had operated against me, and many in my favor, but one was, my Friend General Thomas was dead, if not, I should make immediate application to him to give me the command of one of the vessels on Lake Champlain, which I knew he would grant. The Major said, "you cannot be more profitably employed than in building them boats, for transporting baggage and everything else from the river St. Lawrence up to Chamberlé, and you will oblige me very much if you will go there, and I shall be there myself as soon as possible." I finally complied with his request. I soon arrived at Chamberlé with a letter from the Major. The man that the letter was directed to, took me to the place where they had commenced the business. One of the boats that was building I preferred to any of the rest and took charge of her in her construction. In three or four days after I arrived there, Major Westervelt came there and said, "he was informed our army had entered the mouth of the river Sorrel, and that the English troops had lately increased, which made it necessary for the American army to continue their retreat as fast as possible until they got to Chamberlé, and it was now too late to build boats for that river, and he was ordered on to Crown Point, and to send the vessels to St. Johns, and wanted me to go and take charge of the fleet if no one had been appointed to that duty. If there was a man, or men as commanders of the whole we would proceed on to Albany as quick as possible." There were several officers with him and we all went on to St. Johns, where we arrived very soon, as it was but three miles. A vessel was there ready to receive us, and we immediately set sail, and the next day we were safely landed at Crown Point, which was a remarkably quick passage. We stayed there but a short time, and proceeded on to Ticonderoga. There the fleet was lying and many men to work on board. A man by the name of Fosdick[37] was sent there as Commodore, and Commanders to every vessel, with a number of seamen.

OBSERVATIONS AND COMMENTS

There are a couple of discrepancies between Prince's account of his service on board the Gaspee *and the documentary record, but these discrepancies can be reconciled by making a couple of logical deductions.*

One discrepancy is Prince's failure to mention the presence of Sailing Master Ryall on board the Gaspee. *According to Prince, in October the* Polly *was moved to Montreal, where he was transferred to the* Gaspee. *The* Gaspee *was a six-gun brig, with a complement of thirty men. Its officers included Lieutenant William Hunter, Midshipman William Bradley, and Sailing Master Maltis Lucullus Ryall. Sometime in August or September, Hunter and several crewmen were sent to man a schooner at Fort St. Johns. When they were taken prisoners there by the Americans on 2 November, Hunter had with him two officers and ten seamen from the brig.[38] Prince says that General Prescott put him in charge of the* Gaspee *until the officers might return, that he and a midshipman were the only officers on board, and that he was in charge when Ethan Allen was sent on board as a prisoner. This accounts for Midshipman William Bradley, but not for Sailing Master Ryall. In his testimony given on 14 February 1776 to the American General David Wooster concerning Allen's treatment on board the brig, Midshipman William Bradley stated that in "pursuant to Orders of Capt Ryall, who then commanded said Ship," he put leg*

---

[37]I.e., Jacobus Wynkoop.
[38]Lt. William Hunter to Vice Admiral Samuel Graves, 16 December 1775, Clark and Morgan, eds., *Naval Documents of the American Revolution*, Vol. 3, 128–29.

irons on Allen.[39] *"Capt Ryall" is clearly Sailing Master Ryall. And in Allen's account of his captivity, published in 1779, he says the captain's name was "Royal," more likely a mistake for "Ryall" than for "Prince."*

A second discrepancy is the failure of Ethan Allen to mention Christopher Prince. Allen writes that the captain was not an "ill natured man" and that Midshipman Bradley generously shared food with his prisoner.[40] *Prince tells the same story of Bradley, but says that he, too, shared his food with Allen.*

An examination of the sequence of events suggests a solution to reconciling these discrepancies. Allen was captured and sent on board the Gaspee *on 25 September 1775, where he was kept for about six weeks. Prince reports that it was in October that he was ordered to the* Gaspee, *and that Allen remained on the brig only a few days. It seems probable that Prince is mistaken that he was in charge of the* Gaspee *when Allen was captured. Rather, Sailing Master Ryall was in command at that date. Then late in October Ryall was needed elsewhere, and Prince was transferred to take his place. Allen, who had already been on board many weeks, was removed a few days after Prince took command, and, hence, had little reason to refer to him in his own narrative.*

If Prince's account of Ethan Allen's imprisonment is interesting because of the way it serves to verify Allen's own account of his treatment as a prisoner, Prince's account of the capitulation of Montreal and its aftermath is even more valuable because of the minute detail he provides that is not found elsewhere.

Until the discovery of Prince's narrative, the only circumstantial description of the battle at Longueuil known to historians was a rather jaundiced account by a Monsieur Sanguinet, a French-speaking

[39]Depositions of Crew Members, HM Brig *Gaspee*, 14 February 1776, in Clark and Morgan, eds., *Naval Documents of the American Revolution*, Vol. 3, 1272–73.

[40]Allen, *Narrative*, 10–11. See appendix 2.

resident of Montreal.[41] *Prince's description of the British procedures in the engagement at Longueuil accords exactly with standard British amphibious tactics, including the building of flat-bottomed boats designed to carry forty soldiers and the employment of flags to signal the boats to advance or withdraw.*[42] *Prince's account is more detailed than, but consistent with, Sanguinet's. Some descriptions mirror each other closely. Both agree that the British had some forty boats. Sanguinet calls the rocks onto which the canoes were swept by the French word* battures, *a specialized term meaning "breakers" or "shelf of rocks." Prince describes the location as "a high and very steep rock on every side." But Prince's descriptions are much more specific than are Sanguinet's. For instance, from Prince we learn the details of the flag signals and come to understand that the reason the Indians' canoes were caught in the current and the boats were not is that those who rowed the boats faced the flag signals in Prescott's boat, whereas those in the canoes faced away from the signals.*

Prince's account makes one major departure from all other accounts of the battle, and here one suspects that Prince is in error, probably from mistaking what he observed from a distance. According to all other accounts, the Americans took two Indians and two Canadians prisoner from the rock.[43] *One of these latter Sanguinet identifies as Lacoste, a barber. This must have been the prisoner taken at Longueuil, characterized as a hair dresser, that Montgomery sent into St. Johns to convince the garrison to surrender.*[44] *Prince, in contrast,*

[41]M. Sanguinet, "Temoin Oculaire de L'Invasion du Canada par les Bastonnois," in M. L'Abbé Verreau, ed., *Invasion du Canada: Collection de Memoires, Recueilles et Annotes* (Montreal: Eusèbe Senécal, 1873), 65–66. See appendix 3.

[42]David Syrett, "The Methodology of British Amphibious Operations during the Seven Years and American Wars," *Mariner's Mirror* 58 (1972): 269–80.

[43]Richard Montgomery also reported two Canadian and two Indian prisoners. Montgomery to Philip Schuyler, 3 November 1775, in Force, *American Archives*, 4th ser., vol. 3, 1392–93.

[44]Harrison Bird, *Attack on Quebec: The American Invasion of Canada, 1775* (New York: Oxford University Press, 1968), 140.

reports that the Americans carried their Indian prisoners, of whom he implies there were many, across to the Montreal side of the river and set them free. In grateful response, the Indians abandoned Montreal the next day. According to Carleton, however, the Indians left him after hearing of the capture of St. Johns, which fell on 2 November.[45]

Prince's memoir agrees with what is known about the British withdrawal from Montreal, but provides many new details. Again, Prince's memoir is important because it is one of very few accounts by someone actually present. In Carleton's dispatches to England, he reports that contrary winds delayed the British vessels retreating from Montreal several days before Sorel. Prince's narrative confirms this.[46] On 15 November the Gaspee reconnoitered the American fort at Sorel, but it came under such heavy fire that it had to turn back with the rest of the flotilla. There is some historical question as to how formidable the American artillery position at Sorel actually was, but if the Americans were bluffing, they succeeded in fooling Prince. That afternoon, according to American sources, Ira Allen delivered on board the Gaspee an ultimatum from Col. James Easton, Continental Army: "Resign your Fleet to me immediately without destroying the Effects on Board . . . , to this I expect your direct and Immediate answer. Should you Neglect you will cheerfully take the Consequences which will follow."[47] According to Prince's eyewitness account of this exchange, an American officer—Prince did not know it was Ira Allen—came on board under a flag of truce and asked to see General Carleton. But General Prescott insisted that he, himself, had full authority to negotiate. The American officer gave Prescott the proposed conditions of capit-

---

[45]Carleton to Earl of Dartmouth, 5 November 1775, in Davies, ed., *Documents of the American Revolution*, 11: 173.

[46]"The 12th one of our armed vessels ran aground which occasioned a considerable delay; in the evening the wind failed us near Sorel and became contrary for several days." Carleton to the Earl of Dartmouth, 20 November 1775, in Davies, ed., *Documents of the American Revolution*, 11: 185.

[47]Quoted in Hatch, *Thrust for Canada*, 94.

ulation and Prescott asked for an hour to give an answer. The American returned at the appointed time and Prescott demanded changes to the conditions; but when the American firmly refused to alter them, Prescott gave in and consented to turn over the fleet at eight P.M. that night. That evening Prince observed the British break the conditions by heaving overboard from all the vessels the powder and nearly all the provisions. Montgomery, himself, complained of this: "I hear Carleton has thrown a great quantity of powder into the river. I have desired a severe message to be delivered to him on that subject."[48] According to Prince, Prescott then gave orders for all the vessels to weigh anchor and to attempt to escape to Quebec, but was prevented by a gale of wind. This attempt having failed, Carleton escaped in a boat, disguised as an ordinary civilian.

---

[48]Montgomery to Gen. Philip Schuyler, 19 November 1775, in Force, *American Archives*, 4th ser., vol. 3, 1683.

CHAPTER THREE

New York

Smallpox and *Chevaux-de-Frise*
July–August 1776

HISTORICAL CONTEXT

In 1977, after a worldwide effort to eliminate the disease, the World Health Organization isolated the last naturally occurring cases of smallpox in the world. Throughout most of history, smallpox had been among the most dreaded of afflictions. Caused by a virus carried from person to person in water droplets expelled from mouth and nose, the disease was highly contagious. Symptoms appeared ten or twelve days after exposure, beginning with aches and a fever of 103 or 104 degrees Fahrenheit. Within a few days, a pimply rash developed, first on the face and then elsewhere. In the course of a week, the pimples increased in size and filled with pus. Over the next few weeks, scabs formed and fell off, leaving patients, if they lived, permanently disfigured. Those who survived would not contract smallpox again, for they had developed antibodies that made them immune to the virus.

Eighteenth-century medical practitioners recognized that smallpox was contagious, although, lacking a germ theory of disease, they did not know the mechanism of contagion. To prevent the spread of the deadly disease, communities isolated smallpox patients in hospitals or "pest houses." In 1796, Edward Jenner, an English physician, developed a vaccine that prevented the disease. Earlier, however, in the 1720s, some American doctors began inoculating individuals by introducing into a cut in the skin of a healthy person pus from a smallpox victim. Usually a mild case of smallpox resulted, leaving the person immune. In a small percentage of cases, however, inoculation proved fatal. General George Washington ordered the entire Continental Army inoculated in 1777–78.

Christopher Prince recovered from his own case of smallpox in the summer of 1776 in time to become involved in the defensive preparations of New York City.

On 8 July a conference of general officers of the Continental Army named a number of merchant ship captains to see to the sinking of navigational obstructions in the Hudson River. They sought to impede British use of the river, by which the enemy could outflank the American forces at New York. The obstructions were to be sunk between Fort Washington on the island of Manhattan and Fort Lee on the New Jersey shore.[1] Some of the obstructions were to be vessels sunk in a line. The vessels were to be fastened together at the stern, two by two, by long timbers. Projecting upward from them at an angle were affixed heavy timbers with iron tips, designed to pierce the hulls of any ship passing over them. Major General Israel Putnam described the obstructions as follows: "The two Ships' Sterns lie towards each other about seventy Feet apart. Three large Logs, which reach from Ship to Ship, are fastened to them; the two Ships and Logs stop the River 280 Feet."[2]

[1]W. W. Abbot, Dorothy Twohig, et al., eds., *The Papers of George Washington, Revolutionary War Series,* Vol. 5 (Charlottesville, Va.: University Press of Virginia, 1993): 238. For a detailed history of this attempt to block the river, see Lincoln Diamant, *Chaining the Hudson: The Fight for the River in the American Revolution* (New York: Carol Publishing Group, 1989), 38–54.

[2]Putnam to Maj. Gen. Horatio Gates, 26 July 1776, quoted in Diamant, *Chaining the Hudson,* 49.

*In the meantime, on 12 July, HMS Phoenix, HMS Rose, and
three tenders penetrated the Hudson River. Untrained townsmen
assigned to the city's south battery fired the cannon at the passing
enemy vessels. Because one gun crew failed to sponge out their gun
after firing it, as they loaded the next charge, the gun went off prematurely, killing or maiming several of the amateur gunners.*[3]

*On 5 August Washington informed the president of Congress that
hulks and* chevaux-de-frise—*submerged navigational obstructions
in which heavy timbers fastened with iron tips project at an angle
beneath water level in order to pierce ships' hulls—were in place and
would be sunk as soon as possible.*[4] *The first of the hulks to be sunk
were actually sunk that day or the day before. Vice Admiral Lord
Howe's secretary on board the British fleet observed the hulks being
towed into place on 4 August.*[5] *In a letter dated 4 August, an anony-
mous writer reported that "last night four ships, chained and boomed,
with a number of amazing large* chevaux-de-frise, *were sunk close by
the fort, under the command of General Mifflin."*[6]

*On 6 August Brigadier General Thomas Mifflin wrote Washing-
ton that he had allowed the "artists" who were sinking the obstructions their own way, without interference, but in the future would
"watch and direct their movements." Mifflin objected to the plan of
sinking the vessels in linked pairs because it involved "the most
abstruse problem in hydraulics to determine of what size the several*

---

[3]"We had six fine fellows killed & 4 or 5 wounded at our Grand Battery,
thro' mere Carelessness, or Ignorance. For, neglecting to swab ye Cannon at all,
or doing it improperly, the catriges took fire, and ye fatal Accidents ensued."
Solomon Drowne, M.D., to Sally Drowne, 13 July 1776, in *New York City during
the American Revolution* (New York: Mercantile Library Association of New
York City, 1861), 100–101; see also Peter Elting to Capt. Richard Varick, 17 July
1776, ibid., 102–3.

[4]Abbot, et al., eds., *The Papers of George Washington, Revolutionary War Series*, 5: 568.

[5]Edward H. Tatum, ed., *The American Journal of Ambrose Serle, Secretary to
Lord Howe, 1776–1778* (San Marino, Calif.: Huntington Library, 1940), 54.

[6]Peter Force, *American Archives*, 5th ser., vol. 1 (Washington, 1848): 752.

ports or holes should be in vessels of different tonnage & construction in order to their sinking at the same time—If one sinks before the other" he observed, "We risque as Yesterday."[7] In fact, as Prince reports, although one pair of his hulks went down together, as planned, of the other pair one hulk sank more quickly than the other, causing the two to part and turn out of the intended orientation. Major General William Heath confirmed the mishap in these words: "Some of the hulks, which were strapped together with large timbers, separated going down. A passage was left open for vessels to pass through; and the British, as it was proved afterwards, found the means of knowing where it was, and of passing through it."[8]

Just before the British landed on Long Island, their warships occupied every water passage out of New York City. British troops, having landed on Long Island on 22 August, defeated the American force stationed there and drove it into the confines of Brooklyn Heights on 27 August. Through the night and early morning of 30 August, Washington withdrew his force across the East River to Manhattan. Contrary to Prince's account, the American troops executed the withdrawal across the river without loss.[9]

---

[7]Abbot, et al., eds., *The Papers of George Washington, Revolutionary War Series,* 5: 580.

[8]William Abbatt, ed., *Memoirs of Major-General William Heath by Himself* (New York: William Abbatt, 1901; reprint ed., New York: New York Times and Arno Press, 1968), 40.

[9]"Even the American rear guard under Thomas Mifflin made its way to the boats before the British troops could attack." John R. Alden, *A History of the American Revolution* (New York: Alfred A. Knopf, 1969), 267.

The smallpox raged here [Ticonderoga] in a violent manner. There was a pest-house provided for every one that was taken with it, a little distance from the town. I did not feel alarmed on account of the complaint about myself, for I was told by my Captain once when I was a boy, laying at Martinique, that he was sure I had the smallpox. There I was sick for some time, and I was not acquainted with the complaint enough to know whether I had it or not. And many times after that I was much exposed to it and never took it. No one could be more so than I was in Canada at Mr. Badeau's, for it was thick round me on every side. In a family near where I boarded a young man was taken with it which I went to see every day, until the pock turned and he was nearly well. That, with many other exposures convinced me I had it in the island of Martinique. One day I took a walk out to the Pest House about half a mile from the landing. Many were there in different stages of the disorder. I did not enter the house, but passed it very near. Nature compelled me to go out of the road a little distance, and entered some underbrush, where I remained some time. When I rose to go away, I heard an uncommon noise of rattling very near me on the right hand, and looking down from where I stood I saw a RattleSnake coiled up with his head about eighteen inches above his coil leaning towards me. He was about eight feet from where I was, and where I had been for fifteen minutes. I was so confounded at the sight I did not know what to do, for I had often heard of that venomous creature, but had never seen one before. I fixed my eyes on him and retreated backward until I considered myself out of his reach unless he sprung three times his length. I dare not take my eyes from him until I considered I was safe let him do what he would. He did not alter his position. He ceased his rattles, and rather inclined to draw his head within his coil. My mind began to be composed in respect to the dangerous situation I had been in, and took my eyes from him to examine his size and length. I considered him to be six inches in circumference, and his coil as he then laid would nearly fill a peck measure. I then wanted to see his length. I took my eyes from him and looked around me not more than two seconds, before he turned his head round and drew out his length, and moved off very slowly, and I was sure he could not have been less than six feet long. He was soon out of my sight. It was some time before I could move from that place. Serious reflections came into my mind while I was meditating on the perilous situation I had been in. My mind was filled with horror and amazement. I lifted my eyes to Heaven and thanked the Lord who had delivered me in a wonderful manner from death, yea an awful death which had been within eight feet of my body not less than ten minutes, and he was not permitted to go one inch nearer, by the Preserver and Protector of my body and my life. I could not dismiss those feelings while I was returning to the landing, and I did not want to do it, for the Lord alone had often delivered me from seen and unseen dangers, which had kept me from death and an awful eternity.

That kind interposition of Divine Providence brought to my mind many others that had brought me within a hair's breadth of death: and one was in a voyage once to St. Lucé,[10] where I fell from the upper deck of a large brig into the bottom of the hold, one tier of hogsheads excepted, in a dark night, and all hands asleep. There was a protecting hand of the Almighty which saved me from death, although I was in the arms of death for some time.

As the fleet was laying between Ticonderoga and Crown Point on account of the smallpox, I did not board them. They were nearly ready to proceed on to Fort St. Johns. We soon took our de-

---

[10] *St. Lucé:* Saint Lucia, French West Indies.

parture to Lake George, where we arrived in a wagon with all our baggage. Major Westervelt conducted all the business connected with our journey. He had ordered a boat to take us across the Lake, which was an open Shallop, already to receive us, which soon landed us on the opposite side of the Lake in safety. We was there but a short time before we had a conveyance to Albany through a long tract of woods, and not a house in sight for many miles, and a number of places trees had fallen across the road which prevented us from going on for many hours. After many hindrances and fatigue, we arrived at Albany. The Major took me to a house where I was to remain until I could get a passage to New York. The Major soon called on me and told me a vessel was going to New York, and he had provided a passage for me and wished me to go on board, and gave me a letter to Messrs. Broom and Sands, and several others, and said, "they will all be your friends, and I shall be there in a few days, and you shall not be out of employ."[11]

I went on board, and found by the information of the Captain, that Major Westervelt had put on board a ham and other provisions for my passage. We had not been long from Albany before I was taken unwell. I was stupid and sleepy, but no fever or pain. I continued so until the day we arrived at New York, which was three days passage. On that day I was taken down with a violent fever and very sick. They landed me at the Old Slip, and took me

---

[11]Wooster arrived in New York City by 17 June and set out for Philadelphia on 20 June. George Washington to John Hancock, 17 June 1776, and 20 June 1776, in Abbot, et al., eds., *The Papers of George Washington, Revolutionary War Series,* 5: 22, 57. "Broom and Sands" may be John Broome and Comfort Sands, both of whom were members for New York City of the New York Provincial Congress, and the latter of whom, at least, was an active member of the New York Committee of Safety. Prince later signed on to serve in a New York privateer belonging to Broome. See note 17, below.

to Mrs. Thompson's, who kept a boarding house, and two or three of the passengers went there with me. As soon as I entered the house I requested them to show me the room where I was to lodge in for I was unwell. A Miss Savage, a daughter of Mrs. Thompson's, conducted me to a room, as soon as I entered it I requested her to bring me a glass of wine and water with a piece of toasted bread in it. I waited for it as I supposed an unreasonable time and went below and told them I was sorry they would not let me have what I wanted, and got into a passion, and said many things which made some of the boarders smile as they were going to sit down to dinner. I saw Miss Savage toasting the bread, when I entered the room. I stood by her, waiting for it until I was out of all patience. It is an hour since I asked you for a glass of wine and water, and I have not got it yet. I am sorry you are such an unfeeling girl. She smiled and said, it is not more than five minutes. I left the room and went upstairs and threw myself on the bed. She soon followed me and gave me the glass of wine and water, and sat down.

I asked her why she did not go to dinner.

She said, "you are too unwell to be left alone."

"Who are you?"

"I am Mrs. Thompson's daughter."

"What is your name?"

"Amelia Savage, I am nineteen years old. My father has been dead for many years, and my mother married a man by the name of Thompson, and he is dead, and she is now a widow."

I told her I was afraid I was a sick man but I did not know what the matter was.

"I know you are sick, and I cannot leave you alone."

I undressed, and turned in, but she would not leave the room. When night came on, her mother wanted her to go to bed and she would stay with me, but Amelia would not do it, and stayed there all night. I was taken with a severe relax,[12] which kept me in motion nearly all the night. She would often say, "O, I wish it was daylight. I would go and get a Doctor." I got asleep, and how long I do not know, but she awoke me and said, "you have got the smallpox, your face is full, and I must go for a Doctor as soon as possible." She soon left the room and a Doctor came and said, "you have got the smallpox, and you must be immediately carried down to Mantelezure's Island, at Hurlgate,[13] at the Smallpox Hospital." At ten o'clock I was sent on board the boat, which took me there in a short time.

As soon as I arrived I was carried up stairs into a room, where I remained more than four weeks. The complaint increased to that degree, they had no hopes for my recovery, so much so that they made a coffin for me three days before the Pock turned. That night it turned, my nurse was sitting by me, expecting every minute that I should expire, which continued until twelve o'clock, as he told me afterwards. "For a long time you was a struggling at a great degree, and sometimes you did not breathe for nearly a minute: expecting for some time that every breath you drew was the last, and this you continued until about twelve o'clock, and all at once you lay entirely still and almost lifeless, but your breath was soft and regular and I was sure you would recover, and I went down and told the Doctor what I believed." This he told me after I had recovered. I then told him the situation I was in that night. I was placed under a sand bank, and there was a number of people over me throwing down sand that often covered me. I then struggled until I got my head above the sand and breathed. But they continued shoveling it upon me until I thought it would be im-

[12]Diarrhea.
[13]*Mantelezure's Island:* Montresor Island, today called Randall's Island, in the East River. *Hurlgate:* Hell Gate, a narrow part of the East River, New York, New York, between Long Island and Manhattan Island.

possible for me to get my head out and fetch my breath. And the last struggle I made, I was sure it would be the last, for my strength was nearly gone. They stopped; I looked up to them and they all laughed and went away, and I was so exhausted I could not move, and fell asleep, and there it ended. I had lost my reason in part before I left Mrs. Thompson's and everything that transpired there and after I got to the hospital was as familiar to me after my recovery, as anything that had ever transpired in all my life when I had my reason. It was nearly a fortnight after I was well enough to go out and play ball, before I was permitted to leave the hospital. I thought I was as well as I ever was, and begged the Doctor to let me go, but he would not. "You are not well enough to go," (as he told me afterwards) because my mind was unsteady and it would have been unsafe for me to have mixed myself with the world, which eventually proved of great advantage to me.

One particular circumstance occurred in the time of sickness that disturbed my mind very much, and made me do and say many things that were very improper. The room I was in being papered with the likeness of men, women, and children, often disturbed me, supposing they were alive and my enemies; thinking sometimes they were approaching me to take my life. Notwithstanding my body was filled with pock in such a degree I could not have anything come near me but linen, yet I often jumped out of my bed and go round the room beating those figures until I supposed I had conquered my enemies. In doing this one time, my nurse entered the room and found my hand very much injured, blood running from almost every finger. In one corner of the room was laying an uncorded bedstead, and I saw a woman open a trap door near where the bedstead lay, and took a women up, and ripped open her belly and took out a child, and threw the knife at me, and took a part of the bedstead and put the woman's head between the two parts, and hung her down the scuttle, and went away. I got up and moved the bedstead and let the woman drop and shut down the scuttle. I went down stairs into the Doctor's room where he was sitting and took his sword hanging by the side of the wall, and went into the kitchen above ground, and drew the sword to run through a woman standing there making bread. The Doctor had followed me, and while I was making that attempt he took hold of my arm, and stopped me from killing her, and asked me, what I was going to do. I then told him all the circumstances that had taken place. He then took me upstairs and moved me into another room, where there was no paper on the walls.

After I got well enough to go out, the Doctor would ask me every day if I still believed a woman was killed in my room. I told him, yes. This he continued to do for ten or twelve days. One day he asked me this question, I asked him if he would let me go into that room for I wanted to see if there was a scuttle and bedstead there which he refused for three or four days, and I often went and looked into the key hole as it was locked. I finally told him I began to think that the murder of that woman was an imaginary thing, and I did not believe it to be true.

"Do you think so?"

"Yes I do."

"If you believe so, I will go and show you the room."

I told him I did not want to see it, I was fully convinced that all I had thought or said on the subject was wrong.

He then said, "get your things ready, for you may go to New York tomorrow."

After I arrived at New York, I went to Mrs. Thompson's as my boarding house, and then delivered my letters of recommendation which were given to me in Albany by Major Westervelt. These letters contained everything necessary for my recommendation or they would not have been noticed as they were. As soon as they were read by Messrs. Broom and Sands, they said, "we have had previous information from Major Westervelt about you, but as we did not see you, we concluded you was not in New York." They soon saw where I had been by my face, which was full of the marks of smallpox. I then informed them of the situation I had been in which prevented me from delivering the letters before. After asking me many questions, they said, "we have many things to do connected with a seafaring life which is out of the power of Landsmen to perform, and one is, we are going to sink four ships up the North River[14] to prevent if possible English ships of war going up to West Point. These ships are to be made Chevaux-de-frise. We do not know all that is necessary for that construction, but that will be performed by Mr. Brown, and Midwinter. Mr. Brown acts as agent for us in all the important duties connected with machinery, and Mr. Midwinter as boss carpenter. Four ships have been purchased by us for this purpose." They then stated the situation they were in, that all their spars and rigging were on them which must be taken away. One of the vessels was a prize ship of seven hundred and fifty tons. The other three were not less than three hundred tons. And as I had to work a part of the time nights as well as days, they would give me one dollar per day, and one for every night I should be necessarily employed. And that they would allow me eight seamen, and the rest must be landsmen. And then gave me a line to Mr. Brown, who would show me the ships, and would superintend all the business. The following day I commenced that important work, and immediately began to unrig the vessels, which were all brought at Crane Wharf, so that all the labor could be under my inspection. In a short time they were all stripped, and all the masts taken

[14]*North River:* Hudson River.

out, but the foremast, in every ship. And while we were doing that duty, many tons of stone were put on board every vessel. In a few days Mr. Midwinter, the carpenter, came on board and informed me the Chevaux would be brought down, which he wished I would take on board as soon as I possibly could, as he wanted to place on the iron.

General Putnam was to give me all the help I wanted except the eight seamen. From eight to ten of the militia were sent on board every day, which were as many as I wanted. While I was fixing these ships, there was a large Ark Chevaux-de-Frise, a building at one of the shipyards. Our pieces of timber made for the Chevaux were about twenty two inches square, and about twenty six feet long, and on the outer end of each piece, iron was placed, on which could not be less than seventy-five pounds in the form of a plough-share. These pieces projected out from the vessels about fifteen feet with an elevation, and well secured on deck. Two ships were fastened together stern to stern about twenty feet apart with two sticks of timber about as large as the Chevaux, and one Chevaux between the two ships. This was done with all the ships fastened two and two. While we were thus employed and had got them nearly completed, news circulated throughout the city that there were two large ships and two schooners below, under full sail coming up to town, and soon discovered they were English ships of war. The south Battery was the place where there were any guns to protect the city. Many of the citizens went to the fort and got the guns in order before the ships got abreast of the town. I was ordered with my eight men to go to the fort. I did not know what it was for. We started and before we got half way there the firing commenced, and some of the shot from the ships were piercing the houses in every direction. As I was entering the Battery, I met a man with one of his arms shot off nearly up to his elbow. I asked him some questions, which he soon answered and said a number of men were laying dead on the platform. They then were abreast of the town, but so far off that nothing but cannon balls could reach the city.

As soon as I got on the Battery, I was requested to take one of the guns, which I did, and by the time I fired three shot the ships were out of reach. We then examined the men that were shot, and we found seven who were blown all to pieces by imprudence. The man I met with his arm shot off had the direction of one of the guns. After he had fired once, he hauled her in from the embrasure under the fort, and placed her fore and aft the platform. It was no doubt neither sponged nor wormed, for as soon as he put the cartridge in, and was ramming it down, it caught fire and took his arm off, and blew all of them men to pieces who stood before it. Their legs, arms, and bodies were all separated, so much so we put them all on two hand-barrows, and carried them up to the Bowling Green, and dug a hole and put all their remains in it and covered them over, where they remain no doubt to this day.

Many houses were very much injured by the shot from the ships. One of the ships was the *Rose* of forty guns, and the other was the *Phoenix* of thirty, and two tenders. They were soon out of sight as they had a fair wind. We all knew that we had enemies around us on every side, communicating to the British Army and Navy, everything that was going on relating to the war, and that it might be these ships had come in to prevent us from sinking those Chevaux-de-frise. But we were determined to do it, and in two days after the ships had gone up the river, we commenced our departure and hauled off into the North River. Such a sight was never seen in America as was seen in them ships, stern to stern fastened together. From bow to bow was not less than two hundred and twenty feet long, 21 Chevaux-de-Frise on each two ships, elevating 45 degrees. General Putnam asked me how many men I wanted to carry the ships up the river. I told him twenty, to weigh

The PHOENIX *and the* ROSE *Engaged by the* ENEMY'S FIRE SHIPS *and* GALLEYS *on the 16 Aug.ᵗʰ 1776.*

Engraved from the Original Picture by D. Serres from a Sketch of Sir James Wallace.

FIGURE 9. In New York City, Christopher Prince heard reports of the attack by American fire ships on the British warships in the Hudson River.

the anchors, and keep watch, and to tow the ships with boats ahead. He sent them on board with two Lieutenants. I lashed the four ships together, so that I could have the management of the whole, and that no separation should take place. We had but two masts standing in the four ships, on which we hoisted a foresail when we had any wind in our favor. But the flood-tide was the only time we could move up the river. The Ark-Chevaux-de-Frise came down and anchored near us. We were all loaded as deep as possible with stone ballast. As soon as the flood made, we weighed our anchors. Mr. Midwinter who had conducted all the carpenters business on board in the Chevaux-de-Frise, port-holes to let the water into the ships to sink them, was my carpenter and pilot. He was a man I esteemed very much. That night when the ebb made down, we came to anchor, called all the boats on board, set the watch, and took a little nap. The flood commenced again about three o'clock in the morning. I called all hands to weigh the anchors, but all the soldiers did not come up on deck. I asked the officers to order the men up, but they did not nor would not come up. I put my head down the gangway and told them the ships were sinking, and begged they would come up in a moment or they would all perish, and in less than a minute every one was on deck. I told them to take hold on the cable, and some of them swore and some grumbled, and it went on pretty well until the next night. We then came to anchor within a few miles of the place where they must be sunk. As soon as the flood made, I called all hands, and I could not get enough up beside my seamen to heave up the anchors. I told the Lieutenants, if they did not do their duty I would go on shore and go to New York, and tell General Washington, Putnam, or some one, of their conduct. They went below and talked with their men for some time before one would come up. But enough came to enable me to heave up the

Anchors, but many of them went down again into the hold, or between decks, in consequence the boats were weak manned in towing the ships. I could not refrain from speaking my feelings and sentiments to the officers who felt so unconcerned about getting the ships where we were to sink them, whose duty ought to be as faithful to the public as mine. They said, "Militia were an ungovernable set of beings, and it was out of their power to govern them." That eased my mind very much, and said no more on the subject. This tide commenced about four o'clock in the morning, and about nine we arrived at the place destination, which was about half a mile above York Island,[15] where the channel is narrower than any part of the river from New York to West Point. There was a large encampment on shore abreast of where we were a going to sink these ships, under the command of General Mifflin, and many officers had got there from New York, to see how the ships were sunk, and how I performed the duty committed to my charge and care. As soon as we got on the spot, I separated the ships and extended them across the river, and let go an anchor from the bow of every ship that secured them.

My desire was to sink the ships at slack water while they were in a correct situation. It was with difficulty I could get the soldiers on deck to assist me in mooring the ships in a proper position. They refused to come up and help us, at least ten or twelve. I told them we were a going to sink the ships then. "This is not the first time you have told us so, and we do not believe what you say," and some of them would not go on deck until they saw the plugs out and the water running in. We had two large boats, one was large enough to take all the soldiers on board to New York, the other was a pinnace of eight oars. I ordered the soldiers all out of

---

[15] *York Island:* Manhattan Island.

the vessels, and after they got into the boat, I asked the officers if they had got them all there, and they said they had, and went off. I ordered my men into the Pinnace, and everyone to be at the oars to take us on board when the ships were a going down. Mr. Midwinter was on board of one ship, and I on board of the other. After we had taken out some plugs we came on deck to examine the situation of each vessel, for as they were fastened together by string pieces, they must both go down at once, for if there was any difference of time they would separate. The two first were sunk within two seconds of each other. We sprung into the boat, while they were agoing down. They were beautifully sunk. The ebb tide then began to run. We went on board the other two ships and opened all the plug holes we could, for I was afraid the tide would drag the anchors, or part the cables, and bring the ships into an angular situation. Notwithstanding the tide bore upon us very heavy, we found they would sink in two minutes. I had a great coat in the cabin and ran down to get it, and when I entered the cabin, the water was half leg deep, and I saw one of the soldiers laying on the transom. I caught hold of him and hauled him off and told him to go on deck, and he would not, and when I went up, I saw the other ship was agoing down, and in an instant the cable parted from that ship we were on board of, which carried her bow round about thirty degrees before she struck the bottom. In about half a minute after I left the cabin we sprung to the boat, and the vortex was so great it was with difficulty they could prevent the boat from following the ship, although they sprung at the oars with all their might. My endeavor to save that man below brought us all in a perilous situation. She was the large ship of seven hundred and fifty tons. The torrent of water that rolled in upon her all around is indescribable, and the water that came from her gangway ascended nearly twenty feet into the air, which must have dashed that man to pieces against the quarter deck.

I got on shore about three o'clock P.M. I was met by many officers who saluted me in a very friendly manner for sinking those ships as I did. The Ark-Chevaux-de-Frise was sunk off the Point, about half a mile below us. I was invited to General Mifflin's tent, where I had a good dinner. And as I had not slept but very little for two nights, and very much fatigued, I laid down and slept until low water. We then went off and cut away the masts on board the ships below the surface of the water, so that they could not be discovered by any one unless there should be a remarkable low ebb.

I never saw a more faithful experienced man as a carpenter, and other qualifications than Mr. Midwinter was, so much so I consulted with him in many of our movements and duties. After he had cut away the masts, all our duties connected with fixing and sinking the Chevaux-de-Frise were finished. Mr. Midwinter and my men were all provided with tents and victuals during the night. I continued in General Mifflin's tent. My intention was to go to New York very early in the morning. I went down to the boat soon after daylight, where I found all my men, but Mr. Midwinter was not there. I sent some of my men after him up to the encampment. I saw some gun boats laying at anchor, a little distance from the shore which I knew had been up to annoy the English ships and prevent them if possible from coming down and frustrate our purposes in sinking the Chevaux-de-Frize's. I went on board of one of them, where I saw an awful sight! Blood and brains laying about the deck. They then told me they took up with them, two fire ships, and went above the English vessels close under the western shore, and after dark they went off into the river where the tide would carry them down to them without sails or oars. They had got very near them and set fire to the fire craft, and in five minutes four or five boats came from the ships and hove grapplings into them and towed them off from the ships

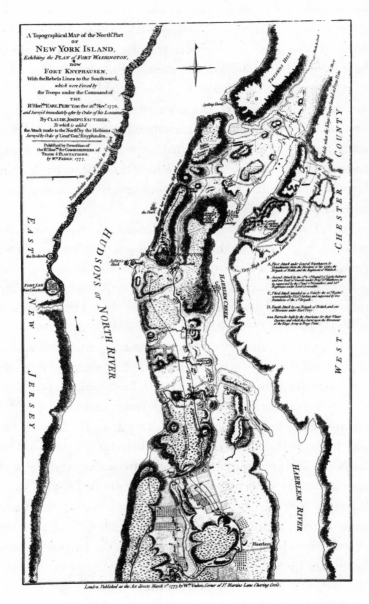

FIGURE 10. Northern Manhattan Island and the Hudson River.
Christopher Prince directed the sinking of ships to block
navigation between Fort Lee and Jeffery's Hook.

so far they could not set them on fire, which threw them in great confusion, for they towed them into their tract, which obliged them to go so near the ships they threw grenades into them, which burst and killed and wounded nearly half on board the boat, which was about one o'clock that morning.[16] This awful catastrophe produced feelings on my mind, which I never felt before. I got into my boat and went on shore meditating on the disposed will of Divine Providence. A state of despondency prevented me from putting all my hope and confidence in God, who alone was able to make us conquerors, and more than conquerors, over all our enemies. My men returned to the boat and said they could not find Mr. Midwinter. I then went up myself, and I could not find him. While I was conversing with some of the sentinels about him, a countryman was coming into the encampment with some produce from his farm. And while I was describing him in size and dress, the countryman said, at sun rise this morning I saw a man of that description get into a canoe, and go on board of the English ships. I thought it almost impossible it should be so, yet it soon proved to be true. I went to my boat and took my departure for New York. As I had eight smart men with eight oars, we got there about twelve o'clock.

For a few days after I settled my account with Broom and Sands, I was idling about the city, but I did not enjoy an idle life but a few days. Privateers at that time was all the ships of war in New York, and I did not know what was going on in any other port. At this time, there was a large sloop of eighteen guns fitting out as a privateer, called the *Harlequin,* Captain Shaw.[17] I see she

[16]On the night of 16 August, two American fire ships attacked HMS *Phoenix* and HMS *Rose,* destroying the latter's tender. See Clark and Morgan, eds., *Naval Documents of the American Revolution,* Vol. 6, 206–8.

[17]On 14 August 1776 the owners petitioned the New York Convention for a privateering commission for the sloop *Harlequin,* and three of the owners, John Broome, Thomas Crab, and Daniel Shaw, took out a privateering bond. The

would go to sea very soon. I went on board, she lay off in the East River. In conversing with Captain Shaw about going with him, he said all his officers were engaged, but none of them had as yet been on board to do their duty, and the sailing master in particular, and if I would enter on board as a master's mate, that office would be safe, and if the Sailing Master did not come on board, I should have his place. I entered immediately on those conditions, and took up my residence on board. She had but as yet but few men. When the time had arrived for our departure, as we were complete in everything on board. We heard that there was a large fleet below, and had entered within the Hook.[18] Captain Shaw then concluded to go through Long Island Sound, and that as soon as possible, and while we were getting a pilot to carry us through Hurlgate, we were informed an English Frigate had come to anchor near the Gate, which stopped all intercourse with the Sound. The next day we heard the English fleet had got up to the Narrows, which threw New York into great confusion. General Washington had about two thousand men on Long Island who were seen about sunset coming from Brooklyn Heights towards the ferry. A few were rapid in their retreat, but the main body slow. A number of boats were sent from New York over to Brooklyn. Before it was dark a heavy fog covered us in every direction, so thick during the night we could not see anything ten feet. Boats were crossing the river all night in getting the soldiers to New York, but that was almost impossible, for after they left one shore to the other, they could not see where they were going, either by wind or lights. If nothing prevented them, all would have been safely landed before daylight.

sloop is described as of about seventy tons, mounting fourteen four-pounders, and manned by ninety men. Daniel Shaw (ca. 1742–98), of New London, Connecticut, was named as the commander. Force, *American Archives*, 5th ser., vol. 1, 954.

[18] *The Hook:* Sandy Hook, New Jersey.

As we lay in the river where the boats passed every time they went or returned, but we could hear them sometimes a great distance from us. After the sun rose it was foggy. They could not make any more progress, and they had nearly a thousand men at Brooklyn. It continued so until eight o'clock. It then began to clear away, and soon as the fog was gone we saw the heights of Brooklyn covered with English troops, and as soon as they could see where they was and who they had to contend with, they rushed down to the landing. About three hundred American soldiers were still there and some boats which were filled, some of which plunged into the water to get into the boats which could not take them because they were so full. Some got hold of the gunwales and was towed across the river, and some were drowned, and those on shore were made prisoners. It was an awful sight.

Nearly all on board the *Harlequin,* officers and men, went on shore, and took their baggage with them, for they knew we could not make our escape into the Atlantic in the sloop. There were some of the marines and seamen on board did not know what they should do, or where they should go if they went on shore, and myself for one, for I was never in New York before, and entirely unacquainted with Long Island Sound and the sea-ports that bordered upon it, such as New Haven and New London. There were about twenty of us on board; I asked Captain Shaw what he was a going to do with the sloop; he said, "he was a going to take her into Harlem River and perhaps sink her, if he could not go through small Hurl Gate in safety from the British Frigate." I then asked him some questions about New Haven and New London, which he gave me such a description of, I preferred going to one or the other than to Philadelphia, where I had previously been, as it was such an interior port and so far from the ocean, I could not be employed in my occupation.

As the English troops had no field pieces, and nothing to annoy us, and had retreated from the shore, and secured themselves in houses and other places, we had nothing to fear from them, and it appeared that there was not more than fifteen hundred of them. We had as I have already observed, two thousand, but were principally militia, that made them incapable of contending with one thousand Englishmen. The Lord sending that heavy fog, and continued it so long, prevented nearly all from being made prisoners, and many numbered among the dead. This interposition of Divine Providence, could not go unnoticed by the greatest infidel.

Movements were making on shore to leave the city, drums and fifes sounding in every direction. We found ourselves unsafe by laying there any longer; we hove up our anchor and made sail, and before we doubled Corlear's Hook,[19] we saw the English fleet coming up, but we soon lost sight of them, and they of us. We soon passed Hurl Gate and entered Harlem Creek[20] and arrived at the place where she was to be sunk. We soon took out everything but her guns and some barrels of beef and pork, and sunk her.

[19] *Corlear's Hook:* Point of land on southern Manhattan Island, New York, on East River, opposite Wallabout Bay.
[20] *Harlem Creek:* The upper portion of Harlem River.

CHAPTER FOUR

The Connecticut Navy
September 1776–June 1777

HISTORICAL CONTEXT

In the hope of capturing several British supply ships reported to be sailing from England for Halifax, Nova Scotia, without an armed escort, the Continental Congress voted on 13 October 1775 to procure, fit out, and man two fast-sailing warships. Out of that small beginning grew the Continental Navy. Within four months of the original vote, Congress had appointed a naval committee to administer the Navy, authorized the construction of thirteen frigates, and sent to sea a small fleet. Because the Continental Navy was too small to protect the American coastline from British depredations, and because the Continental Navy served the purposes of the united war effort, individual states could not rely on it for merely local defense. Many of the revolutionary governments of the colonies (states, after independence was declared) established their own navies to protect their ports, coasts, and trade.

Eventually, eleven of the thirteen states possessed some form of naval force.[1]

Connecticut was among the earliest of the revolted colonies to establish a navy. In July 1775, months before the creation of the Continental Navy, the Connecticut General Assembly "Resolved that two Vessels ... be immediately fitted out, Armed and furnished, with Officers, Men, and necessary Warlike Stores, for Defence of the Sea Coasts in this Colony, under the care and direction of The Governor and Committee of Council."[2] *The Connecticut Navy's first warships were the brig* Minerva, *which the colony soon returned to its owner, and the schooner* Spy. *As a result of the General Assembly's determination of December 1775, the colony next purchased the brigantine* Defence, *which was armed and ready for sea in April 1776 under command of Captain Seth Harding, and contracted for the building of a ship that would be named the* Oliver Cromwell *after the Puritan leader who overthrew the British king in the British civil wars in the seventeenth century.*

Christopher Prince arrived in New London early in September 1776, just when the Connecticut Navy's newest and largest warship, the Oliver Cromwell, *was fitting out and recruiting seamen. She was a full-rigged ship, eighty feet on keel, with a twenty-seven foot beam. Built at Saybrook, she was launched in June and on August 20 arrived at New London to complete her fitting out.*[3]

The captain, William Coit (1742–[1802?]), had no reputation as an accomplished seaman, but had established himself as something of

---

[1] Charles O. Paullin, *The Navy of the American Revolution: Its Administration, Its Policy and Its Achievements* (Cleveland, Ohio: Burrows, 1906; reprint ed., New York: Haskell House Publishers, 1971), 315.

[2] Clark and Morgan, eds., *Naval Documents of the American Revolution*, Vol. 1, 714.

[3] Louis F. Middlebrook, *History of Maritime Connecticut during the American Revolution, 1775–1783*, 2 vols. (Salem, Mass.: Essex Institute, 1925), 1: 80.

a hero. *A graduate of Yale College, class of 1761, this New London merchant and sea captain had, during the autumn of 1775, commanded the* Harrison, *one of several armed schooners George Washington employed to intercept transports supplying British forces stationed in Boston. Before leaving service in Washington's fleet, he captured two provision vessels, as well as a forage transport and a fishing schooner carrying four Tory pilots who were waiting to direct British transports into Boston Harbor. "Tall, portly, soldierly in bearing, frank, jovial, somewhat eccentric and very liberal," Coit seems to have been popular with his crew, but had difficulty attracting able subordinates or skilled seamen.*[4]

Discontent among the officers and crew erupted in tragedy about New Year's Day 1778, when John Dennis, boatswain's second mate on the Oliver Cromwell, *struck seaman William Garrick of the* Oliver Cromwell *on the head with a hoe, fracturing his skull. Garrick later died, and during the last week of March, the Superior Court at Norwich convicted Dennis of murder and sentenced him to death.*[5] *Thus the ship lost two skilled seamen. During the course of the winter of 1777–78, many of the crew, unhappy about the quality of the officers, deserted, while the officers were displeased by Coit's inability to recruit and retain a crew large enough for them to put to sea. Several of the able officers resigned their commissions to go privateering. The most serious loss occurred when highly respected Lieutenant Michael Mellaly left in March. In April, hoping to improve the possibility of dispatching the ship on a cruise, the state council discharged Coit*

[4]Henry P. Johnston, *Yale and Her Honor-Roll in the American Revolution, 1775–1783* (New York: G. P. Putnam, 1888), 226; William Bell Clark, *George Washington's Navy: Being an Account of His Excellency's Fleet in New England Waters* (Baton Rouge, La.: Louisiana State University Press, 1960), 21–23, 37–45, 66–67, 80–85; quotation from Clark, 21–22.

[5]New London, *Connecticut Gazette*, 10 January and 4 April 1777; Clark and Morgan, eds., *Naval Documents of the American Revolution*, Vol. 7, 914, 1284–85.

and appointed Seth Harding to command. Most of the officers then resigned. In June 1777, Harding, having recruited a new crew, took the Oliver Cromwell out on what proved to be a very successful cruise.[6]

Captain Shaw then told me where I must go to Connecticut and New Haven. Before I left him, a man by the name of Wyer, a Lieutenant of Marines, 21 years of age, more than six feet tall, and otherwise well proportioned; he was an uncommon large man, very agreeable in his conversation, and had an excellent disposition. As I was a going away, he asked me where I was a going. I told him I did not know, but Captain Shaw had told me where, and how I could find New Haven. He then said, "I am a stranger to everybody and every part of the world. I was born in the country, and a part of my days brought up on a farm, and served my time at the Saddler's trade, and could not get my living there at that trade. I have left my father's house to earn my own living some how, and I am willing to see what I can do on the ocean, and that is your occupation. I wish you would accept of me as a companion." I told him I would, and Captain Shaw carried us across the creek, and landed us on Harlem side. It was nearly sunset, and we were fatigued and took up our lodgings. We went on our way very early in the morning. About eight o'clock A.M., we saw a number of troops but a little distance from us, in the road we had to pass. I stopped and said to Wyer, "we do not know whether

<hr />

[6]Middlebrook, *Maritime Connecticut during the American Revolution*, Vol. 1, 81–83, 88–91.

they are friends or foes, for we are so near the Sound. They may be English landed from some transport we have not seen." We stood for three or four minutes, and saw the officers looking at us and we were within pistol shot. They were exercising the men, and we were soon convinced they were Americans, and we went on and came up to them and they took but little notice of us for they were busy. We passed on by them about three hundred, and when we had got to the end of the whole, I saw my brother Kimball, an Orderly Serjeant.[7]

We recognized each other the first sight. For many years I had not seen him nor he me, as he was an apprentice to a man in New Bedford at the Mason trade, where he went when he was fourteen years old, and he was born two years after I was. He quit his duty for about five minutes to converse with me. I cannot now describe the feelings I then had in seeing one of my brothers engaged in such a laudable work, not only corresponding in our feelings and sentiments in respect to the freedom of our country, but informed me about our parents, brothers, and sisters, who was enjoying the blessings of health, all of which he had seen a few weeks past, and about the English leaving Boston for some other port and perhaps for New York.[8] I then told them of their arrival at New York, and in a minute we were surrounded by all the officers, who were entirely ignorant of their arrival. After we had related all the circumstances that had taken place, we separated and went on our way, in which they helped us much in our distance to the main road, where we wanted to go. As I had left nearly all my things at Badeau's, in Canada, and under no necessity of making any

---

[7]Kimball Prince served in the rank of sergeant in New York regiments. See *Record of Service of Connecticut Men in the I.—War of the Revolution. II.—War of 1812. III.—Mexican War* (Hartford: Connecticut General Assembly, 1889), 636; Frank A. Prince, *Princes: Records of Our Ancestors* (Franklin, Mass.: 1898), 37.

[8]British forces evacuated Boston and sailed for Halifax on 17 March 1776.

FIGURE 11. A view of New London, Connecticut, Christopher Prince's residence during his career in the Connecticut Navy and as a Connecticut privateersman.

addition, as I had one dozen of shirts and cravats, and some stock-ings, I could carry all I had in a handkerchief, except a surtout[9] that I had purchased, nothing more as the weather was warm, and Wyer had but a few articles. We walked off as fast as possible, and soon got the Sound all in sight. About four P.M., we saw a sloop laying in a harbor, and we went on board of her, where we found a man and boy, which was the ship's company. We asked them where we was.

They said, "the Blackrock."[10]

"Where are you bound?"

"To New London."

"When are you going to sail?"

"In an hour."

"What kind of a place is New London, is there any vessels?"

"Plenty, there is a large State ship of twenty nine pounders fit-ting for sea, called the *Oliver Cromwell*."

"Will you carry us there?"

"With pleasure."

We soon got under way with a fair wind, and the next day we arrived at New London.

After we got on shore we went round the town on every wharf where there was a vessel. I was surprised in seeing such a place. Many vessels were fitting for sea, and many coasters. We then went through the town, where I saw many elegant houses and many inhabitants. I soon saw it was a place for business of every kind, for seamen and landmen. We saw some Taverns, but I did not want to go there, or any of the boarding houses. After we had seen what we could, among which was the ship *Oliver Cromwell*,

---

[9] *Surtout:* A man's long, close-fitting overcoat.

[10] *The Black Rock*: The outermost point of Penfield Reef, 1.4 miles south of Black Rock Harbor, active with shipyards at the time of the Revolution, east of Fairfield, Connecticut.

which Captain Lattimore who carried us there had named, we went to a private house we had passed and noticed as a suitable place for us to put up at if they would receive us, or inform us where we could be accommodated in a private family. After we had entered it, we saw a middle aged woman and girl about nineteen years old, and asked them if they were willing we should stay there that night, and give us a supper and breakfast, for we was never in New London before, and had not seen one person we had ever seen before. The woman and daughter looked on each other without giving us an answer. I told them as we were strangers, they would oblige us much in letting us stay with them. If not convenient, I wished they would tell us where we might be accommodated in a private family. The woman then said, "I believe we can accommodate you for a few days." We told them it was not known to us how long we should remain in New London, and was very much obliged to her for letting us stay there that night. We then went on board the sloop we came in, and got our things and went to our lodgings. We stayed in the room where we was to sleep until we was called to supper, which was early in evening, just at candle-light. We there found a man, and another girl about fifteen years of age, and some smaller children. We then asked them what their names were for we should consider that place our home as long as we stayed there. "My name is Copp, and that is my wife, and these are all my children. And what are your names?" We told him, and where we had come from, and the situation we had left New York in. We found him a very intelligent man, and we sat and conversed on different subjects until bedtime.

Next morning we got up very early and took a walk. I told Wyer I wanted to go on board the *Oliver Cromwell* and examine her and see what situation she was in, for I had some thoughts of going in her if I could get any office. Wyer said, "Oh, my dear friend, if you go on board that ship, I do not know what I shall do. You know I have no money, and no prospect of earning a penny." I told him to enter on board of her as a Marine, for he would be nearly as well off there as he was on board the *Harlequin*. We would go down on board and examine into every particular, and that was what I was a going for. I examined the ship fore and aft, and I found her a complete ship of war below and aloft. Her Quarter Deck was about forty feet long, and her forecastle as many as twenty, and a gangway each side from the Quarter Deck to the forecastle so wide three men could walk abreast, and all these man height, which provided a shelter fore and aft on the gun deck. She was man height between decks, where the crew hung their hammocks, and the after part had an excellent wardroom for officers to eat in, and many state rooms, and abaft of them the Steward's room, adjoining to a bread room, and many other articles, but no light from any part of the ship, but a lamp was always burning. I liked the looks of one of the Master's Mates, for I was sure he had been wet with salt-water. I took him one side and asked him how the ship was provided with officers and seamen. He said he did not know of one vacant place on board for an officer even from the Captain to the Cook, but he knew some of them could not do the duty they entered to perform. I then asked him about the Marines. They were full, officers and men, "but we have but very few seamen. We want at least one hundred of them." I then asked him about the wages and rations. He gave me a very correct information of everything. We then went up and got our breakfast, and after that Wyer and I had a long conversation on the subject of going on board. He said, "if you ship as a seaman, we shall be separated in our mess, and in everything else, for I must enter as a landman, and I shall not have one minute enjoyment if I have not you as a companion." I told him it was hard for me to enter as a landman when I knew my duty from the trucks to the keel. I then told him what our duty would be as waistmen. It would be too humiliating for him and me, and for me in particular. We should be continually employed in washing, scrubbing, and swabbing decks, and every other drudgery. And I should lose two dollars per month, for seamen had eight, and landmen but six. Not only that, our prize money would be in the same proportion. I was two or three days before I could reconcile myself to go on board in that capacity, but I finally went to oblige Wyer, for he was an amiable young man, none could be more so.

After we entered our names on the books,[11] we went to work and never waited for orders, for I knew what my duty was without having a word said to me, and would often call on the waistmen to go to work.

The third day after I went on board, the Boatswain came where I stood and said, "you have certainly been on board of a ship before now, what did you ship as a landman for?"

"Do you disapprove of my doing my duty without being drove to it?"

"By no means, but we are destitute of seamen, and if you are one I want your work as such."

I had not been on board long before I saw many of the officers were an imposition on the public. Captain Coit who commanded her never made any profession of seamanship, but he had been in Massachusetts in 1775, and took an active part in the war and obtained much credit. He was a part of the time in Plymouth, and he prevailed with some of the owners of a vessel to let him have her and go into Boston bay, and take something that would aid them in the implements of war. He filled the vessel with men and went out, without any guns but Muskets, and in two days he re-

[11]The *Oliver Cromwell's* shipping articles indicate that Christopher Prince and Josiah Ware signed on board on 17 September 1776. Clark and Morgan, eds., *Naval Documents of the American Revolution,* Vol. 6, 872.

turned with a brig loaded with powder, guns, shot, and bombs, and many other articles. They then put carriage guns on board and sent him out again and brought in several vessels bound to Boston with ammunition and provisions, which became so serviceable to the American Army, he got a great name throughout the country, and they built that ship for him, and gave him the command of her. The first and three Lieutenants were complete seamen, but the other was not. The sailing master was no seaman, but he had long been a fishing about the Vineyard and Nantucket. Two of his mates were seamen, and one or two of the midshipmen. The Boatswain was completely accomplished for all his duties.[12] There were about thirty men who had entered as seamen, and not more than seven or eight were able to do their duty as such. Quarter Masters and Quarter Gunners ought to be seamen, but it was not so on board that ship. One day a number of us were in the hold, fixing the shifting plank, and levelling the ballast, and stowing water casks. We went on very well for some time and yet I disapproved of what he was a doing in my own mind. I saw he was unacquainted with his duty as a Quarter-Master,[13] in stowing away a water-cask without beds or coins. I said nothing for some time, until he was a going to quit the cask. I handed him some pieces of boards.

[12]Michael Melally, John Chapman, and John Smith were the first, second, and third lieutenants; Silvanus Pinkham, whom Prince identifies below as the third lieutenant, was a midshipman; Levi Young was the sailing master and Robert Newson the boatswain. See "A List of Officers & Seamen Belonging & Have Belong'd to the Ship *Oliver Cromwell*," in Clark and Morgan, eds., *Naval Documents of the American Revolution,* Vol. 7, 1283–87.

[13]The *Oliver Cromwell* had three quartermasters, one of whom was named Job Bunker; by 25 February 1777 Job Bunker had deserted; Clark and Morgan, eds., *Naval Documents of the American Revolution,* Vol. 7, 1284. Note, below, how the seamen used the term "Jo Bunker" to deride men devoid of seamanship. "Joe Bunker" was a nickname for an American. Mitford M. Mathews, ed., *A Dictionary of Americanisms on Historical Principles,* 2 vols. (Chicago: University of Chicago Press, 1951).

"What are they for?"

"For bedding the cask."

"What do you mean, you Jo Bunker, you know nothing about it."

"Will you not bed and coin the cask?"

"Do you hold your tongue, Jo Bunker, or I will stop your mouth, for you shall not dictate me."

We was all waistmen in the hold at work, and Wyer among us, and I came out pretty bold, and said many things which produced considerable confusion, and brought some of the officers below. I told them the reason why I handed him the pieces of boards, and whether he or any one ought to abuse me for so doing, and they said to him, "O, for shame! You have done wrong. That casks must have beds under it." The officer said to me, "since you and the Quarter Master have fell out, go up on deck, for I want some work done there." After I went on deck, one of the officers asked me how I knew anything about stowing casks in a ship's hold. I told him I had often heard seamen talk about beds and coins for stowing away casks, and I had often seen in Boston vessels loaded with molasses and rum, and pieces of boards under every cask, and in some instances where they were not properly bedded, the casks were nearly empty. He turned away and smiled. One day some running rigging was to be rove, we were ordered to go between decks and bring up a coil. I took off the bands, and handed a sailor the end from inside the coil. He refused to take it, and took the end outside the coil, which brought a kink, every time it left the coil, which was impossible to prevent. The Boatswain said, why do you not keep the kinks out of the rigging. I told him the reason why it could not be done. As soon as he saw it he told him to let the rope drop, and gave him the one I wanted him to take. And when he got up to the futtock shrouds he went up through the lubber hole. I then said, I was sorry to see a lubber-hole sailor on board the ship. Several of the officers and seamen laughed at what I said, and asked him what he went through the lubber hole for. Captain Mullaly, first Lieutenant, "I know Prince is a seaman from what I have heard him say before now."

After I had been on board about three weeks, and many scenes had taken place, it came on to rain one day, and a number of us was placed under the forecastle to work, the seamen knotting, splicing, and strapping blocks, and Landmen to picking Oakum. And while we were there a seaman sat on my starboard hand, and Wyer on the larboard. I saw the seaman making knots to secure the cable on deck when the ship was at anchor, as there was no windlass on board. He had made one or two without my taking any notice of what he was about. My curiosity led me to fix my eyes on him as he took up a stopper to knot it, which I knew was of more consequence than any knot made on board the ship, for it must have a thrible [triple] crown. If not, it was a useless stopper knot. And it must be crowned before a loop is made. I saw he began with a loop first, and went on and finished, and laid it by with one crown.

I then asked him if he knew that knot was not made right.

"What do you mean, you Jo Bunker. Say no more about it. If you do, you will be sorry for what you say."

"I say that knot is not made as it ought to be."

"Say so again if you dare."

"I say it is not made right."

He then sprung up to strike me.

I told him, "don't you touch me. If you do you will repent it, for if you say again that knot is made as it ought to be, you are no seaman."

Several of the seamen got up and came there and asked him what I had said. He told them. They took up the stopper and looked at the knot, and said, "never mind what he has said, the knot is made right." I said it was not made right. Three or four stepped up to me, and told me to hold my tongue. Wyer sprung up and said, "I advise you not to touch this man. If you do, you will be sorry for it." By that time several of the Quarter Deck officers came forward and listened to what was said. The Boatswain came among us and said, "what do you mean by this confusion, go to work." The man who made the knot said, "I will have satisfaction from that rascal before I go to work." I then said to the Boatswain what I said before, the knot that man made was good for nothing, and took it up and showed it to him, and told him to examine it. He took it and said, "who has made this knot." "I made it." The Boatswain said it was good for nothing.

I then came out pretty boldly, and said, "I have examined the seamanship on board this vessel fore and aft, but I will leave the Quarter Deck for I have no business there, but there is but seven seamen on board this ship, forward of the mainmast." I then named every one, "and all the rest are ordinary seamen, and I can teach them their A.B.C."

The second Lieutenant said, "Boatswain, make that man prove what he has said."

I told him no man on board could make me do that as long as I was a Landsman on board. I then had a long conversation with the Boatswain, and told him why I entered on board as a green hand, and I was willing to do any seaman's duty if they would place Wyer on the seamen list, and I would perform his duty and my own, if the Captain would ship us both as seamen. I never saw such an alteration on board of any vessel as there was then, the seamen in particular. I took the knot and carried to Bob Hill who was a complete seaman, and said to him, "now Bob I will convince you that what I have said about this knot is not right," and took it to pieces, and it convinced him that I was a seaman for I made it as it ought to be.[14] "Ah," said Bob, "I was always sure you had followed the sea, but I did not know why you shipped as a green hand."

The next day Captain Coit was on board and sent for me on the Quarter Deck, and said, "I understand you have followed the sea for many years. Why did you ship as a Landman?" I then told him, and said to him everything about Wyer I wanted to, and told him I would make him a seaman, and a useful hand on board, if he would only receive his name on the seamen's book and add to his wages two dollars. The first Lieutenant said, "If you will net one side the Quarter Deck, as well as Bob Hill who is a going to do the other, we will place you both on the seamen's list." I asked him if he would let Wyer work with me as I must have some one. He said he would. We immediately went to work, Bob Hill on the Larboard side, and I on the Starboard, with nine thread ratline. There was no Quarter boards fore and aft the Quarter Deck. Nettings were to be made from the quarter rail each side down to the water board and filled in with cork fore and aft. Then there was a bag netting above the quarter rails on armed irons, to receive hammocks in the time of action. The quarter deck run to the gangway forward of the mainmast, which made it very long as may be seen in the 47th page.[15]

After we had finished the cork netting from stanchion to stanchion, fore and aft, and all filled in with cork, where a musket-ball could not pass through ten feet from the ship, which was about half man height. The carpenter then fixed in the iron armed stanchions. I run through the ridge ropes, and Wyer leathered them complete. We then made the bag nettings that went

---

[14]*Oliver Cromwell's* rolls list no Bob Hill, but a boatswain's mate named James Hill, and a seaman named John Hill. Clark and Morgan, eds., *Naval Documents of the American Revolution*, Vol. 7, 1284, 1286.

[15]P. 119, above.

from the ridge ropes down to the quarter rail. That completed that job to the satisfaction of every one on board and on shore. I could not keep my eyes from Bob Hill, for I knew there was no man could exceed him in any work on board of any ship. We soon became as intimate as two brothers. In about twelve days we completed that important work, and we was never called off to any other duty on board, and every evening after dark we was exempt from all duty, and went on shore if we was a mind to go, when all the rest were deprived of that privilege. Captain Coit then complied with my request and received Wyer's name on the seamen's list. After we had finished the nettings, the Boatswain asked me if I would or could point the Tiller rope, and splice, moss, pancy and strap the tiller blocks on the same side I had finished the nettings, as Bob was going to do them on the Larboard side.[16] That I consented to do, but I could not keep Wyer with me, which kept me about six days to perform that work. Bob Hill and I sat together all the time in doing that job, for it was as nice work as could be done on board. After we had done everything necessary on the quarter deck, Captain Coit called Bob and myself to him and said, "Prince, I appoint you Captain of the Main Top,[17] and Bob, I appoint you Captain of the Fore Top. Captain Mullaly will tell you what is to be done there." He then asked us if we knew

---

[16]*Point a rope:* To unlay, taper, and weave some of the outside yarns of the end of a rope, for neatness, to prevent wearing out, and for convenience in reeving through a block. The tiller rope ran several turns around the barrel of the steering wheel; each end then ran down through holes through the decks through vertical sheeves to sheeves in blocks strapped on each side of the midships, from which each end was then directed to the fore end of the tiller. *Moss* may mean *mouse*, as in "mousing a hook" (as attached to a block): Taking several turns of spunyarn round the back and point of a hook, and fastening it, to prevent its unhooking. *Pancy* may mean to install a *panch*, a thick mat used to reduce chafing.

[17]*Captain of the maintop:* The seaman responsible for the men posted in the top of the mainmast.

what was to be done. We both told him what ought to be done as a ship of war. "Go and complete the Tops." We then requested iron stanchions and everything we wanted. I took Wyer up with me and we did not finish short of three weeks. We netted the top about four feet high. We then thrummed, fringed, and torseled the fore part of the top.[18] We then made a crow-foot, from the main stay to the top, which extended as far as was necessary to keep the foot of the sail from getting under the top; that is necessary on board of all ships. I had to fix the Mizzen Top, but that wanted no netting, but everything else the same as the main top.

While Wyer and I was in the main top, which was for many days, we had an opportunity of conversing on any subject we had a mind to for we were out of the hearing of every one on board. I told him what induced me to ship as a Landman with him. I had spent many hours in meditating on that duty on board of a ship that I was able to command. It is a long time since I have been before the mast, and if I entered as a seaman, I might remain in that situation as long as I continued on board, and should deprive you of my company, both on deck and mess. But if I shipped as a landman I was sure of promotion, and take you with me as I went along, which has now proved to be true, for I have gone from a landman to a seaman, and did not stop there, for you see I am Captain of this top, which is nearly as honorable as a midshipman, and I shall not stop here. You shall not go unnoticed by me as long as we remain on board this ship. We have signed the articles to remain on board for twelve months, and longer if we have a mind, and in that time I can teach you to perform your duty as a seaman.

[18]*Thrum:* To insert short pieces of rope yarn or spun yarn in a piece of canvas to make a rough surface or a mat that can be wrapped about rigging to prevent chafing. In the tops, such mats were employed to reduce chafing of topsails against the top rim. *Torsel:* tassel.

While I was at work on the quarter-deck, Captain Coit often asked me where and how I obtained the knowledge of seamanship. I told him along by degrees, for I did not want to tell him at once all my experience, and in particular, of my being in the English Navy for twelve months, that was, six months on board the *Asia,* and six in the river St. Lawrence, for it might bring some jealous feelings on his mind. But after conversed with the Steward. He was not a Steward only, but Purser and Steward, which made it a very lucrative office. His name was Lampheer. A very respectable man, he had been several voyages commander of a vessel to the West Indies. One day I told him he was often imposed on by some of the messes, in victuals and liquor, and was very sorry to see it. He asked me, "in what?" I told him that there were many messes which were deficient in the complete number. Some had but three in the mess, and they drawed for six, some four or five, who did the same, and it was for liquor and not for food. From one day to another he lost more than a gallon of rum but the provisions they could not consume. He thought it "impossible." I told him then to show me his book. He took me into his room, and when I saw it I told him I was astonished at his book.

"For what?"

"Why you have no numbers to your messes. Everyone ought to be numbered from one to everyone on board, except the officers, they number themselves. But here you have the only names of the head of every mess, many of which would rob you every day of many rations which you will be accountable to government for. If you give one hundred rations per day to seamen, and there is but ninety, what would be your loss per month?"

He said, "I have not neglected my duty in that. I have visited the messes, and I have not discovered one instance where I have been imposed on. If I did not find them all there, they satisfied me they belonged to the mess."

I then pointed to him from his own book the names of several heads of messes which I knew was not complete in their numbers, and he had granted to every mess six rations. We then went to one which he had granted six rations per day, and he had but one beside himself. There was four rations per day lost in one mess. He then asked him to name all in his mess as he had done to him before. "There is Tom and myself is two, and there is John, 3, Josephes, 4, John Josephes Joe, 5, and Portuguese Joe, 6." His name was, John Josephes Joe, a Portuguese. He added four names to himself when there was but two in the mess. They were both Portuguese and Roman Catholics. A similar deception was found in several of the other messes but not to that extent. I then told him where I had been in the English Navy, and all the rules and regulations they had in many things, and that which was connected with the stewards in particular. "They had a list of every name on board the ship from the Captain's Clerk. And that was not all. Every mess on board must have their names wrote on a piece of paper. Number one, two, three, and six to everyone on board, and the Clerk's name must be upon it. Beef, Pork, Bread, and every eatable article is weighed out to every mess on Monday only, and no other day in the week. Liquor is given every day, which is the principal duty the Steward has to perform through the week, except Monday, and on board this ship that might be done in two hours. This alteration may be made in a few hours, and if I was in your place it should be done immediately, and as you are shipping hands every day. The Clerk must add their names to the number that are not full, as no mess is allowed more than six."

He made all these arrangements and many things more that I named to him; he informed the Captain and some of the officers what I had said to him, how I was acquainted with all the rules and regulations on board of the British Navy.

After Bob and I had finished the Tops, we were sent into the sail-loft to thimble and fix the sails, which proved to be an excellent job to me, for while I was there I became acquainted with many on shore. Mr. Deshon, who had a large family and some beautiful daughters, and Mr. George Colfax, a young man, only four months older than I was, conducted all the business in that loft.[19] Colfax served his time with Deshon, and after his time was out, he went to sea a few voyages to the West Indies, and then entered into partnership with Deshon.

Bob Hill was a wonderful man in the seafaring life, and amiable in his disposition. Although he was a full blooded seaman, he was modest in his conversation, not a profane word proceeded from his lips, and thus it was with Wyer. This example with those I had for many months before kept me within the limits of rectitude in what I said. But there was much profanity on board the ship, and from Captain Coit in particular. I took Wyer with me to the sail-loft to tar parslin, twine and sew on leather, which was of much advantage to him.

Colfax and I got to be so intimate, we kept together almost ev-

---

[19]John Deshon, Jr. (b. 1727), a wealthy merchant, had led New London's pre-Revolutionary resistance to British trade restrictions and served on numerous Revolutionary committees. In July 1777 Congress appointed him to the Navy Board of the Eastern Department, which oversaw the operations of the Continental Navy. Only Nathaniel Shaw, Jr., and Thomas Mumford had greater investments in New London's privateers. Frances Manwaring Caulkins, *History of New London, Connecticut* (New London: H. D. Utley, 1895), 506; Robert Owen Decker, *The Whaling City: A History of New London* (Chester, Conn.: Pequot Press, 1976), 44, 48. George Colfax (b. 9 Feb. 1752) would serve for a quarter century, 1784–1812, either in the common council or as alderman of New London. See Lucius Albert Barbour, "Barbour Collection of Connecticut Vital Records" (Salt Lake City, Utah: Genealogical Society of the Church of Jesus Christ of Latter-day Saints, n.d.), eighty-one reels, microfilm of alphabetical card file in the Connecticut State Library; Caulkins, *History of New London*, 619.

ery evening. His father was a shipmaster out of New London, and died when he was thirty eight years old. His mother was alive and still a widow. She had six sons and four daughters. One of his brothers followed the sea, and two had entered into the Continental army. One of his sisters was married, and lived at Weathersfield and had two daughters. As I was much attached to George, I became much so to his mother, and brothers and sisters, which were in New London.

While I was at work in the sail loft, Lampheer the Steward, was applied to by his Uncle Deshon, (a merchant who owned vessels, and whose employ he had sailed in before) to take charge of a vessel and go to St. Eustatia, for a load of warlike materials, for our armies and ships of war. Lampheer told Deshon he wished to go if Captain Coit would discharge him from the *Oliver Cromwell*. When he had his application to Captain Coit to discharge him, and for what purpose, some objections were made. But Lampheer removed them in a moment.

"Prince is more capable of filling the office of Purser and Steward on board this ship than I am. I recommend him to you to supply my place."

Coit: "Prince is a stranger to us all, and we do not know whether he is honest or dishonest, and how he will proceed in the office, and further, we have but few seamen on board who are capable of performing that important duty."

Lampheer: "I should have lost many dollars if it had not been for him, for I have been imposed on by many messes, and I did not know how to prevent until he told me, and I am much obliged to him for it."

I was sent for on board, and when they told me all that had passed between them, Captain Coit asked me if I would accept of the office of Purser and Steward of the ship. I asked him on what conditions?

"The same of Captain Lampheer."

"What is that?"

"Fifteen dollars per month."

I then told him the perquisites of Stewards in the British Navy and Navies of other nations in addition to their wages. And that was, all the bread dust which was not eatable, all the salt remaining in the provision casks after the meat was taken out, and there were always some on board who drank no liquor, and the Steward had the liberty to purchase it of them, which became his own property, and do what he had a mind with them, to sell them, or charge them to the government.

"Are you willing, Sir, to give me these perquisites?"

"I cannot answer you now."

"You can Sir, when I tell you, I am accountable to you, and the state of Connecticut, for every pound of beef and pork, bread, sugar, tea, coffee, meal, flour, butter, &c., on board, and for every gallon of spirit. Many of these article turn the scale but once, and I have to turn them hundreds of times. Sometimes the bread-dust and salt does not more than compensate the Steward for his loss on all these articles. Now, Sir, if you will not make me accountable for any of these articles agreeable to the number of men and officers on board, I will have no reference to my request."

Coit, "all this is new to me. I will grant it, and I now appoint you Purser and Steward of this ship."

"I must have a correct weight and proportion of every article on board before I can commence this duty."

Coit, "Captain Lampheer, you will or must comply with Mr. Prince's request before you are discharged."

We then went to work, and ascertained the amount of everything committed to my charge, and I commenced this duty about two months after I entered on board that ship. I put Wyer in head of the mess I was in, and aided him in the performance of many of his duties.[20]

All the commission and warrant officers were boarded on shore. Captain Mallaly, the first Lieutenant, then invited me to make his house my home. I should have a room to myself. Captain Pinkham the 3d Lieutenant there and he wished me to accept the offer. I had been at his house and was much pleased with his family, for he had none there but his wife and one daughter about eighteen years old. She was all the child he had, and she was a beautiful girl. I immediately took up my board and lodgings there.[21] A more pleasant house and family I could not have found in the city. Mrs. Mullaly was nearly connected with the widow Colfax and her family, where I soon became acquainted with many other connections which were in many parts of the city, that led me on from one family to another, until there were but few of good reputation I was not acquainted with. One qualification I had then carried me forward very rapidly, and in particular among young people, that was in singing songs, some of which were of the first quality, but none that was trifled with in composition. I could and did sing nearly forty. For a long time, I would bring a new song in every evening. I continued this amusement for some time, and then relinquished it by degrees.

My duty on board every day except Monday was always per-

[20]In confirmation of Prince's story, the *Oliver Cromwell's* crew list dated 25 February 1777 gives Christopher Prince as the present steward and James Lanphere, Jr., as former steward now discharged. The same list shows Prince's friend, Josiah Ware, as having deserted—an event Prince overlooks in the retelling. Clark and Morgan, eds., *Naval Documents of the American Revolution*, Vol. 7, 1284, 1285.

[21]"Michael Melally's Bill Against the State of Connecticut," of 12 December 1776, charged the state of Connecticut for boarding and lodging Prince fourteen weeks, Midshipman Sylvanus Pinkham eighteen weeks, and several others various lengths of time. Clark and Morgan, eds., *Naval Documents of the American Revolution*, Vol. 7, 459.

formed in about an hour. I had a deputy allowed me, a young man, who did all the labor under my inspection. I kept every article under lock and key. There was an agent on shore to whom I applied to for all the articles I wanted. I would not allow no man anything to eat or drink without a numbered ticket, with every man's name in the mess signed by the clerk. As we were daily shipping hands, I was obliged to examine the clerk's book, and kept a list of every name on board. As we were laying alongside of the wharf, some of the crew left the ship and never returned again. That I was obliged to examine every day.

In December we moved the ship from the cove into the river, about a quarter of a mile from the shore, as we were to sail in a few days.[22] Before the winter set in we took our departure. The wind was at S.W., which prevented us from laying our course out without a tack or two. We got nearly on the leeward reef and the Pilot ordered the ship about. The Sailing Master said, "every man to his station." They immediately said, "all is ready." I was standing by the Sailing Master and he gave no further orders. The Pilot then said, "if you do not put the ship about in ten seconds, she will be on the shore." The master then said, "Captain Mullaly I wish you would order the ship about," which he did in an instant, which saved the ship from going on shore. And after she got on the other tack, the Pilot said we were not more than two rods from the reef. The Pilot was one of the quarter gunners, for that reason he had no power on board as a Pilot, but to tell the Sailing Master when we were in danger, while we was on pilot ground in that port only. After we had tacked ship and got near to the windward reef, he said again, "you must put the ship about." Mallaly waited for no request, for there was a violent N.W. squall not far

[22] On 28 January 1777 the Connecticut Council of Safety instructed Capt. Coit to sail on a cruise as soon as possible. Clark and Morgan, eds., *Naval Documents of the American Revolution*, Vol. 7, 1051.

from us. No orders was given by the Sailing Master to take in sail. The Captain said, "Mr. Young, that wind will be on board of us in a minute. Why do you not order the sails taken in." The words had not been uttered but a few seconds before the squall struck us, and carried the ship almost on her beam ends. Everything on board that could move was carried to the leeward. For five minutes there was no prospect of her coming back on her bottom. Some of the weather guns carried away their breechings and tackles and moved a distance from their places. Not a word proceeded from the Sailing Master. The Boatswain ordered the topsail sheets off. Some of us on the quarterdeck brailed up the mizzen and let go the mizzen topsail sheets. She then began to right. The squall abated, so that she began to move through the water, but wanted three strakes of being upright. The Foretopsail sheets were hauled home, and Providence had directed us abreast of the Hommoc Islands, which enter into Fisher's Island Sound,[23] and she was ordered down between the Hommoc's to Stonington, where we arrived safe before dark and came to an anchor. The Sailing Master's ignorance and inability of performing his office threw the ship into great confusion. He was a nice man, but no seaman. He would have made everything harmonious if he had been one of the Lieutenants. We lay there several days and got the ship in order again. I spoke my mind very freely to all the officers, that the ship was over-sparred[24] and an unsafe vessel to go to sea.

The ship being overmasted and unsafe was taken into consideration by some experienced shipbuilders were sent for to examine the hull and spars. They pronounced her to be oversparred. Her lower mast only which ought to be reduced at least twelve

[23]*Hommoc Islands:* Today known as North Dumpling and South Dumpling, rocky islands north of the western end of Fishers Island, at the northeast end of Long Island. *Fishers Island Sound:* Passage between the south coast of Connecticut and Fishers Island.

[24]In place of "over-sparred," the manuscript has "ever spared."

feet. Their judgment was decided on, and as many of her sails, standing and running rigging must be altered as well as the masts, it was necessary we should go back to New London. When we got there, the Winter set in and made so much ice in the river we were obliged to lay alongside of a wharf. In a few days we had the masts reduced twelve feet, at least the lower masts, standing and running rigging fixed. But there was not one day but some of the crew left us until more than one half was gone, which prevented us from going on our cruise. Such a winter I never spent in all my life, not one night but what we had dancing frolics and other amusements. Several of us took up our board and lodgings at Captain Coit's. He had four daughters, three of which were old enough to go with us to our dancing frolics. One evening Mrs. Coit asked me if I would take her youngest daughter with me. She was about eleven years old. I made some objections and the girl burst out a crying in such a degree it was a long time before I could pacify her after I told her she might go. They were all very amiable girls. The oldest was about eighteen years of age. He had but one son which was his youngest child. Before the winter ended I quit them dancing meetings for I see too many loose characters among the girls that met with us. Some of the officers who boarded there liked the meetings, which was of no advantage to their reputation. After I quit, Mrs. Coit would not let one of her daughters go, when I told her what prevented me from going. After that I visited families who I knew from experience were as reputable as any in the city. I wanted different qualifications to converse with those who live on shore than what I had, and there was no other way that I knew of that I could obtain it. And I never was placed among ladies and gentlemen before as I was then. I was often ashamed, abased and confounded, for I knew I could not speak nor act as I ought to. I had made considerable improvement while I boarded at Captain Mallaly's, and was daily making some progress where I then was at Captain Coit's, not by him, but by his wife and daughters. Although I was not free from profanity, yet Coit often made my heart tremble, and as he commanded the ship, I was much exposed to the sound of his voice, not at his house, for he was but seldom there even at meal times.

I found George Colfax as useful companion as any in the city, he lived with his mother where I often went, and among his sisters there was one that made me feel as I never felt before at the sight of a female. As I knew I was in no situation to marry, I dismissed those feelings as much as possible.

We could not get any addition to our ship's crew during the winter, about one hundred deserted, and on board there was much confusion. One man, a seaman who had a family in the city, he became jealous of one of his shipmates by believing he had intercourse with his wife, and one night he struck him on the head and wounded him so much he died in eight days, and the murderer was hung in a few days after that. They were able seamen, which was a loss to us. As soon as the river was clear of ice, we hauled the ship off. That was about the first of March 1777. We then used all our exertions to get men sufficient to go to sea, but all in vain.

The impression made on my mind about the salvation of my soul for many months past could not be entirely dismissed, and still I had no real conviction of sin, yet I disapproved of profanity, drunkenness, and debauchery of every kind, and gambling among other vices. I felt full of depravity, which gave me anxious thoughts about the turpitude of transgressions which I daily committed. There was no minister of the gospel there. The Sabbaths were but little noticed, but not openly profaned. Although I had no religion, my heart rejoiced in seeing it in so many houses I visited. Modesty, morality, and virtue, which I saw, kept a check on all my inclinations and actions. As my duty on board the ship was so trifling, I but seldom stayed on board more than six hours in twenty four.

I often heard from some of the officers and men who were acquainted with a seafaring life some reasonable objections of the ship a going to sea under the command of Captain Coit, and Mr. Young Sailing Master, both of which I corresponded. And yet I plead the ability of both. Coit was a hero, he had done much for our country, and he might forsake his present vices when he got on the ocean, and had an enemy to contend with; and Young had some qualifications, which might prevent him from being entirely useless, and obtain knowledge of his duty every day. Early in June we had so many men on board we was making preparation to sail. We got everything in complete order. All of a sudden, Captain H _____[25] came on board the ship, and asked for Captain Coit. We told him he was on shore. He then said, "the Governor of this State has sent me a commission and orders to come and take charge of this ship, in the room of Captain Coit who is discharged. You are all strangers to me, and I wish to converse with every officer on board, in every station, hoping we shall all agree, except two or three the Governor has appointed, notwithstanding, the decision of all is left with me." It threw us all into great confusion. After he had examined every qualification on board, and distinguished every individual, he went to the first Lieutenant. "Will you remain on board in the station you are now in?" "No." So he went on until he came to me. I then told him "I had no objection of being a Steward, but there I must remain without promotion, and that was hard for one brought up to the sea from a boy, and nothing but necessity had brought me into that office now, and I must say with the rest, no." The men were obliged to remain until their time expired. Nearly all the commissioned and warrant officers left the ship.

[25]Seth Harding.

CHAPTER FIVE

Privateering
June 1777–1781

HISTORICAL CONTEXT

Between the spring of 1777 and late 1781, Christopher Prince sailed as an officer in a series of New London privateers, many of which made profitable cruises. For most seamen, sailing on board a privateer was much more attractive than was enlisting for naval service. In a privateer a seaman signed on for a single cruise, faced laxer discipline, and had the prospect of prize money in addition to his pay. What is more, a privateer captain was less likely than a naval captain to take his ship into deadly combat with enemy warships, since the goal of the owners of the privateer was to make a profit by preying on enemy trade.

Privateers were privately owned armed vessels whose captains held permits, called letters of marque, issued by their governments to capture vessels and property of the enemy. Privateersmen were not pirates, but were bound by the internationally recognized laws of war. They were required to post bonds as guarantees of proper conduct. Although they could fly false flags as a ruse de guerre, *they were required to hoist their true national colors before engaging the enemy. They were expected to treat prisoners humanely. They were required to respect the rights of neutrals. Having captured a vessel, a privateer captain would place a prize master and prize crew on board with orders to bring it into port to be tried in an admiralty court, which would determine whether the captured vessel was a lawful prize. After deductions for court costs, prize money would be divided among the owners, officers, and crew according to a formula agreed to before the cruise.[1]*

Vessels carrying letters of marque but sailing on commercial voyages were usually also called letters of marque.

The Continental Congress authorized privateering in March of 1776. By the end of the war, it had issued some 2,000 letters of marque. Privateers came in all shapes and sizes, ranging from boats carrying a few swivel guns to frigates of twenty-eight guns, but the principal vessel types were ships, brigs, schooners, and sloops. Some privateers brought fortunes to their owners. Others were less successful. Many were captured.

Because privateers were privately owned, few privateer records, aside from bonds and admiralty court proceedings, have been preserved in government archives. Most privateer owners disposed of log books, muster rolls, sailing instructions, and like documents soon after their purposes had been served. Fortunately for us, Christopher served in several privateers owned by leading merchants of New London whose records have survived.

The one physical description we have of Christopher Prince appears in one of these extant privateering documents. On the back of the letter of marque for the brigantine Marquis de Lafayette, *dated 13 June 1781, following a description of the commander, Elisha Hinman, is that of his first lieutenant: "Lieu^t· Christopher Prince, is aged*

---

[1] Donald A. Petrie, *The Prize Game: Lawful Looting on the High Seas in the Days of Fighting Sail* (Annapolis, Md.: Naval Institute Press, 1999), provides a useful introduction to the law of maritime prize.

*Thirty Years, five feet four inches high—well sett—dart [dark] Eyes
and dark complection—pitted with the Smal Pox, short brown
Hair—and is Stoop Shouldered."*[2]

   *These privateering records, along with contemporary newspaper
reports and Louis F. Middlebrook's study of maritime Connecticut during the Revolution,*[3] *among other sources, enable us to verify Prince's
account and to correct chronological and other errors. Citations to records that confirm or correct Prince's account appear in the notes; appendix 4, "Christopher Prince as Privateersman," attempts to reconstruct
the actual order of events recounted by Prince.*

There was a privateer fitting out called the *American Revenue,*
a Bermuda built sloop of fourteen guns, commanded by O
Champlin, and owned by Nathaniel Shaw, the richest man in
New London.[4] A number of us went to Mr. Shaw's and engaged to
go in the *American Revenue.* Mr. Pinkham and I had some conver-

   [2]Letter of Marque for the brigantine *Marquis de Lafayette,* 13 June 1781.
Washington, D.C., National Society Daughters of the American Revolution,
Americana Collection., No. 2526.
   [3]The most important such collection belonged to Nathaniel Shaw, Jr. (1735–
82). Under the listing "Shaw, Nathaniel," in *Dictionary of American Biography,*
edited by Dumas Malone, Vol. 17 (New York: Charles Scribner's Sons, 1943); Er-
nest E. Rogers, *Connecticut's Naval Office at New London during the War of the
American Revolution* (New London, Conn.: New London County Historical Society, 1933), *New London County Historical Society Collections,* Vol. 2; Louis F.
Middlebrook, *History of Maritime Connecticut during the American Revolution,
1775–1783,* 2 vols. (Salem, Mass.: Essex Institute, 1925).
   [4]The Connecticut sloop *American Revenue,* fourteen guns, seventy men, was
commissioned on 9 October 1776 and was commanded by Samuel Champlin, Jr.
Charles H. Lincoln, *Naval Records of the American Revolution, 1776–1788* (Washington: Government Printing Office, 1906), 225.

IN CONGRESS,

APRIL 3, 1776.

RESOLVED, That blank Commissions for private Ships of War, and Letters of Marque and Reprisal, signed by the President, be sent to the General Assemblies, Conventions, and Councils or Committees of Safety of the United Colonies, to be by them filled up and delivered to the Persons intending to fit out such private Ships of War for making Captures of British Vessels and Cargoes, who shall apply for the same, and execute the Bonds which shall be sent with the said Commissions, which Bonds shall be returned to the Congress.

By Order of Congress,

John Hancock PRESIDENT.

sation on the subject before we went to Mr. Shaw's, and said to me he was almost sure he was a going as Sailing Master, and wanted me to go his mate, for he should not be allowed but two mates on board that sloop. Mr. Pinkham was third Lieutenant on board the *Oliver Cromwell,* and he was a complete seaman, and I agreed at once to go in the sloop if Mr. Shaw gave us the offices. Mr. Shaw was much pleased with our application, and we shipped immediately, and in four or five days she was completely manned, and sailed on a cruise.[5] She had a round-house only. A large steerage was built that accommodated a goodly number of officers. The men all slept in the hold. We had been out about twenty days before we saw any vessel. When we was in the trade winds about four degrees eastward of all the West India Islands, a very pleasant day, laying to under easy sail early in the morning, the man at mast head said he saw something due west from us which he believed was a vessel. A man went aloft and said there was nothing in sight. The man who was stationed there insisted upon it there was a vessel in sight. I went aloft, and I saw in a moment something which I knew was the topgallant sails of a vessel. We bore away and made all the sail we could. The wind was light, it did not exceed a six knot breeze. I kept aloft until I saw the topsails of the ship, and she was seen off deck. At twelve o'clock, meridian, we was alongside of her. After we boarded her we found by her bills a cargo of £50,000 sterling. She was called the *Lovely Lass.* In one hour we put a Prize Master on board her by the name of Thompson, and sent her to New Bedford, as the safest port she could go to.[6]

[5]Two undated crew lists for the *American Revenue,* Samuel Champlin commander, have Silvanus Pinkham and Prince down as sailing master and first master's mate. New Haven, Connecticut, Yale University Library, "Shaw Papers," packet 35, #3 and #11.

[6]*American Revenue* captured *Lovely Lass* on 31 March 1778, and prize master Nathaniel Thompson brought her into Boston for trial. Samuel Champlin to

As all our seamen were obliged to sling their hammocks in the hold, we could not take more water with us than a two month's cruise. The quarter master had not been as prudent in that one article as he ought to have been, brought us under the necessity of going to some island for water. Myself and some others knew there was no island could be compared to Martinique that we could go to where we could get water free from expense. After cruising about fifteen days longer, and saw nothing we dare to encounter, we bore away for Martinique, where we arrived in a few days. We had not been there but a short time before we was informed that the smallpox was raging in a great degree on shore and many had been to the river after water, and in other parts of St. Pears.[7] We began to be alarmed at the fatal consequence of the disorder it might produce on board. Nearly all the officers on board had been inoculated or had it the natural way. We went on shore to the Theater almost every evening for amusement, and other places, while we were waiting to see how many of the crew were going to be confined with the smallpox. In about twelve days many was taken down with the complaint. About forty on board we was sure would go through the remediless disorder, which kept us there until some had recovered and some died. We lay there about twenty days, and then sailed for our native places, for we was visited by the chastising hand of the Almighty, for his Holy name was taken in vain too much on board by some, and not one spark of religion in one heart from the Captain to the Cook. After we left Martinique, we had so many sick and dying we gave ourself but little trouble about cruising the ocean for our

---

Nathaniel Shaw, 1 April 1778, New London, New London County Historical Society, "Shaw Papers"; and Middlebrook, *Maritime Connecticut during the American Revolution*, Vol. 2, 51. Prince reverses the order of this cruise of early 1778 and one in mid-1777.

[7] *St. Pears:* St. Pierre.

enemies. In truth it was a melancholy place for me, not on any account only the sickness on board. My duty on board that sloop was comparatively nothing. I had bought a quadrant and marine books, in keeping the Log book Journal and the daily latitude and longitude of the vessel was nearly all my labor. The other mate attended with the Boatswain to all the needful duties. Upon the whole it was an idle life to me, but our daily conversation on different topics was an advantage.

About the first of October we arrived at New Bedford. All our hearts rejoiced in seeing the *Lovely Lass*. We soon found that she and all her cargo was sold, and the agent was still there with all the money in his possession and ready to give to every individual on board, which was about two hundred thousand dollars. At that time there was not one cent discount on continental money. Paper money, gold and silver, were all on a par. My prize money amounted to two thousand dollars, which I received.[8] It came into my mind at once to deposit some of it in the Continental loan office in Boston. I communicated my intention to Captain Champlin, requesting him to let me go to Boston while we were laying at New Bedford, which should not exceed four days. "That I will do with pleasure if you will return and take charge of the sloop and carry her to New London, for I am a going there immediately, for I am informed some English ships of war are in Gardners Bay,[9] which makes it unsafe to carry her there now, and Mr. Pinkham and the Lieutenants are a going likewise, but one must remain on board until you return, and I will inform you as soon as possible, as Mr. Hatfield you know is very sick with the small-

---

[8]A share in the *American Revenue*'s mid-1777 cruise was about $1,000. As master's mate, Prince owned two shares. See Simon Wolcott to Thomas Shaw, 22 October 1777, New London County Historical Society, "Shaw Papers."

[9]*Gardners Bay:* Gardiners Bay, inlet of Long Island Sound on east end of Long Island, New York.

pox, and no hope of his recovery." Mr. Hatfield was a master's mate; he and myself were the only ones on board. I set out on foot, for I dare not ride a horse for fear he would throw me off which had happened several times, unless it was one who would not start and become unmanageable. My father lived but twenty miles from New Bedford, where I knew I could get a horse I could ride in safety. I soon arrived there where I had not been for five years. Such a reception as I had into my Parents arms, throwed me into much confusion.

"My son! my son! has the Lord spared your life? for many years we have not known whether you was dead or alive, or whether you was a friend or an enemy to your country where you was born. O, we are happy to see you, and we hope the Lord has not spared your life in vain."

"Have you not received a letter from me?"

"We have not."

"I wrote to you a letter in January 1776, to let you know where I was and the situation I was in" (as may be seen in the 31. page).[10] "I hoped you would receive it. I know the conveyance of letters since the war commenced has been very uncertain."

After we had some conversation on different subjects, I told my Father I wanted to go to Boston the next day, and whether he would let me have a horse that would carry me there safe, and would not throw me from him. For that reason I had walked from Bedford for fear I should have some of my limbs broken, and perhaps killed!

"Yes, my son, I will let you have a horse that will carry you safe, go where you will. When do you expect to return?"

"Next day after tomorrow."

[10]P. 72, above.

"So soon, what are you a going there for?"

"To give some money to my country, and deposit it in the loan office."

"Who sent it?"

"No one, it is my own."

I then told him how I got it, and he was astonished.

"Why, there is not ten men in Massachusetts can spare as much money to their country as you."

I told him, I intended to deposit seventeen hundred dollars only, out of the two thousand, and that would bring me in six per cent interest per annum.

"You are a going to do that which is right, and I am glad the Lord has blessed your labors."

The next morning I set out very early, and arrived at Boston in season. I went to my Uncle Job's house, and was received there almost as affectionate as I was at my Parents. I told him what I came for. He went with me to the loan office, where I deposited $1,700 and took a loan office certificate, and got ready to depart the next day.[11] I stayed that night at my Uncle Job Prince's house. My Aunt and cousins treated me as formerly, as though I was one of the family. Early in the morning I took my departure, and arrived at my Father's before night in safety, where I stayed until the following day. My Father then took a horse and chaise and carried me within six miles of New Bedford, where he had some business to transact for himself, and in a short time I arrived and went on board the sloop, where I found the second Lieutenant the only officer, Mr. Champlin, a connection of Captain Champlin, who set out immediately for New London.

I found Mr. Hatfield very low, but he had his reason so he

[11]Prince bought five Continental loan certificates valued at a total of $1,700 on 17 September 1777. Rogers, *Connecticut's Naval Office at New London*, 326.

could converse. We were under the necessity of carrying him forward before I went to Boston. He talked to me about death and eternity.

"O, what shall I do or say to obtain eternal life? I shall soon appear before the judgment seat of Christ."

"You are not a very wicked man."

"I am wicked! I am not fit for Heaven. Do pray for me."

I saw his pock had all sunk into his skin, and I was sure it would soon end his existence. An uncommon feeling rushed into my mind at what he had said about death, and wanted me an awful sinner to pray for him. I went aft and took an Episcopal Prayer Book which we had on board, examined it and found the prayers which were made for any one placed in his situation.

I took it forward and said unto him, "you want prayers to Almighty God for the salvation of your soul. We must both pray in earnest or it will be needless for us to pray at all."

"O, I shall pray in earnest and sincerity of heart. I have prayed, but I want you to pray for me and with me."

Although his face was much swelled, I saw tears flowing from his eyes. I then opened the book and read the prayers. I read them slow and as solemn as possible. I saw his eyes were closed and a motion on his lips, I never felt so before. After I had ended the prayers, he opened his eyes and fixed them upon me. I was so affected I could not speak to him. He then lifted his eyes to Heaven. I went aft and left the prayer book there, and soon after I went forward again and found him dead. We were under the necessity of burying him as soon as possible.

I had about twenty men left on board. The rest had gone to the place of their nativity. In about ten days, a letter and a Pilot came, and I made sail immediately, and arrived safe at New London in about twenty four hours. I was welcomed by near one hundred of my acquaintances. I was ordered to carry the sloop into the cove, where I hauled her alongside the wharf, stripped her of her sails and rigging, which was soon done. Captain Mallaly told me to board at his house, where I found Pinkham had married his daughter. I could not help making some observations on what he had done so soon after his arrival.

In a few days after that, Captain Mallaly says to me, "Mr. Shaw is a going to put a new bottom on the *American Revenue,* which is a critical and laborious undertaking, and he has appointed me as an agent to have her done as soon as possible, and to employ you in superintending all her movements, for she will have to lay on her beam ends after she is hove down for a long time, for her plank must be taken off, and new ones put on before she can be righted. And you shall be well paid for your labor." I moved her so far up the cove that no wind could disturb her when she was hove down. We soon went to work, and began at her keel. I was allowed as many men as I wanted, not less than four at the pump on board at night and day, and many others.

We went on very well and soon finished one side. I had no opportunity of visiting any of my acquaintances, for I was obliged to be on board all the time the carpenters were there. One day I was passing the street, I met Lucy Colfax, the one who had received all my affections before, so much so I could not bear to see her, it gave me so much distress. She was in company with one of her sisters. Before I came up to them, Lucy said, "Why Nancy, that is Mr. Prince," and run up to me, and took hold of my hand and said, "I am glad to see you."[12] She saw I was very much confused, and said in an instant good bye. What constructions she put on

[12]Lucy Colfax, b. 21 March 1755; and probably Ann Colfax, b. 12 April 1760. Lucius Albert Barbour, "Barbour Collection of Connecticut Vital Records" (Salt Lake City, Utah: Genealogical Society of the Church of Jesus Christ of Latter-day Saints, n.d.), eighty-one reels, microfilm of alphabetical card file in the Connecticut State Library.

my countenance I could not tell, I became in an instant like a statue, almost lifeless. I walked on to the sloop as a stupid creature, and such conflagrant feelings, they could not go unnoticed by any one who see me or had any conversation with me. I dismissed my feelings as much as possible, and when I went home in the evening I conversed with Mr. Pinkham and his wife about her, as she was a cousin to Mrs. Pinkham, and a Mr. Halister was present, who boarded there and had been a prize master with us our last trip in the *Revenue*.[13] They all laughed at what I said. They told me she was one of the best girls in New London, but she was a going to be married to Mr. Lord, who was Captain clerk on board the ship *Oliver Cromwell*, and it was needless for me to say anything to her on the subject of marriage.[14] I fell into a state of despondency.

We was all together up in one of the chambers, and while they were a laughing at me, I got up and went to Mrs. Pinkham and said to her, "Nancy, if Mr. Pinkham loves you as I love Lucy Colfax, you may deal with him as you please. And I have no doubt he loves you as much as he ought to. You nor no other girl on the face of the earth has ever altered my feelings but your cousin Lucy."

"Well go and see her and talk to her."

"You say she is a going to be married to Lord! What can I say?"

"Well he is now in the Continental army and he may never return home."

Mr. Halister went with me to Mrs Colfax's, where I found some I never saw before, Mrs. Rose, her oldest daughter who was

---

[13]Giles Hollister was listed as a steward on the *American Revenue*. Yale University Library, "Shaw Papers," packet 35, #3 and #11.

[14]George Lord. "A List of Officers & Seamen Belonging & Have Belong'd to the Ship *Oliver Cromwell*," Clark and Morgan, eds., *Naval Documents of the American Revolution*, Vol. 7, 1284.

married, and lived at Weathersfield,[15] and one of her sons who belonged to the army, and three other daughters, and George my particular friend. Such an evening I never spent before. I got perfectly composed, and was able to act as a rational creature after I had been there a little while. Mr. Halister was intimately acquainted with the family, and related in a small degree. He gave some obscure expressions to Miss Colfax about me. But one thing I knew was imprudent, I could not keep my eyes from her, which I see she noticed. When we left the house, George said to me, "come again, we shall be happy to see you." That was a delightful evening. It lulled my mind down to that degree, I was able to go on from day to day in my avocation. I continued to spend every evening at that house until Mrs. Rose went to Weathersfield, for she and I was more familiar in our conversation than any of the family. And before she went away she told me she was going to Weathersfield, and she would be much pleased if I would go there and spend a few days with her. Lucy was a going up with her, and George was a going up in a short time to be married to a girl who lived there, and wished I would go up with him.[16] I was much pleased with that friendly invitation. I told her what my feelings were in what she had said to me, and never should forget it as long as I lived, whether I went there or not, but I should certainly go if nothing prevented me. They soon departed, and I felt very lonesome, and had to go to Taverns, and spend evenings improperly.

About the first of December the sloop was completely planked in bottom and deck. I hauled her down to Mr. Shaw's wharf at the mouth of the cove. George Colfax told me he was going up to Weathersfield, and he had promised his sister Rose to carry me up with him, and wanted me to get ready as soon as possible. I men-

[15]Sarah Colfax, 1751–1801. "Barbour Collection."
[16]George Colfax married Mary Robbins of Wethersfield on 2 October 1777. "Barbour Collection."

tioned my desire to Captain Mallaly. He said I could not go, for the sloop was to be immediately fitted out and I was to go in her as Sailing Master.[17] That with some other things he added, I thought it would not be prudent for me to go, and I told Colfax I could not leave the sloop not more than two or three days, and he went off and left me. I had after that some conversation with Captain Mullaly and Captain Champlin about going to Weathersfield, and no objection was made, and I got a horse and commenced my journey. When I arrived, Mr. Colfax was married, and Lord had been at Mrs. Rose's to see Miss Colfax, and had gone up to Detroit to get his discharge from the army, and come down and marry immediately. I conversed with her on the subject. If she was bound by oath or any other way to marry him I would not say a word, if not I advised her not to have any connection with him, for I was intimately acquainted with him, and he was a very intemperate young man, and he would in all probability make her live a wretched life. "You tell me nothing new, Mr. Prince. I do not want to marry him, and I told him so the last time I saw him, and he said if you will not let me be your husband, I will murder myself in your presence, and now before I go away I will give you twenty thousand dollars for I am too rich. I told him I would not receive a penny, and he obliged me to say what I was unwilling to do, to be his wife when he returned." After remaining there about ten days, we all returned to New London. I found but very little had been done on board the sloop in my absence.

About the 20th of December, news came to New London that Mr. Lord was dead. He got his discharge from the army as a Lieutenant, and on his passage home he had a fit and died. I then expressed my desires to Miss Colfax, and wished she would engage

[17]"A List of Men belonging to *American Revenue*," undated, lists Prince as master. Yale University Library, "Shaw Papers," packet 78, #7.

to be my companion after my return from the trip I was a going to make soon. She told me, if I wanted to marry her, the sooner it was done the better, "for I have too many applications for that important change." As the law obliged to advertise two Sundays in the church our intention, before we could be united, I was obliged to commence that duty at once, which detained the sloop six or seven days, for we could not marry until the 11th of January 1778,[18] and they let me remain with my beloved wife a few days, before they compelled me to go on board. I was nearly half a mile from the river, and when I got there, the sloop was under way laying off and on, and the boat was ashore waiting for me. As soon as I got on board we spread all sail and soon left the city where I left my heart. Never did I leave a port and go to sea under such feelings before; there was a magnetic power I cannot describe.

When I left my wife, a more healthy woman could not be, but she had never the smallpox which prevailed considerable in New London. A Pest House was provided at the mouth of the river for all who were inoculated or had it the natural way. I advised my wife to be inoculated when I left her. She went through the operation, and her life was nearly extinguished, no hopes of her recovery. After many weeks she was partly restored to health, but a poor emaciated woman.

In May 1778 we returned from our cruise not very successful. We took some vessels but not very valuable. I did not receive more than a thousand dollars. I began to be dissatisfied with that sloop. She was a smaller vessel than I was in a habit of going to sea in, and not a fast sailer. In truth she was disapproved of by nearly all that was in her.

I found my wife so reduced in health and flesh I thought it my duty to do something for her restoration. She was not laboring

---

[18]New London vital records confirm this date. See "Barbour Collection."

under any complaint, but was weak and unable to do anything, nor walk any distance. I had made some arrangements to carry her to my parents and to Boston, and while I was a doing that, news arrived that General Burgoyne and his army was taken in the State of New York.[19] It made such joy and rejoicing among us we could not let it pass by unnoticed, but testified our feelings in having a banquet provided for eighty of us who combined to assemble and celebrate the day when so many Englishmen had fallen into our hands. Such a dinner I never saw, and such harmony of sentiments in our toasts. Mr. Shaw presided as Chairman. He and several at the close of the meeting were obliged to be sent home in coaches, for they could not walk. Wine never has that effect on me if I drink a gallon, but is not so with every one. None of us drank less than two quarts. It was a wonderful luxury. Mr. George Colfax had got to keeping house and I boarded with him, as his mother lived too far from my daily duty.

Soon after that feast, a vessel arrived at New London from Rhode Island, mounting eighteen four pounders, a sloop, one hundred and eighty tons, commanded by a Captain Pierce, on purpose for a Sailing Master. He immediately applied to me to accept the office. I had but a short conversation with him on the subject, and agreed to go, and took my things on board and sailed immediately. As the supplement of his crew was at the Vineyard,[20] we went there and took them in and commenced the cruise. We had one severe action, and met several powerful enemies, which obliged us to escape rather than contend, and took but one ship and she was a heavy letter of marque, but no lives

[19]Burgoyne surrendered his forces to Maj. Gen. Horatio Gates at Saratoga, New York, on 17 October 1777. News of this event would have reached New London shortly after Prince returned from his first cruise in the *American Revenue*. Since Prince reversed the order of his first and second cruises, he also misdated the surrender, moving it from the autumn of 1777 to the spring of 1778.

[20] *The Vineyard:* Martha's Vineyard, Massachusetts.

were lost on either side. In about three months we arrived back again to New Bedford, where we found the prize had arrived, and sold. I went on to New London the first opportunity, and found my wife in better health, but still much debilitated. I made my arrangements at once to take her to my parents. As I could not get a horse and chaise in New London that suited me, we went up to Norwich in a boat, and there we was well pleased with an excellent horse, and soon took our departure. After we arrived at Providence, I went down to Bristol, and got my prize money from the owner of the sloop, *General Gates,* which was the name of the last sloop I was in.[21] Money began to differ in its value, there was nearly ten per cent discount on Continental money. The prize we went in brought but little either to the owner or crew.

I returned back to Providence again that night. As soon as I entered the house, my wife introduced me to a man. "Mr. Prince, this is Captain Peter Richards, born in New London, a particular acquaintance of mine." He informed me he had been taken and carried to England, where he had been confined as a prisoner twelve months and finally exchanged, and had lately arrived in Boston, and was bound to New London, and was determined to have some revenge on the English for their ill-treatment of him and his crew since he was taken.[22] I told him I had been six months a prisoner, though not illy treated, yet I would be willing to go with him and aid him in seeking his revenge. Early next morning we parted, and me and my wife arrived at my parents in

[21]Perhaps Rhode Island privateer *General Stark,* commissioned 5 April 1778, Benjamin Pearce, commander. See William P. Sheffield, *Privateersmen of Newport, an Address Delivered by William P. Sheffield, before the Rhode Island Historical Society, in Providence, February 7, A.D., 1882* (Newport, R.I.: 1883), 60.

[22]Peter Richards was a lieutenant in the Continental Navy ship *Alfred,* Elisha Hinman, commander, when she was captured 9 March 1778. He eventually escaped from confinement in Forton Prison, near Portsmouth, England, and returned via France to New London in the spring of 1779. Middlebrook, *Maritime Connecticut during the American Revolution,* Vol. 2, 151.

the afternoon the same day. I visited all my connections and stayed at Kingston about ten days, and then we went to Boston, and remained there about as long. In about a month after we left New London we returned back there again, my wife considerably improved in her health.

When I was married and before, I told my wife I had made up my mind to make Boston my home, which she had no objection to, and after we returned to New London, she said she was sorry in hearing there was such a depreciation in Continental money, and it might continue, and I would lose much or all of mine I had on loan, and advised me to purchase a house, and named one. I soon took her advise and went to Mr. Green the owner, who told me what I should have it for. I wanted him to take my bond of seventeen hundred dollars as payment, and be accountable to me for the remainder after he had given me the deed. He asked thirteen hundred dollars for his house and lot, and was unwilling to take my bond or loan for that sum. That disturbed my feeling very much, that seventeen hundred dollars, with one year's interest would not pay the sum of thirteen hundred. I went to Mr. Shaw and carried my loan certificate with me, and asked him how much he would give me for it. After a few minutes he said, "I will give you thirteen hundred and fifty dollars for it."[23] I accepted the offer, took the money and purchased the house, without any intention of living in it. My wife then told me I had better lay out my money for furniture which we should want, and I might save many hundred dollars by it, for the continental money was depreciating every day. I gave her all my money, about a thousand dollars, and do with it as she thought best.

Captain Peter Richards, who I saw at Providence, was married

---

[23]On 30 March 1780, Nathaniel Shaw, Jr., initiated action to collect the interest due on Prince's $1,700 worth of Continental loan certificates. Rogers, *Connecticut's Naval Office at New London*, 326–37.

in a few days after his return to New London, to Thomas Mumford's daughter at Groton, who he was engaged to before he went to sea the last time.[24]

Mr. Mumford owned some vessels, and one he had built which had never been sent to sea, about one hundred and thirty tons, as she was built for a horse-jockey, and use her for that purpose. She had been laying by for many months. It was suggested to him she would make a good privateer. It was some time before he took any notice of what was said to him about her. He finally told Captain Hinman to fix her up in sails and rigging, and carry her into the Sound and try her, and let him know whether she was fit for a vessel of war. That was done and he pronounced her to be an excellent vessel for the purpose. He ordered her to be fitted out as soon as possible, and they were at work on her when Captain Richards arrived, and was nearly finished. Mr. Mumford appointed Captain Richards commander of that sloop, which they then called the *Hancock,* after that respectable name and character which stood so high in the National Council.[25] As soon as I had returned to New London, Captain Richards called on me, and said I must go with him agreeable to my promise as first Lieutenant. I accepted the offer, but as I had but little duty to do on board, I was not prevented from purchasing the house and some other necessary duties. As soon as we had got her complete, we hauled her off into the river and hoisted the flag, for shipping our crew, and in three days we had more applications than we wanted. Captain Richards was but seldom on board, and I had little or no opportunity to know what kind of a man he was, but I

[24]"MARRIED . . . At *Groton,* Mr. Peter Richards, a Lieutenant in the Continental Navy, to Miss Catharine Mumford, Daughter of Thomas Mumford, Esq." *Connecticut Gazette,* 29 April 1779.

[25]John Hancock (1737–93), Boston merchant, president of the Continental Congress, 24 May 1775–29 October 1777, major general of Massachusetts militia.

discovered he had much friendship towards me. He was a heavy, corpulent, and inactive to all appearance, but was sure he was resolute and determined in all his duties. He was about four years older than me.

We sailed about the first of November, and the third day we fell in with a brig loaded with salt, commanded by Captain Blanch, bound to New York. We manned her and sent her in, and we soon took several other ships and brigs, so that in twenty days after we sailed we had more prisoners on board than those who belonged to the *Hancock,* and had to return, for an arrangement was made by a Lieutenant of the British Navy, one of the prisoners, to take the vessel from us, which would have been done if it had not been for Captain Blanch, who revealed it to me about one hour before they were a going to commence the mutiny. Many lives would have been lost without any doubt. We was not out more than twenty four days before we arrived back to New London, and found all our prizes but one, landed our prisoners, and sailed again in a few days, which happened to be on Friday, which Mr. Mumford protested against. We was a lying off and on, waiting for Captain Richards, and when he came on board he said Mr. Mumford and many others said we never shall return again if we go out today. I told him I despised such predictions, and every officer on board said the same. Captain Richards then said to the Sailing Master, "Mr. Rider, make sail," and said to the gunner, "fire a departing gun." The sloop *Jay,* Captain Havens, had sailed about one hour before. She mounted sixteen guns. Before she had got to Montaque Point,[26] we came up to her and agreed to cruise together for a day or two. The weather was pleasant for the time of year. We went out under very easy sail all night. Early in the morning we was still in sight of Long Island,

[26]*Montauk Point:* Point on eastern extremity of Long Island, New York.

and kept under easy sail. About meridian, we saw a large ship standing to the westward. She passed us about three miles off. She showed twenty guns. Captain Havens requested to attack her first, and if she made any resistance, to treat her as she deserved. He soon came within gun shot, and the ship hove too, and hauled up her courses, and fired a broad shot into the *Jay,* and struck her colors. We soon boarded her, and in examining her bills of lading, we found ninety-seven yards of Osnaburgs,[27] and seven hundred barrels of beef and pork, and various other articles, and bound to New York. The Captain was a stubborn fellow. We put two prize masters on board, with men and sent her in. We then both stood off under easy sail, the wind at S.E. At twelve o'clock at night the wind shifted to S.S.W. As it came on very sudden, Havens took his larboard tacks, and we the starboard, and soon lost sight of each other. It was my watch on deck at four o'clock. At daylight I saw a square rigged vessel standing by the wind, head on. I could not tell whether she was a ship or a brig, or vessel of war or a merchantman. I ordered the sloop about, and went below and told Captain Richards what I had seen and what I had done. He said, "go on, I shall not go on deck at present." Soon after that she saw us and bore away. I saw at once she was a brig and no guns. I tacked at once, and stood for her with colors at mast head, and in twenty minutes I was alongside of her, hoisted out the boat, and went on board while the sun was making its appearance. I went on board the *Hancock,* and told Captain Richards we had taken a brig with 307 pipes of Madeira Wine.[28] I sent a[29] Prize Master on board with men, and told him to make sail immediately, which

[27] *Osnaburg:* A rough coarse durable cotton fabric in plain weave.

[28] 2 June 1780, *Hancock,* Capt. Peter Richards, captured British brig *Friendship,* with 306 pipes of Madiera. Middlebrook, *Maritime Connecticut during the American Revolution,* Vol. 2, 107. *Pipe:* A large cask of varying capacity used especially for wine and oil.

[29] The manuscript reads "to."

he did. The wind had got at S.W. but we was out of sight of the *Jay,* and all the property was ours. The wind was so light we found the brig made but slow way ahead, and she was such a dull sailer we began to fear she might not get in for many days, and as she was such a valuable prize, we was unwilling to lose her. We run along-side and took a hawser on board and took her in tow. But the wind was remarkable light, and did not make Montaque Point until Thursday. As soon as we got up with the Point we cast off the tow rope, and went into the Sound to see if there was any English ship in Gardner's Bay. We found none and returned to the Brig at daylight on Friday morning and took her in tow again, and at one o'clock P.M. we arrived safe at New London, only eight days ab-sent, and brought Mr. Mumford not less than $40,000 worth of property, equal to silver and gold. The success throwed away the superstition of many about a vessel sailing on Friday.

We sailed again very soon. A few days after we got out, we saw a vessel at the eastward, standing towards us, with a light wind at N.E. After she came within three miles of us, she luffed[30] up to the wind; we saw she was a large Virginia built schooner of sixteen guns. She hove out signals as we had done, which neither of us understood, which convinced them and us we were enemies. We made sail and stood for her, and found she sailed remarkably fast. Before dark we found we had not gained on her but very little, which made us more anxious to get her. It proved to be a dark night, and very little wind. We got out our oars and kept sight of her by glasses and eyes, until an hour before daylight, and did not see her again until the day dawned. She was then as much as three miles from us, about west. We doubled our exertions to take her. A slight breeze came out at S.W., but we kept our oars at work un-til we got within a mile of her. She wore round and fired a broad-

---

[30]The manuscript reads "loosed."

side at us. Some of the shot fell short of us, and some passed. Before she luffed to, we had gained upon her considerable. She wore round again and fired another broadside. By that time we was so near her, some of her grape fell around us. We made no alteration, but kept our oars a going with all our might. She luffed to the wind, loaded her guns, and wore round again. Our gunner was ordered to fix one of the bridle port guns. As soon as the schooner wore four points on her heel, our gunner fired, which dismounted one of their guns, killed three men, and wounded two. He loaded it again and fired into her, and killed two men and wounded three. By that time we were not more than 300 feet from her. The oars were ordered in, and every man to board the schooner. We saw but one man on deck, and he was the Sailing Master. He begged as a favor we would not board them with the whole crew, "we confess ourselves all to be prisoners of war." When I went on board I was astonished in seeing the five men dead on deck, and four badly wounded, the other was slightly wounded, no risk of his life, but not so with the four. Three of them died after they arrived at New London, where we sent her immediately, well manned. She was a beautiful vessel, about sixty on board. She was 160 tons and mounted sixteen guns.[31] They told us they believed there was not another vessel in the world that would outsail her. When they saw us the night before they knew we was a privateer, and did not want to have anything to do with us, but felt no more concerned about being taken than if they were in New York, for they never saw a vessel of any kind that could sail as fast as they. As we had so many prisoners on board and the weather began to be boisterous, we did not mean to stay out but a few days. We stood on with the schooner that day and night until

[31] 2 September 1780, *Hancock,* Capt. Peter Richards, captured British privateer *Hibernia,* ten guns. Middlebrook, *Maritime Connecticut during the American Revolution,* Vol. 2, 107.

we got near Montague Point, and then quit her and stood off to the southward. The next day we fell in with Captain Havens in the *Jay*. The wind came out at N.E. with a heavy mist. We could not see but a short distance. We were laying to under easy sail, and saw two Brigs to windward coming down before the wind under easy sail. We hove out our signals, but they did not answer them, but luffed to. We saw one of 16, the other of 14 guns. We made sail for them. They were about two miles from us. They made sail. All of us were on our larboard tacks. In about one hour we found we was gaining on them, in eating them out of the wind, but not in any other way. The 16-gun brig rather outsailed the other, and we outsailed the *Jay*. The wind and rain increased, and the sun was not more than an hour high, when the large Brig bore away and run down athwart our forefoot within gunshot, and made all the sail she could. The *Jay* bore away after her, and they were soon out of sight. We was gaining on the other. The wind and sea increased. We got within shot of her and fired a few guns, but to no effect. She was carrying such sail her lee guns were all under water. She could not fire anything but muskets. Our weather guns at last opened so heavy upon her, she struck her colors, but the wind and seas was so heavy we could not board her. They were both from Halifax. We ordered her to wear and bring her starboard tacks on board. We all had to reef our sails, and it soon came on very dark. We both had lights out, but the gale increased to that degree, we lost sight of her and hove too, and saw her no more. As soon as the gale decreased, we directed our course to New London, where we soon arrived. We was received at New London with joyful hearts and hands. The schooner we sent in was sold at an enormous price, for she was purchased for a privateer, and called the *Minerva*. I settled my account with my owner, and received about ten thousand dollars in money and goods, equal to silver and gold.

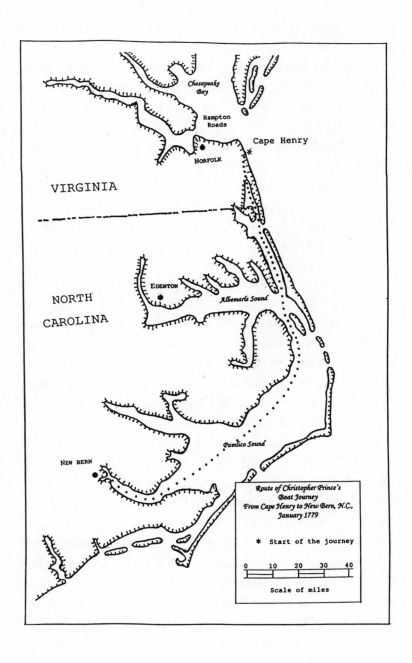

Chesapeake
Bay

Hampton
Roads

Cape Henry

● NORFOLK

*

VIRGINIA

NORTH

CAROLINA

EDENTON
●

Albemarle Sound

Pamlico Sound

NEW BERN
●

Route of Christopher Prince's
Boat Journey
From Cape Henry to New Bern, N.C.,
January 1779

* Start of the journey

0   10   20   30   40

Scale of miles

Flour was very scarce in New London, and meal of every kind. Mr. Guy Richards had a sloop about sixty tons, which a number of citizens wanted to send to Virginia for a load of Flour, and wanted me to go in her as commander. It was some time before I consented to go, and then, not without some one who was acquainted with navigation to go with me. They could not get one for some time, at last a man by the name of Moore offered to go if he was allowed as much for the voyage as I was. I and they received him on these conditions, and each of us had the continental money sewed and quilted in the back of our vests. We took two men before the mast only. We made sail early in January 1779, and had an excellent passage to the mouth of the Chesapeake. We passed Cape Henry about sunset, not a vessel in sight. The wind was light and the tide against us. At 10 P.M., we were in sight of the lights in Hampton Roads, and in three fathom of water. All of a sudden we saw two schooners astern of us, as the moon was setting. We saw they were under full sail. We began to feel uneasy about our situation, because they were not in the channel but in pursuit of us over the banks. In a few minutes one came alongside not more than one hundred feet from us, and poured in a broadside. We ordered the two men below, and Moore took the helm, and I went in the gangway. She wore off and the other one came up and fired cannon and musket shot into us. I was then at the helm. I was in hopes we should get into such shoal water they could not come so near us again. The other was a coming up, and but a few rods astern of us. Our men came out of the cabin and told us the sloop was a sinking, the water was above the cabin floor. Mr. Moore went down and saw the water coming into the vessel in torrents, and ran up on deck, and told me she would sink in a minute. The schooner astern of us was not more than her length from us. I requested them to take in sail and come alongside without firing a gun as we wanted to go on board of them. We took all our things out of the cabin on deck, and in five minutes they were alongside. We hove our things on board of them in an instant, and they took our boat on board of them, and one cable and anchor, and as we had nothing in the hold, they set fire to her and made sail. We were not more than two miles then from Hampton Roads.

These schooners both belonged to New York, twelve guns each. Moore and I was on board of one vessel, and our two men on board the other. They got out about ten miles from the Cape, and hove too under very easy sail. Nearly all on board were asleep in the morning, but a very little wind, but a heavy swell from the N.E. At Breakfast the Captain then conversed with us about our voyage, but never intimated any suspicion from what we said we had any money about us or in our chests. I made myself so ignorant about guns and other implements of war, he thought I never was on board of a ship of war before, and laughed at my ignorance. Moore and I had talked about getting our liberty to go on shore, in the boat they took out of the sloop, and he wanted me to use every means to obtain that liberty. I began first about my ignorance in respect vessels of war, and after I got through with that, I asked the Captain what was a going to do with us?

"Why carry you to New York, and put you in prison."

"For what?"

"Because you are rebels."

"We were a going to try and get some flour for the people in New London, and we would do the same for you if we could. I wish you would put us on shore, and let us go to work and earn our living, for we do not care anything about such vessels as these."

About eleven o'clock he consented for Moore and I to go on

shore. He would give us our own boat. I told him I wish he would let my men go with me for it was too far for us to row ashore, we are twelve miles off.

"Do you want to kill us, or suffer us to loose our own lives? We know not what the weather will be before sunset, and we are as much as sixteen miles from the bay we must go on shore in the surf. Do let me have my men, or I must remain on board, for I dare not go in the boat without them."

"I will ask the Captain on board the other vessel," and made sail.

She was about one mile from us. When he first asked him he refused, but in a few minutes he consented. The boat was hoisted out and we went on board and took our men, and bid them all good bye, and set off. They gave us a small sail to help us along.

We made for the beach about eight miles south of Cape Henry, and arrived a little before sunset. The surf was so high we considered it to be unsafe to go on shore. While we were meditating on this, a Grampus came up within ten feet of the boat with his mouth open wide enough to take the boat and all of us into it. That alarmed us so much we thought we would make our attempt while it was daylight, for the weather began to have the appearance of a storm, which would prevent us from going to the Chesapeake, or Roanoke Inlet. We found the third surf was the safest, the second broke as much as fifteen feet high, the third not more than eight or ten. We got on the second surf and was just on the edge of the third, when it commenced to role, and it carried the boat almost perpendicular until she was on the beach. We all jumped out about knee high, and held the boat until the water left us, and then hauled her up on dry ground, where we were safe. We did not see any house, neither did we expect to see any man, for that is a barren beach from Cape Henry, south one hundred miles. We knew there were some wreckers who lived there, but we did not want to see any of them, for they were robbers as well as wreckers. But in a few minutes a man came to us and asked us where we were going. We told him into Pamlico Sound.

"How are you a going to get your boat there."

"We do not know. Have you got a horse?"

"I have."

"Will you drag it over?"

"I will if you pay me."

We agreed with him, and he carried it by his horse[32] into the head of a creek, and as it was low water we could not go into the Sound. The night was cloudy and very dark. We asked the man if he would give us something to eat. He told us he would. We all went to his house, and got what we wanted. His house was small, one room and a small loft. He had a wife and one or two children. The land was so barren it could not produce anything they could live on. We asked him if he was alone, whether there were any other men that lived near him? He said, "not within many miles." We went down to the boat about fifty rods from the house and requested our men to stay at the boat, and watch the tide, and as soon as it came in to float the boat, to let us know. Moore and I went up to the house and asked the man if we could lay down any where in the house and sleep, for we had not slept any for 48 hours? He told us there was straw in the garret where we could lay warm and comfortable. There was a ladder to get into the loft. We went up and lay down. I told Moore I did not like the looks of that man nor his wife, and I could not sleep quietly, for some unfavorable impressions were made on my mind about them. "So it is with me," said Moore. It was not long before I fell asleep, but I did not know it, and Moore shook me and said there were several men below, and were talking in a low voice, and believed they

[32]The manuscript reads "house."

had some unfavorable designs in view. We then began to deliberate on what ought to be done and concluded to go down and see who was there, and if it put on an unfavorable appearance, to make our escape if possible. Moore went down the ladder first, and I followed him, and as soon as we got down, we saw five large men beside the landlord.

He said to us, "what is the matter?"

"We feel uneasy about our men. We told them to stay in the boat and let us know when the tide comes, so we can go into the Sound, and we feel uneasy about them, and are going down and let them come and sleep on the straw up above, for they may get asleep in the boat and get sick."

We saw the most rugged countenances in them men we ever saw. They were ragged in their dress, and uncouth in their countenance. Not one of them said anything to us but looked upon us with vengeance. The landlord said, "we will go down with you." We told him we was much obliged to him there was no necessity. We wanted our great coats and the men, and should return in twenty minutes, and wished him to make us a sling of rum and water if he had any, for our men must be chilled. We went very fast down to the boat. As soon as we got there, we told our men, we were not safe. We would haul the boat down the creek. We jumped into the creek, two on each side of the boat, and sometimes we went knee high in mud and water. It was very dark. We had not got down more than a quarter of a mile before we saw all them men but a little distance from us, coming on as fast as possible, and they were not more than ten rods from us when we passed another creek which they could not in safety get over, for the water was so deep we got into our boat, and they said many words we did not understand, for we was a poling our boat on very fast with our oars. If they could have passed that creek, I do not know what would have been the consequence. In a few minutes we were out of their sight, and was able to row the boat, and got into the Sound about twelve o'clock. We rowed across for the main as quick as possible, for the mud and water we had gone through made us feel very uncomfortable. It was the 28th day of January 1779.

About one o'clock in the morning we found ourselves in a cove and alongside of a wharf where some boats were laying, and in three minutes three or four large dogs came down barking which prevented us from going on shore. In a few minutes we saw a light, and then a lantern coming to us. A colored man came to the boat and asked us what we wanted? We told him. He ordered the dogs away, and we walked up to the house, an elegant building. We passed one or two large barns and outhouses, and when we came to the house, an elderly gentleman was a standing at the door, and invited us in, and as soon as he saw our situation, muddy and wet up to our waists, he ordered a large fire to be made, gave us something to drink, called up several negro women, and told them to make a fire in the kitchen immediately, and hung on a large quantity of water and warm it. Very soon a large bathing tub was filled with warm water. I stripped off my clothes, got in, washed myself and put on clean clothes which was taken out of my trunk brought up from the boat. Thus did Moore. The men he gave clothes to from his own family, for they had none fit to put on. Our dirty clothes were all ordered to be washed, which was done and dried before eight o'clock in the morning. After we had related to him every circumstance that had taken place, he said he had no doubt but it was the intention of them men to murder us. Government could not prevent it. They were placed in that dreary place to accommodate those who should be cast away on that shore, but many unfavorable informations had been given, but no evidence as yet was ever known. On the 29th January our eyes saw what they never did before, and that was the Peach and Cherry trees were full of blossoms and an unusual change in nature, in almost everything, which was not seen before at that time of the year.

We thought it would be more safe to get home from Newbern, North Carolina, than from Norfolk. We communicated our intention to the gentleman we was with, and he gave us letters to several gentlemen the whole length of the Sound. It was impossible for us to have fallen into the hands of a more benevolent man than he was in that country. He was immensely rich. He had as many as a hundred negroes, and a beautiful farm, and buildings of every kind. When we left him, he gave us a bottle of Peach brandy and provisions enough for two or three days in boiled ham and bread. We took our departure. The weather was very pleasant, as we had food on board and the wind in our favor, we did not stop until we came to the house described to us, about forty miles from where we started, and a letter wrote to the owner who lived there, and was a Member of the Legislature. As soon as he read the letter, he said we must not go any further until the next morning, for we could not be accommodated with lodging as at his house. We agreed with his friendly request as it was four o'clock P.M. He treated us in such a feeling and affectionate manner we was astonished. Next morning we started early as the wind and weather was very favorable, so much so we passed all the rest of the houses we had letters to, for our friend who wrote them thought it almost impossible to go the whole length of the Sound with a fair wind and weather. Before the sun set, we got to the point of land that forms a part of the Sound that leads up to Edenton. My eyes then saw what they had before, for I had been there, and acquainted with every foot of channel, creeks, sounds, and ports.

We went on shore and was accommodated that night, and in the morning we started for the marshes which separate the Pamlico, from the Albemarle Sound. We arrived there about two P.M. We then had to go more than one hundred miles to the mouth of the river that leads up to Newbern. While we were passing through the marshes, which is about one mile, the weather had an unfavorable appearance, the wind at about east and very cloudy, and not less than sixty miles from any house in our power to get to in safety, for it was but a little difference from the ocean in entering the Albemarle Sound. We finally concluded to go as the wind was much in our favor, and our sail would carry us six and seven knots an hour. We quit the marshes, and was soon out of sight of land. The wind increased to such a degree, the sea began to comb and break, the boat was unsafe. We had to bear away before the wind with a small piece of sail up. Night soon came on, and although the moon had passed the first Quarter, yet it was very dark. About twelve o'clock at night all at once we found ourselves in smooth water, and saw the marshes on each side of us, and soon found ourselves in a creek, among a large flock of wild geese which rose all around us in such a manner they struck us with their wings and we were obliged to lean down in the boat to keep out of their way. We finally got up so far we got out of the boat and went on the marsh to try to get some fresh water, for we were distressed with thirst. We found some, we drank and it brought on a fever in ten minutes. We secured the boat and went on until we found the high land and a house, and awaked up those who lived there. They opened the door and let us in, we told our situation, and begged them to do something for us. They made us some herb tea which we drank plenty of and it removed our fever. We found ourselves about forty miles from Newbern River. About nine o'clock in the morning the wind and weather abated so much we got under way, and about nine o'clock in the evening we entered the Newbern River very much fatigued, for we were obliged to row all the way. We went on shore, and entered a log house, and begged them to let us sleep there. They accommodated us and we all turned in on some straw. We had not been asleep but an hour or so before the house got on fire and we all had to make our escape. A man who lived but a few rods from there, told us to go to his house. We took our trunks, and went there, but the house that was on fire was soon consumed. Early in the morning we took our departure and got up to Newbern that day. We soon found there was no prospect of ever going home from there, and finally concluded to go back to Norfolk, and go home by land.

A prize had been brought in there loaded with brandy, and was to be sold in a day or two at public sale. Moore and I concluded to buy ten pipes each, and hire a vessel to carry it up to the head of Pimlico Sound within three miles of Norfolk. When the sale came on we purchased them, got a vessel, and went on with it, and in a few days we got it at Baltimore. Our seamen did not go with us; we left them at Newburn. I soon sold mine at a good profit. I cleared about two hundred dollars clear of all expenses. Moore's conduct was a little singular after we arrived at Norfolk. Although he had a wife at Groton, he got linked in with a girl at Norfolk, and I could not get him to sell his Brandy and go home with me.

A sloop was a going to Baltimore, and a number of passengers, the day before I was ready. They all consented to wait until the next day, and then we all embarked and made sail and arrived after a short passage. One of the passengers bought my trunk and gave me ten dollars for it. I got a passage at once in a packet up to the head of Blackwater Creek, and a conveyance to Philadelphia.

While I was walking through the street, I met Captain Wheeler belonging to New London, taken by a British privateer, and put on shore near the Delaware, and he was on his way home and had just arrived. We went off together and arrived at Princeton that evening. We went on very well and found it a great favor in falling in company with each other. We passed through General Washington's camp at Pompton, where I saw one of my wife's brothers, Lieutenant in the General's guard.[33] We spent a few hours with him and then passed on. We had to pass the North River above West Point, and then direct our course to Middletown.

The day after we crossed the North River, Wheeler and I entered a tavern to get a dinner. It was late in the afternoon. We went into the back room and sat down. Before we got half through, a Continental officer entered the front room, and passed by the door several times where we sat, and fixed his eyes on me, which confused me. He walked up to me and asked me if my name was Prince. I told him it was.

"You married Lucy Colfax."

"I did."

"Do you not remember my countenance."

"I do not recollect I ever saw you before."

"I was at your wedding. My name is Hallem."

I know there were several there I never saw before and did not

---

[33]William Colfax (1756–1838); ens. 1st Connecticut, 1 January 1777; 2d lt., 1 January 1778; 1st lt., 18 March 1778; detailed to Commander in Chief's Guard in March 1778; transferred to 5th Connecticut, 1 January 1781; transferred to 2d Connecticut, 1 January 1783; capt., 1 April 1783; retained in Swift's Connecticut Regiment, June 1783, and served to 3 November 1783; commandant of the Commander in Chief's Guard, 1780–82. "Barbour Collection"; Francis B. Heitman, *Historical Register of Officers of the Continental Army during the War of the Revolution*, new revised and enlarged edition (Washington, D.C.: The Rare Book Shop Publishing Co., 1914), 165; John C. Fitzpatrick, ed., *The Writings of George Washington from the Original Manuscript Sources, 1745–1799*, 39 vols. (Washington, D.C.: Government Printing Office, 1931–44), Vol. 16, 393n; 23: 62n.

know them afterwards. I then told him, "I had often heard that Captain Robert Hallem was at my wedding. Are you the man?"[34]

"I am."

I then rose and took hold of his hand. He then said, "You must ride my horse half the way from here to New London." I made some apology. One was that Captain Wheeler would be left alone. But Captain Hallem and Wheeler insisted on it, and I immediately mounted the horse and rode fifteen miles, where we all put up that night, and early next morning Wheeler and I set out and Hallem overtook us about eight miles, and told me where I would find his horse. When we arrived there, I mounted the horse and left Wheeler to walk alone, which was not pleasant to me. Captain Hallem and I did not arrive at New London more than twenty-four hours before Captain Wheeler, but it was an indescribable favor bestowed on me, for even then, I could hardly walk. This friendly act will never be forgotten.

It was about the 25th of February when I arrived at New London. I was immediately called on to get the *Hancock* ready for sea. My wife had furnished my house complete and moved into it, which I was very much pleased with. Mr. Mumford lived at Groton, where he kept the *Hancock.* My house stood on a water lot. I bought a canoe to go and come when I was a mind. I soon got the sloop ready, hauled her off in the river to ship our hands. They were fitting out the schooner *Minerva*, Captain Fosdick was a going as Commander,[35] and the sloop *American Revenue*, Captain Champlin.

[34]Robert Hallam, d. 1835; sergeant in the Lexington Alarm, April 1775; 2d lt. 20th Continental Infantry, 1 January 1776; 1st lt. 4th Connecticut, 1 January 1777; capt., 31 July 1777; resigned, 20 May 1779. Heitman, *Historical Register*, 268.

[35]Nicoll Fosdick, of New London, commanded several privateers during the war, including brigantine *Defiance*, commissioned 27 November 1779, and sloop *Randolph*, in 1780, 1781, and 1782. Middlebrook, *Maritime Connecticut during the American Revolution*, Vol. 2, 68, 180–85.

We all sailed together, and as it happened we did not separate after we got out. We stood westward until we saw Sandy Hook. One night we stretched off under easy sail, and the first thing we saw in the morning was a frigate under full sail between us and a large fleet coming out from New York. She was not more than three miles from us, the wind at the westward. We had the day before a heavy gale from the S.E. that lasted about two hours, which made a heavy sea and left a heavy and large swell. There was that morning about an eight knot breeze from W.N.W. and we found after we saw the frigate and fleet, we were out of sight of land. We all made sail and bore away before the wind, while the sun was rising in a clear and cloudless sky. The frigate got alongside of the *Revenue,* Captain Champlin. The *Minerva* then took her starboard tacks on board and hauled up by the wind, and was soon out of gun-shot of the frigate. By the time she had taken full possession of the *Revenue,* and made sail, we were nearly three miles from her plunging into the swell ahead in such a degree we expected every minute to see the topmast go over the bow, and did not feel easy about the Mainmast. We got preventer stays on them both, the topsail and studding sail halyard continued chafing and giving away, which kept us often destitute of sail we stood in need of to make our escape. We found the ship gained upon us, for the swell did not impede her as it did us. She finally came so near us, not more than one hundred rods from us, and said to us standing forward, "O you Yankee Rebels, we shall soon be alongside of you." We had begun to heave our guns overboard, and we hove over twelve, and four remaining. We started nearly all the water in the hold, and pumped it out. We sawed down the gunwales. The swell only that prevented us from sailing abated so much, none of our Halyards gave way. They remained at that distance from us about twenty minutes, and did not come any nearer, and we expected every moment they would bring her broadside on us, which must have sunk us. We soon found we were gaining from them, and at ten A.M. we were out of gun-shot from them. The wind rather increased. By twelve o'clock we were abreast of Montague Point; by five o'clock we were close to Elizabeth Island, and the hull of the frigate was not seen off of our deck. Joseph Champlin was second Lieutenant, he and myself were the only Pilots across Nantucket Shoals, and before daylight next day we were a past the shoals and close on board Cape Cod, and at four P.M. we arrived at Boston in safety. Captain Richard went on to New London the next day and requested me to remain on board.[36]

Some of our men left us, and some of our Prize masters, but we had about eighty remaining on board when I received orders from Mr. Mumford to carry the *Hancock* to New London. We sailed very soon, and as we was entering on Nantucket shoals a large ship was in chase of us, and she did not give up until we passed Pollock rip shoal.[37] She then had to stop. We continued on safe by Nantucket, Vineyard, and all the islands. The next day we arrived safe at New London, and in ten days we had her complete for a cruise. She was soon manned, and we sailed.[38]

We had not been out but a day or two, before we fell in with the brig *Holker,* belonging to Philadelphia, she, sixteen six

[36]HM frigate *Greyhound* captured the *American Revenue,* Samuel Champlin, commander, in July 1779, and sent her into New York. The sloop *Hancock,* Capt. Lodowick Champlin, in company of *American Revenue,* escaped a close pursuit by heaving her guns over the side. Middlebrook, *Maritime Connecticut during the American Revolution,* Vol. 2, 52; *Connecticut Gazette,* 28 July, 4 August, 1779.

[37]*Pollock Rip:* Sand shoals and ridges with little water over them in places, extending eastward of Monomoy Point, Barnstable County, Massachusetts.

[38]"The HANCOCK will sail again on a short Cruize, in five Days—Some good Sailors have once more an Opportunity to make their Fortunes, by applying soon to Capt. Champlin, at his House, or on Board said Sloop at Mr. Mumford's Wharf, at Groton. Sept. 1, 1779." *Connecticut Gazette,* 1 September 1779.

pounders. We kept together and in a short time fell in with the sloop *Jay.* We had not been together more than half a day before we saw a ship coming down towards us under full sail, the wind about south. She was within three miles of us before she altered her course. She then bore away as much as eight points from the wind. We saw she had twenty guns and many men on board. We all bore away after her when we had consulted together, for we was sure she was a ship of war or a packet. That was about three P.M. We outsailed the *Holker* and *Jay,* and gained fast on the ship. At 5 P.M. we saw Long Island right ahead, and yet the ship would not alter her course, she steered right on for the land. Before we got within gun shot of her, it came on dark, and all of a sudden we was within pistol shot of her, and all her sails standing. We luffed too in an instant and struck the bottom. She still went on and struck three times before we was clear of the shoal which made off from Fire Island Inlet. We came to anchor within one hundred rods of the ship, for we knew she was on shore, although we could not see the land. In about half an hour, the brig and sloop arrived and came to anchor, for we hoisted lights that they might be directed to us in safety. The *Jay* came very near the shoal, by not taking in sail in season. We all came to anchor close to the ship not knowing whether she was a ship of war or not. Not a gun was fired from them or us. Each vessel manned a boat, about twenty men in each boat, and the first Lieutenant of each vessel took charge of each boat to go and man the ship if prudent. We got close under her stern, and saw the Quarter Deck full of men. They said nothing to us, nor we to them. Robert Sheffield, Lieutenant of the *Jay* was very near me. I told him I did not think it prudent to board her. We all agreed to return on board our vessels. Before daylight we saw them going on shore and at the dawn of day we boarded her and not a person was there; and there was not less than thirty boarding pikes laying on deck, as many loaded muskets, and her carriage guns all loaded. But we saw at once she was a packet. We found by the mess list on board, there were 108 men, 72 were British soldiers. She was loaded with silver and plated ware. We took out of her about five thousand pounds sterling each on board our vessels. As it was low water when she went on shore, we had some prospect of getting her off. We took out an anchor, and got her afloat, and while we were getting her in order, to make sail, we saw a fleet go over the bar at Sandy Hook and one of the ships bore away for us, which we knew was a frigate, which would prevent us from getting the ship off safe, and not only that, all our vessels were unsafe. We cut the ship's cable and let her go on shore again, and we made sail and stood off by the wind until we got clear from the island, and she chased us until twelve meridian, but we all outsailed her.[39]

We did not stay out but a few days after that on account of the sloop was rather too heavy loaded to sail well. We parted from the *Holker* and *Jay,* and arrived at New London, discharged the articles we had, and sailed again, and soon fell in with the *Holker* and *Jay,* which had not taken anything after we left them. The second day after we met, at 3. P.M., we saw a large ship steering in for New York, the wind at S.S.E. but very moderate. She was as much as six miles to leeward of us. We saw she was a heavy letter of marque. She had twenty-four guns, and many men. We crowded sail for her. We were all before the wind, and gained fast on the ship. I kept forward with a spyglass to watch her motion. At 5 P.M. I saw

---

[39] "Yesterday returned into port from a cruize, the *Hancock, Experiment,* and *Young Beaver* Privateers. At 11 o'clock last tuesday night [23 May 1780], the above privateers, in company with the brig *Holker* of Philadelphia, fell in with the *Arteriel,* a packet from Falmouth, bound to New York, commanded by Charles Newman, mounting 20 guns; at which time the ship being near the east point of Sandy Hook, ran on shore, by which they carried off the mail. The prize would soon have been got off, but a fleet of 20 sail coming out of the Hook the next morning, the privateers were obliged to leave her, after taking out a few articles." *Connecticut Gazette,* 26 May 1780.

them hoist their Pendant at the main royal mast head, and the halyard fastened below the truck and cut away, so it was impossible to strike that color, then hoisted the Ensign over the stern on the flag-staff, and cut them halyards away. I then told Captain Richards what they had done. We was about two miles from them then. We pressed on with all the sail we could set. The other vessels were two miles astern of us and a fog increased which kept us almost out of sight of each other, but Richards said, "we can and will take that ship." We got within shot of her, and she veered twice to bring her broadside on us, and she could not do it without bring her sails aback. We were so near her stern we could have fired a musket ball into her, and she into us. I saw a boy going aloft, after he got there he cut the Pendant off within three feet of the Royal masthead, and it flew away on the water, and they could not strike the Ensign, they hauled it in, and rolled it around the staff. By that time our Jib boom was not more than forty feet from her taffrail or stern.

Captain Richards came forward and asked them where they were from.

They said "from Barbadoes."

"Where are you bound?"

"New York."

We hauled up our Square sail, clued up the topsail, and told them to clue up their topgallant sails: They did. "Lower down your topsails, and clue them up": They did. "Clue up your courses": They did. "Starboard your helm and luff to the wind": All was done in a few minutes. We hove too under her lee, hove out the boat. I took two loaded pistols in my belt and hanger, and went on board. The gang-ladder was put over the side, and one man each side. When I got on the gunwale, I stood for half a minute looking fore and aft, and saw she had a complete set of guns fore and aft, matches lit, and the deck full of men, so much so I could not go into the cabin. It was foggy and commenced to be dark. I then told them to open a way for me to pass: They did not more than two feet wide. I went down on deck and passed through them into the cabin, where the Captain and owners sat. I asked them for their papers. As soon as I took them and saw what they were, I told them they were all prisoners of war, and I should deal with them accordingly; and while I was talking with them a man came into the cabin, and as soon as I saw him, I knew who it was. I sprung up to him and caught hold of his hand, and said, "Captain Thayer, is it you?" He dropped his head, and tears started into his eyes, and it was with difficulty he could speak. I asked him how he had been treated by those gentlemen. He said but little, but they said, "we have treated him well." I told him to stay in the cabin for I must go on deck and send the prisoners on board. I ran up and ordered the boat loaded. In a few minutes she returned, and while I was loading her again, the other vessels came too, and their boats were on board directly. It got to be very dark, but we soon had about seventy men out, and put the Prize Masters on board, and about twenty of our men, for she was a large ship loaded with rum and sugar. We all made sail for Cape May, the wind still at S.S.E. and thick fog, but we drove on with all our might for we had a valuable prize with us. About four o'clock P.M. the next day, we made Cape May, and entered the Delaware about five miles up the bay, and came to anchor before dark. We were all so fatigued, we set a watch and turned in. Early next morning we all took some articles out of the ship, rum, sugar, and sweetmeats. I went on board to see Captain Thayer, a man who I sailed with once as his Mate, a long voyage the first time he ever commanded a vessel. I found him out of the cabin in the steerage, and much oppressed in his feelings. He had been taken prisoner as first Lieutenant in a ship of war and carried to

Barbadoes, and put into a prison, where he was taken so unwell after remaining there many months, the Doctors advised the authority to send him to New York by his own request, which they consented to do and put him on board that ship. I told the Steward to bring a bottle of wine and I made him drink near half of it, but it did not raise his spirits much. As he was destitute of money, I gave him an order on my agent at Philadelphia for $400 to buy him a horse and get home to his family in Boston. About ten A.M. we put all the prisoners on board the ship, among which were fifty British soldiers, about ninety in all, and sent them off for Philadelphia, and we laid there until we saw them enter Delaware River, where we knew she would be safe, and then we all made sail and went to sea. We made an excellent cruise in taking several merchantmen and then went to New London.[40]

We fitted out the *Hancock* again very soon, and went on our cruise. We had not been out but a few days before we fell in with the *Minerva*, Captain Fosdick. We were both under sail, head and head. We hove out a signal which he did not answer, and we considered him an enemy, and made all preparation for action, and was not convinced it was the *Minerva* until she was within musket shot of us.

---

[40]"Philadelphia. Yesterday was sent in here the ship *Commerce*, Capt. Coran, of 16 guns, and 80 men, belonging to Liverpool, bound from Barbados for New York, with 350 puncheons and 60 tierces of rum, 60 casks and 150 bags of cocoa. She was captured by the brig *Holker*, of this port, the sloop *Bunker-Hill*, and schooner ----, belonging to New England. On board of the prize was a Capt. and 30 men, belonging to the Royal immigrants, who on their passage from St. John's, in Newfoundland, to Halifax, were blown off the coast and arrived at Barbadoes, from whence they were going to New-York in the *Commerce* when they were obliged to stop at this port." *Pennsylvania Journal*, 24 May 1780. The following issue of the *Journal* identified the captors as brigantine *Holker*, Matthew Loller commander, schooner *Bunkerhill*, Sanford Thompson commander, and sloop *Hancock*, Peter Richards commander. Ibid., 31 May 1780. See also *Connecticut Gazette*, 26 May 1780.

Captain Richards asked Fosdick why he did not answer the signal?

"Do you not know the *Minerva,* what did you heave a signal out for?"

"How did I know but what you had been taken, and in possession of my enemy? I disapprove and despise such conduct!"

Fosdick, "I hope you will dismiss them feelings."

"I will if I can, but I consider myself insulted."

Fosdick, "let us cruise together a few days."

"You may do as you please."

We stood off to the Southward under easy sail. We kept together for two or three days, and we saw a brig bearing down upon us. After she got within 2 gunshot, she hoisted the American signal, which we answered and she soon came alongside. She was from Salem, commanded by Welding. She mounted sixteen guns. We all wondered at his presumption in coming to us, as he did not know whether we were friends or enemies, for he would certainly have been taken if we had been his enemies. We all lay within shot of each other until next day, when we saw a large ship steering to the eastward. When she passed us we saw she had twenty-four guns. The wind was at S.W. We all consulted about attacking her, and Captain Richards in particular. The other two told us if we would go and bring her to action they would follow us, and get under her stern, and compel her to surrender. We made sail and soon got within gun shot of her. She hove too, hauled up her courses. We lay on her broadside within musket shot. She had a boarding netting which went from her taffrail up to her main and foretop, and down to the end of her bowsprit. She had swivels in her main and fore tops. The brig and the *Minerva* had not started an inch when we commenced the action. In a few minutes we had two men killed and much of our standing and running rigging cut away. We soon drove the men out of the tops, and cut her boarding netting all to pieces. We continued our action two hours and a half, and lulled the wind into a calm. The brig and schooner were about six miles from us. After we had been alongside of the ship one hour they made sail, but neared us very slowly. A twelve pound shot went through our mast about fourteen feet above the deck, which throwed us into a perilous situation, for all our stays and many of our shrouds were cut away and nothing to secure the mast, which must be done immediately or we should become a wreck. At that time the brig was close on board of us, and one of our men by the name of Sheffield, a quarter gunner, went on the opposite side and fired a shot into her, which came very near the man at the helm, and cut away a part of the main boom. I ordered him away. Captain Welden asked us what we meant by firing into him? Richards told him to ask no more questions about that, it was unbeknown to him until it was done. He run under the stern of the ship, and commenced a severe fire, which obliged the ship to bear away before the wind. We then went to work and cleared our wreck. We had seven men dead and some wounded. We buried them and went to work to secure the masts, for we could not hoist one sail on board. While we were at work Fosdick came to us and began to ask some questions, which were not answered. After the brig got the ship out of gun shot from us she came back to us and offered us what assistance we wanted. We told him we despised his conduct, for if he and Fosdick had come as they ought to have done, we should have that ship now in possession. As for Fosdick, he had a sufficient evidence he was a coward. By the time we got our mast fished and rigging fixed, a violent gale came on from the N.E. which drove us very near to Cape Hatteras. Before we were in danger of losing the vessel the wind abated and shifted, and we soon arrived at New

London, for we dare not speak with any vessel, for our mast was supported by rigging entirely.[41]

Soon after we arrived, a beautiful brig arrived from Middletown, loaded for one of the West India Islands owned by Mr. Sage. Edward and John Hallem bought one third of her and wanted me to take one third, which I did and gave eighteen thousand dollars continental money; she was loaded with a valuable cargo and 48 horses, and mounted twelve guns; she soon sailed.[42]

Mr. Mumford owned a part of the *Minerva,* and bought some more of her, and turned Fosdick out, and intended to employ the *Hancock* and *Minerva* as Letters of Marques to Martinique and St. Eustatia. The *Hancock* had been built for a man by the name of Chester, but he had Quaker principles which prevented him from doing anything with vessels of war. But when he commenced fitting them out as Letters of Marque, he gave Chester the *Hancock,* and Richards the *Minerva.* As Chester could not nor would not fight, either to defend himself, or take a vessel if she was within his power, they got me to go with Chester as a commissioned officer and do all the fighting. I consented on certain conditions, which we all agreed to. We had about thirty men each, and never separated from the time we left New London un-

[41]"On the 8th instant, Capt. Champlin in the *Hancock,* Capt. Welden in the *Venus,* and Capt. Fosdick in the *Eagle,* fell in with a letter of marque ship of 20 carriage guns, a three decker, which they engaged three glasses, but his force being much superior to them, they were obliged to leave her. The *Hancock* lost three men . . . killed, and 4 wounded, and was much disabled in her rigging and spars. The *Venus* had 2 men wounded." The *Hancock* returned to New London on 25 or 26 September 1779. *Connecticut Gazette,* 29 September 1779. The *Venus,* a 16-gun brigantine, commander Richard Whellen or Weldon, was commissioned in Massachusetts on 9 August 1779. Gardner Weld Allen, *Massachusetts Privateers of the Revolution,* Vol. 7 of *Massachusetts Historical Society Collections* (Cambridge, Mass.: 1927), 315.

[42]Brigantine letter of marque *Delight,* owned by Comfort Sage, & Co., of Middletown, Connecticut, mounting 8 carriage guns. Middlebrook, *Maritime Connecticut during the American Revolution,* Vol. 2, 69.

til we returned in the spring of 1780, except in our passage out for about 24 hours, in a severe gale. We went one day in pursuit of a vessel two days before we arrived at Martinique. She proved to be a Danish Brig.[43]

After we arrived home in February, Mr. Mumford had nearly completed his brig he was a building up at Norwich, but she had no rigging fitted for her. He got me to go up and fix all her rigging. He gave me as many men as I wanted. She was still on the stocks. I went on board and measured her and went to work, and in ten days I got it all complete. She was about 300 tons. She was to mount 18 six pounders. She was built exactly like the *Oliver Cromwell*. In four days after she was launched, I got her to New London completely rigged. About the 1st of April she was ready to sail, 190 men. Richards took command of her and I went out as his first Lieutenant. She was called the *Marquis De Lafayette*. We had not been out but a day or two, until we fell in with the brig *Holker,* and another brig from Philadelphia, and they outsailed us under their topsails. We went to work and trimmed her every way but to no effect. Richards got out of patience with her, and returned back to New London, and would not out in her again.[44]

Mr. Mumford did not know what to do with the brig. She lay there till the first of May. Captain Elisha Hinman, an experienced

[43]The sloop *Hancock* was commissioned 22 September 1778, Thomas Chester, Jr., of Groton, commander; owned by Thomas Mumford; and bonded by Chester and Mumford. She made a voyage to Martinique in late 1779, in company with schooner *Deane*, Capt. Richards, and sloop *Sally,* Capt. Thomson. Middlebrook, *Maritime Connecticut during the American Revolution,* Vol. 2, 106; *Connecticut Gazette,* 12 January 1780.

[44]When the brigantine *Marquis de Lafayette* was commissioned on 7 February 1781, Peter Richards, commander, with 16 guns and 120 men, she was owned by Andrew Perkins & Co. Richards sailed with her and captured a brigantine on 11 March, which was subsequently recaptured. He took a sloop and a ship in May. The brigantine was then sold to Thomas Mumford and was issued a new commission under the command of Elisha Hinman on 13 June. Middlebrook, *Maritime Connecticut during the American Revolution,* Vol. 2, 149–50.

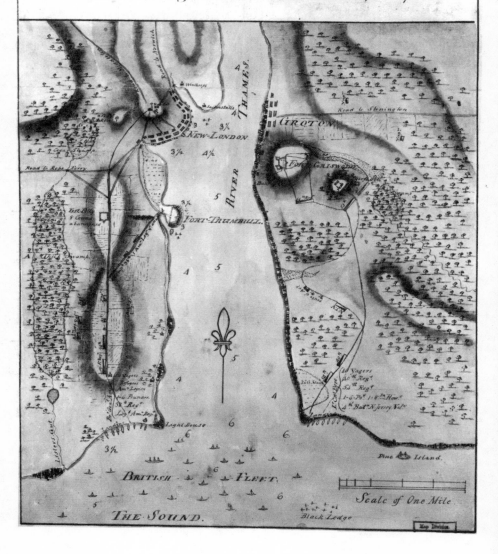

A SKETCH of
NEW LONDON & GROTON
with the attacks made on
FORTS TRUMBULL & **GRISWOLD** by the **BRITISH TROOPS**
under the Command of **BRIGr. GENl. ARNOLD**, Sepr. 6th 1781.

man, said to Mr. Mumford he would try her one trip, which he consented to do, and we sailed, and we soon fell in with the *Holker* and *Delight,* the brigs we saw before. We found she sailed dull, although we had altered the standing of the mast. Captain Hinman exerted all his faculties to no purpose. We were all standing by the wind, we had every rag of sail set, and the two brigs under their topsails. All at once she sprung ahead and was alongside the brigs. They made sail and could not come up with us. Captain Hinman and I saw Mr. Rider, the Sailing Master, casting off the lashing from the main stay around the foremast, and as soon as it was loosed she started between three and four knots. He then made a Martingale and fastened it to the stay. We were then easy in our minds, and went to work and took several prizes and went to New London.[45]

Mr. Mumford was building a brig for Captain Richards of a different construction, and while we were fitting out again, the brig I bought a part of, arrived her second voyage. They brought their bills to me for the cargo they had purchased, which I paid. My proportion of goods she had landed was in Messrs. Hallem's store, sugar, rum, and coffee, worth ten thousand dollars, but as I did not want the money, I let the goods remain. They loaded the brig again and sailed.

We were going on our cruise. A day or two before we sailed, a man came to me from Glossenburg[46] and wanted to sell me his farm of 150 acres, houses, and stock, which I could have bought as easy as I could a pound of tobacco. We went on our cruise but did not get one vessel. When we returned it happened to be in the

---

[45]Elisha Hinman, capt., Christopher Prince, 1st lt., and John Rider, 2d lt., are listed on the *Marquis de Lafayette*'s crew list of 18 August 1781. Mystic, Connecticut, The Marine Historical Association, Papers of the Brig *Marquis de Lafayette.*

[46]Perhaps Glastonbury, Connecticut.

night. The moon was setting when we passed the fort and not a word was said to us, which we thought very strange of. We got abreast of the town, we came to anchor, and ordered the boat manned. Captain Hinman and I got into her to go on shore, and as we approached the wharf we saw fire in every direction, on the wharves and banks. Captain Hinman began to be alarmed. I put my head down and could not see a house. We ordered the boat to stop. Captain Hinman said he did not think it safe to go on shore for the enemy might be there. I told him they might have been there, but if they were there then, we should have seen vessels of different descriptions, and there is not one here now. We went on shore and sent the boat on board and walked up the wharf without saying a word, for our minds were so confused. After we got on the bank, not a house was to be seen. We walked a little distance and saw Captain Mallaly's house, and a few others, and soon saw Captain Hinman's house, that was about 300 rods from the shore. We both went up there about two o'clock in the morning. We awaked Mrs. Hinman, who put her head out one of the chamber windows. "Who is there?" She soon knew her husband was the man. She came down out of the chamber, without one rag of clothes more than what nature requires in going into a bed, and flew into the arms of Captain Hinman.[47] She soon discovered the situation she was in and made some apology, and said to me, "your house is burnt, but your wife is alive and well, you will find her at her mother's." I continued on with a multitude of thoughts on my mind, for it was impossible to dismiss them when I saw such destruction around me on every side. I had not been in the

[47]Elisha Hinman married Abigail Dolebar in New London 1 March 1777. Mrs. Hinman reportedly attempted to shoot Arnold during his raid on New London. Middlebrook, *Maritime Connecticut during the American Revolution*, Vol. 2, 151; Robert Owen Decker, *The Whaling City: A History of New London* (Chester, Conn.: Pequot Press, 1976), 60.

presence of my wife more than a minute before she told me my friend Captain Peter Richards was dead and had 32 bayonet holes in his body. I then felt as I never did before, and I could not dismiss them feelings for many days. Although I lost more than $20,000 in property, it did not give me one moment of uneasiness. And not only Captain Richards, but many others who were murdered at Fort Trumbull on Groton side. After I had been at home some time, it came to my mind about the farm that was offered me: What a different situation I should have been in as it respects property. The depreciation of money, and that conflagration, reduced my property more than thirty thousand dollars. Many valuable vessels were burnt, among which was the brig built for Captain Richards on the same construction of the *Hancock*, in order to make her a fast sailer. Such destruction as was made there by that awful man Arnold, who was born at Norwich, and acquainted with many who were killed and who remained alive, produced much sin that proceeded from many lips. Provisions, ammunition, sail-lofts, and almost every article was destroyed. Near a million of dollars worth of property was destroyed. All business, labor, and exertions became almost inactive.[48]

---

[48]On 6 September 1781, a British force of 1,700 under Benedict Arnold raided New London. They destroyed 143 buildings and 12 ships and captured Fort Griswold, across the Thames River in Groton, after a stubborn defense. The conquerors reportedly bayonetted many of the defenders in the fort after the surrender. Among the destruction was Prince's house, for which he claimed a loss of 1,031 pounds, 7 shillings. "A List of the Sufferers, with an Estimate of their Losses sustained by a Party of the British Troops in their Hostile cruel, and inhumane excursion at New London September 6th 1781 under the Command of Benedict Arnold," Washington, D.C., National Archives, Papers of the Continental Congress, Microcopy 247, roll 66, item 53, page 208.

CHAPTER SIX

Transitions

1782–1806

During the War of Independence, British authorities refused to treat American soldiers and sailors captured in battle as prisoners of war. Because the British did not recognize the United States as a legitimate government, they considered Americans taken in arms against the king to be subjects guilty of treason. This distinction presented the possibility that Americans captured and held for rebellion would assert their rights as British subjects and apply for habeas corpus. *In an action of* habeas corpus *(Latin for "you have the body"), a prisoner forced his jailer to go before a judge to show cause why the prisoner should not be set free. In other words, the government could not keep rebels prisoner for long without trial. The prospect of having to hold hearings for every one of the potentially thousands of soldiers and sailors that would be taken in rebellion was daunting. To escape the dilemma, Lord North, first lord of the Treasury and head of George III's cabinet, introduced into Parliament a bill empowering authorities to commit to prison per-*

sons suspected of, or "taken in the act of high treason, committed in any of the colonies, or on the high seas, or in the act of piracy," and to hold them there without trial or bail. Adopted on 3 March 1777, North's Act was to remain in effect for five years.[1]

Under the terms of North's Act, the British sent thousands of the sailors captured in American warships, whether of the Continental or state navies, or of privateers, to England. There, they held naval prisoners on board prison ships, primarily at the naval base at Portsmouth, and at two building complexes used for housing prisoners of war during previous wars, Forton Prison, near Portsmouth, and Mill Prison, near Plymouth.[2]

American sailors who were found on board trading vessels that were captured by the British fell into a category different from those taken in warships. They could not be convicted of treason or piracy. Rather, their vessels were seized for being in violation either of the Restraining Acts or of the Prohibitory Act, and the sailors were liable to impressment into the Royal Navy. The first Restraining Act, of 30 March 1775, prohibited inhabitants of the New England colonies from trading except with Great Britain, Ireland, and the British West Indies, and excluded them from the North American fishery; the second, of 13 April 1775, extended the law to New Jersey, Pennsylvania, Delaware, Maryland, Virginia, and South Carolina. The Prohibitory Act of 26 December 1775 replaced the Restraining Acts by interdicting all seaborne trade of the thirteen rebellious colonies. These laws authorized commanders of Royal Navy vessels to seize and prosecute the ships and cargoes, but provided no criminal penalties for the crews.[3]

[1]Sheldon S. Cohen, *Yankee Sailors in British Gaols: Prisoners of War at Forton and Mill, 1777–1783* (Newark, Del.: University of Delaware Press, 1995), 26–29.
[2]Ibid., 30–54.
[3]David H. Murdoch, *Rebellion in America: A Contemporary British Viewpoint, 1765–1783* (Santa Barbara, Calif.: Clio Books, 1979), 174–75, 182, 352–53; "Abstract of the bill to Restrain the Trade and Fisheries of the Americans," *Virginia Gazette* (John Pinkney's), Williamsburg, 18 May 1775.

Whenever Christopher Prince went to sea during the war,
whether in a ship of war or in a trading vessel, he placed himself in
danger of being taken prisoner or of being pressed into the Royal Navy.
When peace finally came in 1783 and American independence was
secured, Prince would have experienced capture, imprisonment, and
release more than once.

The Enlightenment and Evangelicalism competed for the soul of
America in the late eighteenth century. Shortly after the end of the
War of Independence, Prince enlisted under the banner of the latter
movement.

Enlightenment thinkers understood the world and mankind's
place in it through the lens of the experimental science of the seven-
teenth century. Believing that all phenomena operated according to
universal natural laws, they judged every intellectual proposition
according to the tests of empiricism and reasonableness. Their attitude
was one of skepticism of anything seeming improbable or unreasonable,
one of questioning of tradition and the authority of the past. The
Enlightenment embraced the idea of progress, trusting in the perfectibil-
ity of mankind, the equality of nations and persons, and the gradual
elimination of superstition and prejudice.[4]

When applied to religion, Enlightenment principles made reason
the test of doctrine, practice, and the interpretation of Scripture. Radi-
cal Enlightenment philosophers in Europe rejected Christianity as
improbable and superstitious, considering the miracles of the Bible as
mere hoaxes. They embraced Deism, a religion of nature and reason.
The Deists' god, like a watchmaker having wound his watch, stood
aloof from his creation, allowing it to run of its own according to natu-

[4]Ralph Ketcham, "The Enlightenment," in *Encyclopedia of the North Ameri-*
can Colonies (New York: Charles Scribner's Sons, 1993), Vol. 3, 151–62. See also
Henry May, *The Enlightenment in America* (New York: Oxford University Press,
1976).

ral laws. While few eighteenth-century Americans subscribed to such radical doctrines, the Enlightenment had a range of effects on American religious beliefs. The movement moderated the strict predestinarian doctrines of some of the Congregationalists, Presbyterians, and Baptists; it promoted beliefs in free will and human ability to work out one's own salvation through reliance on reason among liberal thinkers; and it led to the conviction that Jesus was primarily a great moral teacher and to the rejection of trinitarianism among the more free thinking. By the last decades of the eighteenth century, the Enlightenment in America had laid the foundations of two new religious denominations. Unitarians, pursuing faith in the reasonableness of Christianity, taught that Jesus was a moral teacher but that God is a single personality and not the three-in-one divinity of Father, Son, and Holy Spirit of orthodox Christianity. Universalists, pressing the notion of the equality of human beings, held that Christ died for all and that all would be saved, not just the Elect as in Calvinist doctrine. As convinced rationalist Thomas Jefferson contemplated the future of the United States at the end of the eighteenth century, he expected Unitarianism to "become the general religion of the United States." Jefferson had not reckoned on the resilience of Evangelicalism in America.[5]

The Great Awakening, an American religious movement of the middle decades of the eighteenth century, made local religious revivals familiar to Americans. During a revival, large segments of communities became concerned about religion, particularly about the state of their souls, attendance at worship increased, special revival meetings were held, and several people experienced evangelical conversion and applied for formal membership in the church. It became common for

---

[5]Ketcham, "The Enlightenment," 155–57; for Thomas Jefferson's religious thought, see Edwin S. Gaustad, *Sworn on the Altar of God: A Religious Biography of Thomas Jefferson* (Grand Rapids, Mich.: W. B. Eerdmans, 1996).

*persons to undergo the process of conversion in a matter of days, rather
than the months that had been usual previously. Display of strong
emotions under religious convictions, public testimony from lay persons about their religious experience, and a special focus on the spiri-
tuality of young people came to characterize evangelical religion. In
contrast to the devotees of Reason, evangelicals placed emotions at
the center of religion, upheld the authority of the Bible, and believed
that no real progress was possible for sinful mankind without divine
aid. Evangelicals taught that Jesus Christ, God and man, was a savior and not just a teacher: His death and resurrection, and not just
his moral teachings, were necessary for the eternal salvation of
sinners.*[6]

*A new wave of revivals, part of the Second Great Awakening,
began in New England in the 1790s under the preaching of evangelical leaders who feared the growing strength of Deism in America,
which such works as Ethan Allen's* Reason the Only Oracle of
Man *(1784) and Thomas Paine's* Age of Reason *(1794) were propa-
gating. The Second Great Awakening endured for decades; evangelical denominations flourished; and evangelical Christianity, not
rationalism, became the dominant religious force in nineteenth-
century America.*[7]

*Christopher Prince's education and family background predisposed
him to heed the evangelical call. In a number of episodes throughout
his varied war experiences, Christopher's conscience troubled him*

[6]Michael J. Crawford, "Revivalism and the Great Awakening," in *Encyclopedia of the North American Colonies* (New York: Charles Scribner's Sons, 1993),
Vol. 3, 665–82.

[7]Michael J. Crawford, "Great Awakening, First and Second," in *The Oxford
Companion to United States History* (New York: Oxford University Press, 2001);
see also William G. McLoughlin, *Revivals, Awakenings, and Reform: An Essay on
Religion and Social Change in America, 1607–1977* (Chicago: University of Chicago Press, 1978).

because of his lack of piety. A religious revival in New London a few years after the war provided Christopher the opportunity to answer the call of conscience. His religious conversion brought him back to the pious values inculcated in childhood. Christopher joined the New London Congregational Church in 1787, and his wife, Lucy, joined in 1788.[8] Christopher's religious conversion transformed his life and provided the principles that guided him for the remainder of his days.

A gentleman by the name of Constant, a Frenchman born, brought up in Guadaloupe, but married a woman in New London by the name of Stewart, bought a brig, about 150 tons, for himself and brother who lived in Guadaloupe, a very rich man.[9] She was a Virginia built. He wanted me to take command of her and go to Guadaloupe, load her, and go to Bordeaux. He would put ten four pounders on board, and six wooden guns, plenty of ammunition, and let me have two mates, a boatswain, and thirty men. We agreed, and I went to work on board, got her complete, but in going to Guadaloupe I had to dismount all my guns but four, for we took out 36 horses. Mr. Constant and his wife went out in the brig to Guadaloupe, where we arrived in a remarkable passage—she was a remarkable fast sailer. We loaded her very soon and sailed for Bordeaux. Mr. Constant's brother, who lived

---

[8] *A List of All Those Who Are Known to Have Been Members of the First Church of Christ in New London. From the Beginning to January 1, 1901* (New London, 1900), 17.

[9] William Constant married Polly Stewart in New London in November 1779. *Connecticut Gazette*, 1 December 1779.

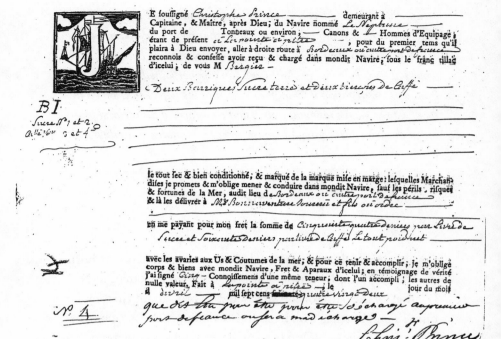

FIGURE 15. A bill of lading, in French, for the brigantine *Neptune*,
signed by Christopher Prince, master, for sugar and coffee taken on
at Pointe-à-Pitre, Guadeloupe, for delivery to Bordeaux, France.

at Guadaloupe, and seven passengers, went with me. Not one could speak English, but at that time I could speak, read, and write French as well as I could English.

In 21 days I got soundings at 12 o'clock at night in twenty fathom water. I knew I was near to Bordeaux by the sand I brought up from the bottom. I run into 12 fathom and hove too, a heavy breeze at the westward, with a mist, that prevented me from seeing the lighthouse after daylight. I soon saw a vessel coming out, which I thought was a pilot. A Danish brig was very near me. She made easy sail and stood in. She got about one mile ahead of me. I saw the pilot boat pass her, as I thought a pilot boat, without boarding her. She stood on by the wind and when she passed us I saw she was a privateer of 14 guns. I made sail to run in, but I could not go in without a pilot. The wind and fog increased. She hove about and stood for me. I was then in seven fathom of water, not more than one mile from the light house, but the weather was so thick I could not see the land. I had to haul off by the wind, and the privateer came alongside while I was brailing up my topgallant sails to hand them, and she discharged as many as forty muskets into us, and I could not send my men aloft to hand the sails, the sea was so heavy and large. He nor I could discharge our carriage guns, and I had no muskets. My topgallant sails I was sure would be blown from the yards if they were not handed, and that could not be done in safety. I ordered all my men below deck and took the helm myself. I struggled with them for near an hour, and they came so near as to fire muskets balls into us six or seven times. The last time they fired there were as many as twenty went within a few inches of me, and one in particular struck the tiller which was on my right abreast of my body, and entered it more than one inch. My owner requested me several times to surrender to them. I finally found I should carry away my mast if I did not shorten sail which I could not do in safety. The wind increased so much I ordered some of my men up to lower down the topsails and clue them up. I then hailed our enemy and told them I had struck to them, and wished they would cease firing until I handed the topgallant sails. That was the first words that was said to them, and they gave me no answer, only they did not fire a musket until my men were going aloft, and they began again. They were as near to us as they dare to be on account of the sea rushing upon us in violence. I then asked them if they would not let me hand my sails. They then said, "no, not until you come on board." Those were the first words they had said to us. I then ordered my boat out, and went on board, and found them all Frenchmen, belonging to the island of Jersey under the English dominions, and had English colors on board. They told me that they had anchored under the Cordwan light house last night,[10] and come out from there early that morning. They took possession of the brig, and the third day we arrived at the island of Jersey. They treated me in a very friendly manner all the time, and all my crew, and let my owner and passengers remain on board the brig. They provided a large house for us and treated us all as friends and not as prisoners.

The commandant of the island was a Bostonian, who left there early when the war commenced, and left all his property, which was considerable, and he was appointed a governor or commander there. He heard my name was Prince.

He came to see me, and said, "I am informed your name is Prince."

"It is."

"Are you related to Captain Job Prince?"

"I am. He is my uncle, and I sailed many years in his employ."

"That is enough, he is one of my best friends. There is no man

---

[10] *Cordwan:* The Tour de Cordouan, at the mouth of the Gironde River.

I esteem more. Whatever you want you shall have within my power, that is clothes and money, but I have nothing to do with your freedom, that belongs to Captain Meserva,[11] but I will get him to do all he can for you."

He had not been gone more than an hour before a gentleman called on me, a naval officer. As soon as he entered the room I recognized him.

"Is your name Prince?"

"It is, Sir!"

"You are Captain Job Prince's nephew."

"I am, Sir."

"You and I have often dined together at his house, and if we had never seen each other before, as you are a nephew to that man, I will do everything in my power. You shall not be a prisoner but a few days. I am going to take you and all your crew to Portsmouth, and I will get Admiral Pye[12] to give you freedom immediately; your owner and passengers shall be sent to France."

After remaining there three days we were carried to Portsmouth. He sent all my men and officers to a mill prison,[13] except my mate. He put us on board of a prison ship. Before he took me on board he went on shore and left me on board the packet for nearly three hours after my men were landed. When he came on board he said he had not accomplished his intention, and that was, I should not be made a prisoner, but go on shore with perfect freedom. But Admiral Pye had promised him I should go on shore that day. As soon as he had ended his other duties, he would order the captain of the Prison ship to send me on shore. And when he took me on board the ship, he said to the commander, "I now commit this man, Captain Prince, into your care, as a friend

[11]Perhaps Francis Messervy, lieutenant, Royal Navy, 16 September 1779.
[12]Admiral Sir Thomas Pye, commander in chief, Portsmouth.
[13]Mill Prison, Plymouth, England.

THE WEST PROSPECT OF PORTSMOUTH IN HAMP-SHIRE.

FIGURE 16. Christopher Prince was imprisoned on board a Royal Navy ship at Portsmouth, England.

of mine and not as a prisoner. Admiral Pye has promised me he shall be permitted to go on shore to day, and if I was not obliged to return to the island of Jersey immediately, I would not go until he had his freedom to go where he pleased." I remained on board three days, and no parole for me came on board. I was a walking the quarterdeck one day, and the Captain came to me and said, "Lieutenant Meserva said you was to go on shore the day he left us. I advise you to write a letter to Admiral Pye. Perhaps he has forgot the promise he made Meserva, and I will see it is carried on shore." I wrote a few lines stating to him what Captain Meserva had said, and I would refer him to Captain Edward Thornburrough, (which may be seen in the 11th page)[14] for my character, with whom I was intimately acquainted, and many other officers in the British navy, and if he would permit me to go on shore, such indulgence should not be abused. As I was not permitted to seal it, I gave it to the Commander. There were 8 or 9 ship masters on board, prisoners. Some had been on board for twelve months. They had used all their endeavors to have their parole, and were not allowed, for many had been paroled and made their escape into France, and Captain Peter Richards, my deceased friend, was one who had told me all the particulars relating to his escape, and seven or eight more with him, and crossed the British channel in an open boat. That was the reason those on board could not go on shore, and laughed at me with sneer and contempt. Two days after I wrote I did not receive an answer. I was taken unwell, but not so much as to prevent me from going on deck, and while I was there the Purser came up to me and told me my letter was still in the cabin, and it had been read by a hundred officers and gentlemen who had been on board, which often made him feel unpleasant. The Captain would not carry nor send it to the Admiral. "I

[14]P. 32, above.

am agoing on shore tomorrow morning and if you are willing I will deliver it to the Admiral myself." I told him he had mentioned that which laid me under an obligation which could never be paid by me, and it never should be forgotten. That night I was taken so unwell, Mr. Thompson,[15] my mate, had to set up near all night with me. Early in the morning the Doctor bled me. I had lost my reason, but after blood was taken from me, I was composed. At 10 A.M. the Captain sent for me. I told Mr. Thompson to go up and see what he wanted.

He saw the Captain standing by the Binnacle with his back to him, when he go to him and spoke, and said, "you have sent for Captain Prince. He is unwell and sent me to you."

"Get off the quarter deck you rascal."

He came down and told me how he was treated. I threw my cloak over me as I could not put on my coat on account of being bled, and went on deck. He was standing by the gangway and as I walked up to him he smiled and said, "the Admiral has wrote you a curious note. Mr. C. Prince, Sir. You have liberty to come on shore, and go where you please, and I hope such indulgence will not be abused. You are no longer a prisoner under my care."

I told him I was too unwell to go, and begged it as a favor to let me remain until I was able to go. He said, "by all means, stay as long as you please." This was on Saturday, and on Monday I was well and went on shore.

Mr. Wren, a minister of the Gospel,[16] came to see me as soon as

[15]John Thompson. Prize case files for *Neptune,* Christopher Prince, Public Record Office, London, High Court of Admiralty 32/409/5.

[16]Thomas Wren, a Dissenting minister, was a member of the British relief committee formed at the close of 1777 for the purpose of ameliorating the conditions for Americans held in British prisons. He advised the prisoners, brought them news, and aided them when they escaped. Sheldon S. Cohen, "The Preachers and the Prisoners," *Essex Institute Historical Collections* 126, no. 1 (January 1990): 1–26.

I had got to my lodging. He was a great friend to Americans, and told me he had spent many days to get Captain Clark, and Mr. Cook's parole on shore, and another Captain whose name I do not remember, and he said I hope they will be with you in a day or two. I boarded at a house where there was considerable piety. He had been a Boatswain in the British Navy for many years, but was now discharged for life. He had an excellent wife and children. I was requested to go to that house in preference to any other in Portsmouth. I went to the Admiral's twice and could not see him, so many officers were there. In about one week, Mr. Wren said he was a going to Admiral Pye's on account of them men above named, and if I was willing he would take my letter to him, but I had better go myself, for he might want to see me. I went with him and stayed more than a hour before Mr. Wren got out, and he could not see the Admiral but would go soon again. In about two hours he came with my discharge and paroles for them men, which were soon brought on shore, and boarded in the same house with me.

Mr. Wren dare not go to the Admiral for a discharge for Clark, Cook, and the other, but wrote a letter to the Duke of York, and one to another gentleman, requesting me to carry them and deliver them myself and obtain a discharge for the above Captains and passenger. I set out at eleven o'clock at night, and arrived in London at one P.M. and took my dinner, and a man went with me to the Duke of York. The man who opened the door took the letter in, and in three minutes he came to the door and said the Duke wanted to see me. I went into the room where he was sitting at the table with about twenty. He rose up, and came to me, and took me by the hand and said, "you are an American born." "I am, Sir." No sooner did the words proceed from my lips, than a young woman sitting at the table lifted her hand up and uttered a loud voice, "is that an American, why he is as white as we are." Someone who sat at the table said, "hush, hush."[17] The Duke went to the table and filled two glasses with wine and brought it himself on a small waiter, and said, "I wish you health and prosperity, and next day after tomorrow you shall dine with your countrymen named in this letter." I was so confounded in seeing and hearing such words and countenance in one of the Royal Family, I did not know what to say, nor how to act. I got so composed when I left the room, "I render you, Sir, ten thousand thanks for your friendship." I have no doubt I looked as foolish as I felt. There was great attention by all in the room when I answered the Duke, to the questions he asked me about my country, and the increase and prospect of independence. He did not make use of one unfavorable or feeling expression. Agreeable to his promise I dined with them men on the third day.[18] Clark and I took our passage to Rotterdam, and arrived there the third day after we left London, and proceeded on to Amsterdam, where we soon arrived by land in a canal boat. I did not stay there more than a week before we sailed for Boston,

[17]Compare this passage with similar passages in two other autobiographical narratives of naval experiences during the Revolutionary War. Having been released from prison, John Blatchford was taken into the home of a lawyer of Portsmouth, England, who had befriended him. There he was brought into the parlor, "to satisfy the curiosity of some ladies, who had never seen a Yankee, as they called me: I went in, and they seemed greatly surprized to see me look like an Englishman; they said they were sure I was no Yankee, but like themselves. The idea they had formed of the Americans was nearly the same as we have of the natives of this country." In his memoir, Nathaniel Fanning observed that the country people who came to gape at the American prisoners at Forton Prison, outside of Portsmouth, England, would exclaim: "Why, Lard, neighbour, there be white paple; they taulk jest as us do, by my troth." *The Narrative of John Blatchford, Detailing His Sufferings in the Revolutionary War, while a Prisoner with the British. As Related by Himself. With an Introduction and Notes, by Charles I. Bushnell* (New York, 1865), 22; John S. Barnes, ed., *Fanning's Narrative: Being the Memoirs of Nathaniel Fanning, an Officer of the Revolutionary Navy, 1778–1783* (New York: Naval History Society, 1912), 11.

[18]The Duke of York, the future George IV, was at this time closely connected with the Whig opposition to his father, the king, which helps explain his friendliness to the Americans.

where we arrived after a short passage. I went to my uncle Job's and told him what had happened to me, and how much I had been favored by being his nephew. I soon arrived at Providence, where I went by water to New London.

I had not been but a few days at home before Mr. Shaw and several others wanted me to go the Brandewynes[19] after a load of flour in a small vessel. I took three men with me and made sail. I took no money nor property, only letters to the owners of flour. When I got to Great Egg Harbor, I hove out a signal for a pilot. I soon saw a boat coming off, which I thought was a Pilot until they got on board or alongside. I soon saw they were an armed commissioned boat, commanded by Devenport, thirteen men. One of the men knew me and called me by name and said, "I am the man that put fire to your house in New London." Devenport stopped him and said, "not another word out of your lips on that subject." He then told me he should take my vessel from me, and send her to New York. I told him he had better let me go and load her with flour first, and then she would be a good prize, but now she was of no value. But all in vain. He put four men on board and sent my three men in her. I had a barrel of rum in the hold covered over with ballast, which was not seen. They took me on shore, and gave me my liberty to go home. A woman was there from the mainland with eggs for sale. As soon as she sold them she took me into her boat and carried me across the bay about five miles and kept me at her house until next morning, and then I began my journey. I went as much as ten miles through the pine woods before I got to any house. It then came to my mind what I had to encounter, for when Wheeler and I passed through the Jersey state before, it was with difficulty we could get a mouthful of victuals, or lodgings in a Dutch family. The same it was then: In some

[19]*Brandewynes:* Brandywine Range and Brandywine Shoal, a channel and bar in Delaware Bay.

houses I could not get bread, milk, or meat, and lodgings was almost impossible, and I had to travel all the way to West Point before I could cross the North river in safety. I was much wore down when I arrived at New London. As soon as I got there, my wife informed me my men had arrived safe in the sloop I was taken in. As soon as they left us, one of them went down into the hold, and drawed out some rum out of the cask, and got the four men so drunk they put them in the hold, and barred them in, and kept them there until they arrived.[20]

It was some time before I could walk out. One day I was going down to see some of my acquaintance, and I came across Captain J. Packwood, an old experienced ship master, who wanted me to take command of one of his schooners.[21] I went and examined the vessel, and told him she stood in need of a breast hook. If he would put one in the whole width of the bow, I would go in her. He was a going to send her to the island of Granada, with a good cargo, and 28 horses. She was a schooner of about one hundred tons. In a few days I sailed, and had one of the most violent gales I ever experienced from the N.W. It was a fair wind and did not vary nor alter for 60 hours. I could not suffer one foot of sail during the gale, and did not lose one horse. I fell in with Barbadoes. I made it at meridian, and hauled as nigh the wind as possible to weather it. I found I could not do it. I made two tacks in vain. I did not gain one mile. I saw many plantations on shore but I knew there was no harbors or vessels. I finally drawed up my resolution to go the leeward. Mr. Chester, my mate, said, "you are a going to carry us into the hands of our enemies, for we shall have to pass all the harbors where there is hundreds of vessels." I told him we

---

[20] "Capt. Prince, in a Schooner from this Port [New London], bound to Egg-Harbour, was taken near that Place, where himself and People were released." *Connecticut Gazette,* 18 October 1782.

[21] Joseph Packwood, shipowner and captain of New London, Connecticut.

should be in sight of the island for two or three days if we attempted to weather it, and some cruiser would come out and take us. I ordered the helm up and bore away, and got close in shore. It soon came on dark, and had a land and sea breeze as much as we wanted. We passed several vessels, and when we went by the harbor, we saw it full of ships of war and merchantmen, and not a word was said to us, for we was by the wind and they supposed we were beating in; and at daylight I was out of sight of all the vessels at anchor in the islands, and by eight A.M. I was out of sight of land.

My mate had commanded a vessel for several voyages to some of them islands. He said he did not believe there was one commander in a hundred would have done as I did that night, and he was astonished in seeing our escape. We had a fine run that day. That night by twelve o'clock, I was in the latitude of the island of Grenada, and bore away. Early in the morning I saw the Grenadillas, and soon saw the Grenada, and at eleven A.M. I came to anchor about one mile from the shore. Before I had furled the sails a man came on board and asked me what I asked for my horses. I told him 24 Joes. "I will give you 18, and run the risk of landing them if you will haul close in shore." I told him I could not give him an answer until I went on shore. He said, "I will not give you but one hour, after that I shall be free from the offer I have made you." I got into his boat, and ordered mine on shore as soon as possible. I entered my vessel, and conversed with some respectable men about him who had made me an offer for my horses." They told me he was the safest horse-jockey on the island. I soon saw him, and told him he might have all the horses. He requested me to land them immediately, which I did, safe, and he paid me for them at once, and then told me I had done as I ought to have done for my owners, for if I had not accepted of his offer I should not have got on an average more than 15 Joes. I then went into the cove where there was 18 American vessels. My old acquaintance Captain Clark, as may be seen in 85 page, was one,[22] and several others I was acquainted with. There were two armed vessels, letters of Marque, one of 20, the other 14 guns, all of the rest unarmed.

The next day after I arrived, a vessel with a deck load of horses, came from New Haven. They were but a little inferior to mine, and could not get but 13 Joes for them. 21 sail had now arrived, and was lying in the cove. We all unbent our sails, covered our vessels with awning and nothing but the lower mast standing, and all dined on board of each vessel in preference to dining on shore. News came to us that some English ships of war was a laying at St. Vincents, to take us all when we took our departure from there, for there were many Englishmen on that island to give a signal on a mountain by day with a flag, and by night with a barrel of tar on fire. Many were ready to sail three weeks before we all got loaded. The armed vessels waited for us more than a week. The day arrived when we were agoing, not any alteration made on board of one vessel until the afternoon, and by the time the sun set, every vessel was ready for sea, and took our departure as soon as night set in, and directed our course for the Mona passage,[23] and the next day or night we passed through that, and the third day we passed all the Bahamas. The sixth day many of us separated and steered for our various ports. I arrived safe at New London, and made an excellent voyage.[24]

I had not been there but a few days before Captain Havens in the *Jay*, who had altered her into a brig, and wanted me to go Sail-

[22]Pp. 203–4, above.

[23]*Mona Passage:* Water passage, eighty miles wide, between Haiti and Puerto Rico.

[24]"Saturday last [22 February 1783] ... arrived here [New London] ... the Schooner *Seaflower*, Capt. Prince, from Granada." *Connecticut Gazette*, 28 February 1783.

ing Master of her.[25] I told him I wished my friends would let me live with my wife a few days; but he was ready to sail, and was obliged to go; but it proved to be an unprofitable cruise to us all. We got home safe and there it ended. He was the most altered man I ever saw, not a day but he was intoxicated. One day we were obliged to take the vessel from him. A British frigate hove in sight, standing for us on our larboard quarter, and we was a laying too making some repairs after a violent gale. The wind then was about a whole sail breeze. I ordered the steering sails booms up. He said, "they shall not be sent up." I paid no attention to what he said. I then ordered the topgallant yards across. He said, "if you disobey me I will go down and get a pistol and kill you." I said nothing to him but went on as fast as possible and made all the sail I could. The Frigate had got very near us. He went below after the pistol. The Doctor followed him down, and when he was a coming up the Doctor stopped him and the Lieutenant went down and secured him below, and we did not stop one hour after that until we arrived at New London.

Soon after that, news came that Cornwallis was taken.[26] We soon assembled and after a little consultation we concluded to have a joyful feast and celebrate the good tidings. We barbecued an Ox, and nearly one hundred joined and spent all day. There was not as much intemperance as there was when Burgoyne was taken. The brig I was concerned in had made seven voyages to the West India Islands, and the net profits coming to me was about three thousand dollars. She was then laying at Middletown. News

[25] The *Jay*, Capt. William Havens, was recommissioned on 6 September 1781, the day of the burning of New London. Louis F. Middlebrook, *History of Maritime Connecticut during the American Revolution, 1775–1783*, Vol. 2, 137. Perhaps Prince made the cruise in *Jay* after returning to New London from his cruise in *Marquis de Lafayette* in September 1781.

[26] Maj. Gen. Charles Cornwallis surrendered his force of about 10,000 at Yorktown, Virginia, on 19 October 1781.

began to circulate throughout the country that our independence was a going to be given to us by Great Britain, which prevented us from going in merchantmen and privateers, and I stayed longer at home than I had done put it altogether after I had been married.

Glad tidings arrived that our war had come to an end, from one period of time to another, in Latitudes and Longitudes. The brig *Delight* I owned a part of had arrived at New London completely loaded all but her horses. My proportionate part of the cargo was about 2,500 dollars, not continental money, but silver and gold. She was ready to sail two days before peace took place in the longitude of the United States, and we sent her out to Barbadoes as the vessel from our country, expecting to make a profitable voyage. She was so deep loaded she could not sail as she had done before. The day after she sailed she fell in with a frigate who took her and ordered her to New York. It wanted but 14 hours of the expiration of the time when she would have been safe. The 8th day after that, she arrived at New London another man's property, and not one cent was insured. That with my other losses amounted to $50,000, which brought me almost level with the world.[27]

Through the whole course of the war I have had two motives in view, one was the freedom of my country, and the other was the luxuries of life. The first is obtained, the other lost, but not out of my *reach* as long as I have health, strength, and inclination. As soon as our freedom got organized, and each state began to assemble, and take into consideration all the important objects which would be beneficial to the public and individuals, the State of

[27] The brigantine *Delight,* owned by Comfort Sage and Co., was captured and sent into New York at the end of October 1782. *Connecticut Gazette,* 1 November 1782; Middlebrook, *Maritime Connecticut during the American Revolution,* Vol. 2, 71. It was not until 4 February 1783 that the British, and 11 April 1783 that the Continental Congress, proclaimed the end of hostilities.

Connecticut passed a law allowing all who suffered any loss exceeding $500 be allowed 12½ per cent on all their loss in land remaining in New Connecticut on the borders of Lake Erie; but this property which was to be investigated by a Committee was different from what many expected. I was called on to give my account of the loss I sustained when the city was burnt. In my account rendered in was about $22,000. As soon as they saw it they told me to give an account of my house, furniture, and what my house contained, and to mention no other article let it be where it was. They finally allowed me $12,000 in land at a certain price, amounting to 1,772 acres of land, which they gave me a certificate for. At that time I considered it as nothing in one sense, and it never proved to be of much value.[28] I immediately built me a house on the lot of ground where my other house stood, which was an excellent habitation, where I spent many happy days.

As I was continually traversing the ocean to various parts of the world, I left all my concerns on shore, in the care of my beloved wife. In the year 1786, I returned from a voyage to South America. The third day after I arrived I went home in the evening and found my wife absent at the south part of the city. On my passage to where she was, I passed near the Court House. I saw some people a going in. I asked them what was going on there? they told me there was a New Light Meeting. As I was unacquainted with the expression and answer, I went in to see what it was. As

---

[28]At its May 1792 session, the Connecticut state legislature voted to compensate residents who had suffered losses from the devastations of the enemy by granting them land from 500,000 acres in the Western Reserve, now part of Ohio, on the shore of Lake Erie. Christopher was to be compensated to the value of £512/4/3, for the burning of his property in the British raid on New London. He would not have been able to benefit from the grant until after he wrote this memoir, for specific lots in the tract were not assigned until 9 November 1808. *The Public Records of the State of Connecticut*, Vol. 7, *From May 1789 through October 1792*, compiled by Leonard Woods Labaree (Hartford, Conn.: State of Connecticut, 1948), 448–49, 468.

soon as I entered the room I saw a number of people on each side, and a man was praying on one side; but on the other I saw many of my acquaintances, and mixed with them.

While he was praying there was perfect silence and solemnity. I saw a number of citizens there as thoughtless and stupid as myself. They then sung a hymn, and while they were singing, a number of us looked on each other and smiled. After they had done singing, they all sat down, about thirty men, women, and youths, and covered their eyes with their hands, which put on a solemn appearance, but it had but a trifling effect on my feelings. They sat in that position for a few minutes, and a boy rose up and fixed his eyes on us. He could not have been more than 12 years of age. He drawed all our eyes upon him, and as soon as I saw that he began his exhortation, and every word he said went to my heart, and brought so many serious reflections on my mind, it gave me much distress, so much so, I had to leave the room. After I got out of the house, everything looked dark and dreary. So much gloom came upon me I could not walk. No other house except the church was within three hundred rods, for it stood on a hill partly out of town. While I was standing under the walls of the house, no human being in sight, I used all my endeavors to dismiss my feelings, and the more I strove, the more my mind was distressed! I could not move from the house. I began to be angry with myself for feeling as I did. I began to ask myself some questions, and I believe it was in a loud utterance. "What does all these feelings mean? Is religion anything?" An answer came home to my heart, "yes it is everything. Is it important? Yes, it is all important." These answers came to me in a loud voice sounding in my ears. I immediately walked off and said if it is so I will never utter another profane word as long as I live, and I will read the Bible, and whatever that tells me to do, I will do it with all my might. I never felt so as I did after I expressed these resolutions. I looked aloft and below, everything appeared different from what they ever did before. O there is a God who has made all these things, and has made me. My parents have taught me from my infancy that I am, and shall be accountable to God for every word I speak, and every act of my life, and if they are wrong, I shall be deprived of his presence and exposed to eternal misery. These reflections brought horror on my mind, which caused much agitation.

When I arrived at the house where my wife was, I found the room full. They received me with much friendship, but I could not sit down. I told my wife to put on her things and go home. All present objected to my request. My wife said, "I expect he is tired for he is unloading his vessel." She put on her hat, and we left the house. While we were walking home, I could not say a word. She asked me what the reason was. I did not say something.

"Have you and your owners disagreed?"

"No."

"What is the matter?"

"Nothing."

After we got home, she said, "you are tired; we will go to bed." I could not sleep a wink all night. My feelings continued the next day. While I was on board discharging my cargo I could not dismiss my feelings; neither did I want to do it. All that conversed with me thought and said they were sorry to see me so unwell. The next night I could not sleep. My wife began to be much alarmed about my feelings and asked me many questions, but I could not give her a satisfactory answer. The second day my feelings continued the same, but never offered up one prayer to God for relief. The importance of prayer came home to my mind, and felt anxious to devote some time at the throne of grace, which I was determined to do before I turned in or went to bed. I did not say a word to my wife on the subject until we entered the bedroom, and then I was confused and confounded. My wife began to undress, and I stood without any motion.

She then said, "I do not know what you mean nor what you want. You never acted so before."

I then told her I could not go into bed without she would agree with me in one thing.

"What is that?"

"I must pray before I undress and go to bed, and you must kneel down with me."

"Pray!"

"Yes, I must pray for I am an undone sinner," and wept much.

Her countenance altered and said, "I will kneel down with you," and I had not prayed more than four minutes before she burst out into tears, which increased my solemn devotion. As soon as I got into bed I fell asleep with a composed mind. My wife could not sleep. She remained in great distress until one o'clock in the morning. She then awoke me and I found her sitting up in the bed. As soon as she saw I was awake she said, "O my dear do get up and pray for me." I complied with her request with joy, after which she seemed to be composed so much she lay down and told me how she felt. Our feelings corresponded in everything connected with our situation and salvation. Prayers after that was the theme of our employment. The next day I was so composed in my mind, I felt like a new creature. Ejaculations could proceed from my heart and lips. In a few days I was accosted by some of my amiable acquaintances, "Why, I hear you are a lunatic, I hope it is not so." I made but few answers to what they said, but continued on my course without any variation. It was not long before I was saluted in a friendly way by Deist and Infidels.

In a short time I was ready to go to sea again. I took a Bible with me, and allowed no swearing on board. That voyage I read my Bible from the first to the last chapter, and the Lord applied many passages to my mind, heart, and understanding, and never omitted prayer. When I returned to New London I found a great alteration throughout the city, prayer meetings held almost every evening, where I went and joined with all in prayers and supplications. There had not been any Presbyterian Minister there since the year 1774. There was seven or eight sermons preached in a year by some ordained ministers, and more by a Mr. Adams who was nothing more than a celebrated Christian. But in 1786, a Mr. Channing was called after we had finished a new church. He had come before I went to sea again, but as I had but a little opportunity to converse with him on the subject of religion, he said nothing to me nor I to him about my proceedings in the cause of Christ. On my return, I found a great increase of a revival of religion there. My wife had joined the church, and entered into a covenant with her Heavenly Father. As I had performed the duty of prayer on board my vessel the last voyage with my crew, night and morning, it had increased my zeal, and strengthened my faith to such a degree I thought it my duty to dedicate myself to him who had made me, and convinced me I was a sinner. The rules and principles of a Congregational Church at that time in Connecticut and all the Eastern States was to notify all the church members, three sabbaths, and not less than two from the pulpit, and written notices on all the church doors, of the names of every one who applied to be united to the church of Christ. I was allowed admittance in two weeks, for I had to go to sea.

In one of my voyages to Baltimore, I saw my friend Pepper, who I was with in Canada at the commencement of the war. I call him my friend although he did everything in his power to injure me, as may be seen in a number of pages including or commencing at 28th.[29]—He was there in an English vessel. I had but very

---

[29]P. 65, above.

little conversation with him upon any subject. As he was taken during the war on board an English vessel and carried into New London, and where he found I lived and sailed out of there, he told the Mayor and many of my acquaintances that he had said many things against me in Canada to the American Officers which was wrong, and he begged them to give him his freedom for he could not bear to see me, for he felt guilty, and I might do him some injury, for he deserved it; and he was sent to New York two days before I returned. When I saw him in Baltimore, I conversed with him on that subject, and told him, if I had been in New London I would have done everything in my power to have made him comfortable. He was so disappointed at what I said, he wept.

The rules and regulations which I always had on board my vessel, in reading the scripture, and offer up prayers night and morning, the voyage before I joined the church and ever afterwards as long as I followed the sea, was pleasing to my crew, and nearly all of my passengers. One time I was in Savannah, and was bound to New York, on a voyage from St. a Croix. I had many applications by passengers, until my cabin was full. After that 21 carpenters from an island, where they had been a long time cutting live oak[30] for the US Navy,[31] and was bound home to Connecticut. As soon as I fell in company with them, I heard some profane language proceeding from several of them.

I said to the master carpenter, "I cannot carry you in my vessel."

---

[30]*Live oak:* A species of timber used in shipbuilding, valued for its density and durability. Beginning in the 1790s, some New England shipwrights spent winters in the South cutting live oak for the United States Navy, returning home in the spring. See Virginia S. Wood, *Live Oaking: Southern Timber for Tall Ships* (Boston: Northeastern University Press, 1981; reprint ed., Annapolis, Md.: Naval Institute Press, 1995).

[31]The manuscript reads "UNS Navy."

"Why not?"

"Because I allow no swearing on board."

"We do not swear much."

"I allow no profane words of any kind, and my cabin passengers have united with me in the rules and regulations I have, and I will not deviate from them."

"What shall we do, how shall we get home?"

"I will take you on one rule and obligation only, and that is, a dollar shall be paid to me for every profane word uttered on board, and you shall be accountable to me for that, by signing an instrument I will draw up for that purpose, and not you only but every one under your charge."

That, they all consented to do. And on our passage to New York and New London, there were but three profane words uttered by them which was heard by me or any of my crew. They all slept and lived in the steerage, and at the close of the passage nearly all confessed that my rules and regulations were an advantage to them, and they never would forget them. All these rules and regulations I never omitted as long as I followed the sea after I knew I was a wicked fellow.

I was then severely attacked with the rheumatism, which continued for many years to such a degree I could not dress or undress myself, and before I got well I was too old to go to sea, at least I thought I was, but never lost my inclination of being a part of my time on the ocean, for I always preferred that life to any other to this moment. This is a brief sketch of my life up to 1806.

C. Prince

OBSERVATIONS AND COMMENTS

British admiralty court records of the trial of the Neptune *enable us to augment Christopher Prince's story of the journey to France on which he was captured and taken as a prisoner to Portsmouth, England. William Constant was a member of a merchant family based in Pointe-à-Pitre, Guadeloupe, married to a New London woman. Constant registered the 95-ton brigantine* Neptune, *Christopher Prince, master, at the New London Navy Office on 19 February 1782. The brigantine had been a prize to the* Young Cromwell *privateer. The* Neptune, *Captain Christopher Prince, departed Guadaloupe for Bordeaux, France, with a cargo of coffee and sugar at the end of April 1782, navigated by a crew of fourteen, counting Prince, and carrying eight passengers, including the owner's brother and a black servant. The* Neptune *had two guns mounted but carried no other arms. On 31 May, near the lighthouse at the mouth of the Gironde River, she was taken by the Jersey privateer lugger* Argus, *Philip Winter commanding, and brought into Jersey, where she was libeled, tried, and condemned as a good prize.*[32]

The portion of Prince's autobiography in which he describes his religious conversion helps clear up a question in local history, that is to say, whether there was a religious revival in New London in 1787. After the death of Rev. Ephraim Woodbridge in 1776, the New London church engaged Rev. William Adams, among others, occasionally to supply preaching. The congregation decided to build a new church edifice in 1784, which was in use by 1787. Henry Channing (1759– 1840), Yale class of 1781, was called to preach at New London Congregational Church on 26 January 1787 and was ordained there on 17

[32]Ernest E. Rogers, *Connecticut's Naval Office at New London during the War of the American Revolution* (New London, Conn.: New London County Historical Society, 1933), *New London County Historical Society Collections*, Vol. 2, p. 7; *Connecticut Gazette*, 1 December 1779; prize case files for *Neptune*, Christopher Prince, Public Record Office, London, High Court of Admiralty 32/409/5.

May 1787. According to Channing's biographer, "a revival of religion begin with his ministry and continued for nearly two years, during which time eighty persons were received to the communion of the church." Silas Blake, historian of the New London church, however, questions "whether the large number of additions in 1788 was due to what we now call a special religious quickening." Blake's doubts may have been inspired by the fact that the church dismissed Channing in 1806 when his adoption of Unitarian views became known. Prince's memoir makes it clear that there was a religious revival following Channing's appointment.[33]

---

[33]Franklin Bowditch Dexter, *Biographical Sketches of the Graduates of Yale College,* 6 vols. (New York: H. Holt and Co., 1885–1912), Vol. 4, 183–86; Silas Leroy Blake, *The Later History of the First Church of Christ New London, Conn.* (New London: Press of the Day, 1900), 200–203, 210–12, 255–57, quotation on 257; Robert Owen Decker, *The Whaling City: A History of New London* (Chester, Conn.: Pequot Press, 1976), 248.

EPILOGUE

In his later life, Christopher Prince assumed a leadership role in the movement to bring religion to seamen. Students of social reform in the early republic, in particular in reference to mariners, will find clues to the sources of that movement in Christopher Prince's autobiography, for the seeds of his commitment to the spiritual welfare of seafarers were planted in his years of seafaring.

Prince ends his autobiography with his retirement from the sea. The final words of his narrative would have made a fitting epitaph: "I never lost my inclination of being a part of my time on the ocean, for I always preferred that life to any other to this moment." This was in 1806, when Prince was fifty-four years old. Prince lived another twenty-six years, and during those years served the secular and religious needs of the seafaring community according to his best notions.

In 1793 Prince was residing in Paterson, New Jersey,[1] but later moved to New York City. There, dwelling near the docks, he maintained a close association with the maritime community.[2] He served for a quarter century as secretary of the Marine Society, founded in 1770 for "improving maritime knowledge and for relieving indigent and distressed masters of vessels."[3] From about 1813 until retiring in 1831 he worked as agent for the United States Marine Hospital in New York. The marine hospitals were the federal government's earliest venture into socialized medicine; by act of 16 July 1798 they were supported by a monthly deduction from each seaman's wages, collected by the master or owner of the vessel on which he served and paid to the collector of the port in which the vessel arrived. Out of the funds thus raised, the president was authorized to provide for the care of sick and disabled seamen.

Members of the maritime community of New York City recognized Christopher Prince as a hoary-headed activist in the seaman's religious movement from its beginnings about the year 1816. Prince worshiped at Dr. Gardner Spring's Brick Presbyterian Church, located on Beekman Street, near Nassau, a few blocks from the wharves. In the summer of 1816, as an outreach program of the church, members of the congregation held a series of prayer meetings at private homes on Water Street. The attendance of some keepers of sailors' boarding houses and of a few seamen at those meetings persuaded Dr. Spring and some members

[1] Hezekiah Prince, *Remarks of My Life,* 27.

[2] He lived at 80 Gold Street in 1825, 38 Cherry in 1827–28, 20 Cherry in 1829–30, and 4 Cortlandt in 1831–32. *Longworth's American Almanac, New-York Register, and City Directory* (New York, 1825, 1827, 1828, 1829, 1830, 1831, and 1832).

[3] Oscar T. Barck, Jr., *New York City during the War for Independence* (New York: Columbia University Press, 1931), 188. *Christian Herald and Seaman's Magazine* Vol. 9, no. 19 (15 February 1823): 604–6, contains an account of a meeting of the society on 18 January 1823 at which Prince was reelected secretary.

of his congregation to institute prayer meetings specifically for sailors.

On 12 February 1817, merchants and shipowners met in the home of Christopher Prince, a member of Dr. Spring's group, to consider forming a Bible society for the benefit of seamen. The Marine Bible Society organized itself at a public meeting in City Hall on 17 March and elected Prince vice president. Appointed by the society in 1819 to superintend the distribution of Bibles, he "spent much time in traversing around the wharves, boarding almost every vessel to inquire after the spiritual welfare of the crew, and supplying such as were destitute with the inspired volume." He continued this work until shortly before his death.

When the New York Bethel Union, a society for prayer meetings of sailors and watermen, was organized in 1821, Prince was elected treasurer. The "aged sea captain" who offered the prayer at the first raising of the Bethel Flag on board a ship in America on 3 June 1821 was undoubtedly Prince, who noted the event in a journal that he kept. For several years, Prince's "Journal of the Bethel Flag," in which he described the Bethel meetings, was a regular feature in the *Christian Herald and Seaman's Magazine,* a religious periodical published in New York.[4]

On the death of Christopher Prince, the editor of the *Sailor's Magazine* observed that he was "wholly wrapped up in his desires for the good of seamen. . . . And he never lost his interest for them, never became a landsman in his feelings, but used to say he did not suppose he had a drop of landsman's blood in his veins."[5]

[4]*Christian Herald and Seaman's Magazine,* 1821–24; Roald Kverndal, *Seamen's Missions: Their Origin and Early Growth* (Pasadena, Calif.: William Carey Library, 1986), 416–17, 422, 430–31; Harold D. Langley, *Social Reform in the United States Navy, 1798–1862* (Urbana, Ill.: University of Illinois Press, 1967), 51–52; *Sailor's Magazine* 8 (1836): 12–13, 34–35.

[5]Joshua Levitt, "Death of Captain Prince," *Sailor's Magazine* 4 (1832): 253; reprinted in appendix 1.

APPENDIX ONE

Christopher Prince's Obituary

DEATH OF CAPTAIN PRINCE

The venerable captain Christopher Prince deceased at his residence in Cortland-street, March 15, 1832, in the 81st year of his age. He was born, in or near Boston, June 22, 1751, His parents were pious, and gave him a religious education; but he went to sea at the age of thirteen, and soon yielded to the temptations incident to that kind of life, as he himself often testified with tears. He served as a midshipman in the British navy before the revolution, and as lieutenant in an American privateer during the war. In 1797 he left the sea, and resided in this city, where he was an exemplary member of Dr. Spring's church. He was secretary of the Marine Society more than twenty-five years, and United States' Hospital Agent eighteen years. In this latter capacity he passed to the hospital more than fourteen thousand seamen. He was never absent from his post at the hospital during this whole time, till he resigned on the 31st of December last.

From the *Sailor's Magazine, and Naval Journal,* published by the American Seamen's Friend Society, Rev. Joshua Leavitt, ed. (New York, 1832) 4 (August): 253. Printed with a black border.

In 1816 he lost his wife. In 1817 he was active in forming the Marine Bible Society, of which in fact he was a principal mover, and was a vice-president, and one of the distributing committee till he died. He was also "the main spoke in the wheel" of the Bethel Union. He was wholly wrapped up in his desires for the good of seamen. After his own conversion, he never went a voyage without having some on board awakened to the subject of religion. And he never lost his interest for them, never became a landsman in his feelings, but used to say he did not suppose he had a drop of landsman's blood in his veins. When through the decays of age his memory was all gone, he never forgot to call at the office for the Magazine. And after he was confined to his bed, as he was for twelve days before he died, he spent almost his whole time in prayer for "that dear class of people," as he called them. He died without a struggle, and enjoyed an unclouded evidence of the favor and acceptance of God, through Jesus Christ our Lord.

L.

To the Editor of the Sailor's Magazine.

Sir—The following lines are sent to you for insertion in the Sailor's Magazine, if of sufficient merit. They were composed by one who was intimate with captain Prince, during the latter part of his life.

E.S.G.

To The

MEMORY OF CAPTAIN CHRISTOPHER PRINCE,
Who died March 15, 1832, in the 81st year of his age.

Thou hoary headed mariner, old ocean's veteran son!
Thy anchor's cast, thy voyage is o'er, thy christian
    course is run;
Thy bark is moored where no rude storms shall ever
    more molest,
She's safely moored within the port of everlasting
    rest.

Thy voyage has been a lengthened one, for fourscore
years and more

Thou 'st been upon the cruising ground, where
stormy billows roar;

Though many a gale did threaten oft thy bark to
overwhelm,

Thou wast unmoved, for thou didst know the Pilot
at the helm.

Thy voice hath many a shipmate cheered when sore
depressed with fear,

And many a gallant tar will long thy memory revere;

For thou hast been a chart to them o'er this world's
stormy sea,

To guide them from this sinful shore to immortality.

Thy needle always pointed true, and guided by that
star

Which rose in Bethlehem to light the nations from
afar;

Through stormy seas and adverse gales thou didst
thy vessel steer,

For thou hadst heard thy Master say, "Be ever of
good cheer."

The glorious gospel was thy chart, the word of God
thy guide,

And in its gracious promises thy soul thou didst
confide,

Thou knew'st that when the cruise was up, thy
gracious Lord would say,

Welcome, my son, enter the joys of an eternal day.

And while the Bethel flag shall wave, thy name shall
honor'd be,

Thou wast a friend and brother too to all who
plough the sea;

It was thy daily wish and prayer that they might
  love and fear
That Master, by whose command thou thy course so
  long didst steer!

Farewell, thou veteran mariner! Old ocean's son
  adieu!
Thou now hast reached the heavenly port thou long
  hast had in view;
The storms of earth no more shall rage within thy
  peaceful breast,
For thou art safely anchor'd in the haven of the blest.

E.S.G.

APPENDIX TWO

Ethan Allen's Narrative of His Captivity

Gen. Prescott then ordered one of his officers to take me on board the *Gaspee* schooner of war, and confine me, hands and feet, in irons, which was done the same afternoon I was taken. I come now to the description of the irons, which were put on me: The hand-cuff was of a common size and form, but my leg irons (I should imagine) would weigh thirty pounds; the bar was eight feet long, and very substantial; the shackles which encompassed my ancles, were very tight. I was told by the officer who put them on, that it was the king's plate, and I heard other of their officers say, that it would weigh forty weight. The irons were so close upon my ancles, that I could not lie down in any other manner than on my back. I was put into the lowest and most wretched part of the vessel, where I got the favour of a chest to set on; the same answered for my bed at night, and having procured some little blocks of the guard (who day and night,

From Ethan Allen, *A Narrative of Colonel Ethan Allen's Captivity, from the Time of His Being Taken by the British, near Montreal, on the 25th Day of September, in the Year 1775, to the Time of his Exchange, on the 6th Day of May, 1778*, 1st ed. (Philadelphia: Bell, 1779), 10–11.

with fixed bayonets, watched over me) to lay under each end of the large bar of my leg irons, to preserve my ancles from galling, while I set on the chest, or lay back on the same, though much of the time, night and day, I set on it; but at length having a desire to lie down on my side, which the closeness of the irons forbid, desired the captain to loosen them for that purpose, but was denied the favour: The captain's name was Royal, who did not seem to be an ill natured man; but oftentimes said, that his express orders were to treat me with such severity, which was desagreeable to his own feelings; nor did he ever insult me, though many others, who came on board, did. One of the officers, by the name of Bradley, was very generous to me; he would often send me victuals from his own table; nor did a day fail, but that he sent me a good drink of grog. . . . I was confined in the manner I have related, on board the *Gaspee* schooner, about six weeks. . . . I was after sent with the prisoners taken with me to an armed vessel in the river, which lay against Quebec, under the command of Capt. M'Cloud of the British.

APPENDIX THREE

Combat before Montreal, 30 October 1775

Finally, on Monday October 30, General Guy Carleton announced that he wanted to make a landing at Longueuil. At that moment he found himself with about 800 Canadian men, 130 soldiers, and 80 savages who embarked in some 40 boats, barges, and long boats. This little army assembled in the court of the barracks at Montreal, where powder and ball were distributed. The general assembled several officers in a room and gave them the order of march to which they were to adhere. Then this little army departed. The boats crossed at Longueuil. They arrived near the land three-quarters of a league above the fort, where they found only a guard of ten men, which was on the point of retreating, but as the boats nearest the land were signaled to retire into deep water, the guard of Bostonians

From M. Sanguinet, "Temoin Oculaire de L'Invasion du Canada par les Bastonnois," in *Invasion du Canada: Collection de Memoires, Recueilles et Annotes,* ed. M. L'Abbé Verreau (Montreal: Eusèbe Senécal, 1873), 65–66. Translated by Michael J. Crawford.

fired on them. Then the boats promenaded before Longueuil—as during the preceding days—outside musket range. During that time, the Bostonians who were in the fort of Longueuil came to reinforce the guard to the number of 140 men—thirty remained in the fort. Finally, tired of the promenade, the General went down to Saint Helen Island and some Canadians with the savages landed on some rocks[1] and began to fire their muskets at the Bostonians, who responded—all the rest were spectators. M. Montigny, the elder, who led one of the boats on which there was a cannon, asked the General what he should do; he answered him that he should go have supper in the city. At 5 o'clock in the evening the Bostonians brought up a cannon, which they had received that morning from Fort Chambly, and commenced to fire on our small army. Then the general returned to the city with all his people. The savages and those Canadians who were with them on the rocks distinguished themselves in this small battle. There were three savages killed and two taken prisoner. Mr. Jean-Baptiste Lemoine and one named Lacoste, a barber, were also made prisoners.

[1]The phrase in the original is "mirent pied à terre sur des battures." *Batture* means *breakers* or *shelf of rocks*. See Robert Burn, *A Naval and Military Technical Dictionary of the French Language,* 2d ed. (London: John Murray, 1952).

APPENDIX FOUR

Christopher Prince as Privateersman

Occasionally in his narrative, Christopher Prince muddled chronology, dates, and names. This was particularly so in his recounting of his privateering cruises. Although Prince usually remembered the names of the privateering vessels in which he sailed, and their commanders, he often mistook the names of those privateering vessels and commanders that sailed in company. His memory transposed the order of the cruises, and even the years in which they occurred. The following chart reconstructs as best as available data allows the facts of Prince's privateering career from 1777 through 1783. Material in parentheses represents informed guesses.

1777

Summer/autumn, Prince's first cruise in *American Revenue*

17 September, Prince purchased Continental Loan Office certificates worth $1,700

2 October, George Colfax wed

1778

11 January, Prince wed Lucy Colfax

Spring, Prince's second cruise in *American Revenue,* Capt. Champlin; captured *Lovely Lass* 31 March

(Late spring, Prince sailed in Rhode Island privateer *General Stark,* Capt. Benjamin Pearce)

1779

(January, Prince sailed as master of sloop of 60 tons belonging to Guy Richards, which was captured and burned off the Virginia Capes; Prince was released by captors and, after numerous adventures, returned to New London on 25 February)

Spring, Peter Richards returned to New London from captivity in England

19 April, Peter Richards wed

July, Prince sailed in *Hancock,* Capt. Lodowick Champlin, in company with *American Revenue,* Samuel Champlin; *American Revenue* captured by HMS *Greyhound; Hancock* escaped

September, Prince sailed in *Hancock,* Capt. Lodowick Champlin, which, with *Venus,* fifteen-gun brigantine from Salem, Capt. Richard Whellen or Weldon, and *Eagle,* Capt. Fosdick, engaged a twenty-gun letter of marque

Late, Prince sailed in *Hancock,* Capt. Chester, which, with *Deane,* Capt. Richards, and *Sally,* Capt. Thomson, arrived at Martinique

1780

(February, Prince in *Hancock* returned to New London)

May, Prince sailed in *Hancock,* which, with *Experiment, Young Beaver,* and *Holker,* chased *Arteriel,* a twenty-gun packet, on shore near Sandy Hook on May 23; and also in May, with *Hancock, Bunker Hill,* and *Holker,* captured *Commerce,* a sixteen-gun ship, from Barbados to New York, and took her into Philadelphia

(Summer and autumn, Prince made several cruises in *Hancock*, Capt. Peter Richards)

(Late, Prince invested in letter of marque brigantine *Delight*), which on November 20 made its first voyage

1781

7 February, *Marquis de Lafayette*, Capt. Richards, commissioned

(April, Prince sailed in *Marquis de Lafayette*, Capt. Richards)

(May, Elisha Hinman tried out *Marquis de Lafayette*)

13 June, *Marquis de Lafayette*, Capt. Elisha Hinman, recommissioned

18 August, Elisha Hinman, Capt., Christopher Prince, first lieutenant, and John Rider, second lieutenant, listed on the *Marquis de Lafayette*'s crew list

September, Prince arrived with Hinman in *Marquis de Lafayette* at New London just after the British burned the town

(Late, Prince sailed in *Jay*, Capt. William Havens)

1782

Spring, Prince commanded William Constant's brig *Neptune*, in trading voyage from New London to Guadeloupe and Bordeaux, which on May 21 was captured by Jersey privateer lugger *Argus*

Spring and summer, Prince imprisoned in England and released

October, Prince captured in a schooner near Great Egg Harbor; brigantine *Delight*, in which Prince had invested, captured

1783

Prince sailed from New London to Grenada and back in schooner *Seaflower*, returning on 22 February

GLOSSARY

adventure A speculation in goods sent abroad to be sold or bartered for profit. Merchant seamen were customarily allowed to carry on board small amounts of goods on their own accounts.

batteau or bateau A flat-bottomed, sharp-ended, clumsy boat, used on lakes and rivers.

beam-ends A ship is said to be "on her beam-ends" when she has heeled over so much that her beams (the heavy transverse timbers, at right angles to the keel, that support the deck) approach a vertical position.

bear away To turn the helm and run off to leeward.

beds Flat thick pieces of wood, lodged under the quarters of casks containing any liquid, and stowed in a ship's hold, in order to keep the casks bilge-free.

bend sails To make the sails fast to their proper yards, gaffs, or stays, and fit all the gear belonging to them.

binnacle A case or box to contain the compass.

boatswain A petty officer having charge of hull maintenance and related work.

brail up To pull on the ropes attached to the after edge of a trysail so as to spill the wind and haul up the sail for furling.

breasthook One of several horizontal crooked timbers fitted inside and across a vessel's stem for tying the foremost frames and generally uniting and stiffening the bow structure.

breeching A large rope attached to a gun or its carriage and secured to the ship's side, to limit the recoil.

bridle port The forward port on the gun deck.

brig A two-masted, square-rigged vessel.

brigantine A two-masted, square-rigged vessel, differing from a brig in that it does not carry a square mainsail.

by the wind As close to the wind as possible.

captain of the top A seaman placed in charge of the seamen stationed in the top.

chevaux-de-frise A submerged, navigational obstruction in which heavy timbers fastened with iron tips project at an angle beneath water level in order to pierce ships' hulls.

clew up To run the clews, or lower corners, of a sail up to the yard.

coin See quoin.

courses The sails that are bent to the lower yards.

crowfoot A number of small lines rove through a long block spliced to a rope attached to a stay; the ends of the lines are spread apart and attached through holes along the forward rim of the top, for preventing the topsails' getting foul of the stays.

crown To finish up a knot by laying the ends of the strands over and under each other so that they will bind and keep the knot from unlaying. To "double crown" a knot is to follow the parts of the single crown a second time with the ends of the strands.

embrasure An opening with sides flaring outward in a wall or parapet of a fortification, usually to allow the firing of cannon.

file or foil A slender, blunt sword used in fencing.

forecastle 1. The part of the upper deck of a ship forward of the foremast. 2. The forward part of a merchantman where the sailors live.

forefoot The forward end of the keel.

foretop The platform at the head of a foremast.

foretopsail The sail above the foresail.

frigate A square-rigged, three-masted warship, with more than one sail per mast, carrying between twenty and forty-four guns on more than one deck.

futtock shrouds Lengths of rope connecting the topmast rigging with the lower mast.

gasket Plaited stuff or a small line used to confine a sail to its yard when furled.

glass The length of time the sand in a time glass occupies in running out. During a shipboard watch, a half-hour glass was used to measure the passage of time; hence "three glasses" equals one and one-half hours.

grampus An animal of the cetacean or whale tribe, distinguished by the large pointed teeth with which both jaws are armed, and by the high curved dorsal fin. It generally attains a length of twenty to twenty-five feet and is very active and voracious.

grapeshot A cluster of small iron balls used as a cannon charge.

gun deck A deck below the spar deck on which the guns are carried.

gunwale The part of a ship where topsides and deck meet.

halliard or halyard A rope or purchase employed to hoist a yard or sail on its mast or stay.

hand sails To furl sails.

hanger A strap or loop on a sword belt by which a sword or dagger can be suspended; a small sword.

haul up by the wind To change a ship's course so that her course lies nearer to the wind.

hawser A large rope for towing, mooring, or securing a ship.

heave to To bring a vessel's head to the wind and adjust the sails so she will remain stationary, or nearly so.

hold The interior portion of a ship below the lower deck.

jibboom A spar that serves as an extension of the bowsprit.

keel The principal timber of a ship, extending along the center bottom from the stem to the sternpost.

larboard The left side of a vessel when facing toward the bow; port. *See also* tack.

lee-side The side of a ship that is farthest from the wind.

leeward In the direction toward which the wind blows.

letter of marque A commission or license issued by a government to a private armed vessel authorizing reprisals on an enemy; a vessel carrying such a commission.

live oak A species of timber used in shipbuilding, valued for its density and durability.

lubber hole The space between a top and the masthead that affords a passage into the top for greenhorns or persons who are unable to climb outside the rim of the top.

luff to the wind To bring a vessel's head nearer the wind.

martingale A lower stay from the jibboom or flying jibboom used to sustain the strain of the forestays.

mizzen Of or relating to the mast aft or next aft of the mainmast in a ship.

mouse a hook (as attached to a block) To take several turns of spunyarn round the back and point of a hook, and fasten it, to prevent its unhooking.

panch A thick mat used to reduce chafing.

pipe A large cask of varying capacity used especially for wine and oil.

oakum Bits of old cordage untwisted and picked to pieces, used principally in caulking seams.

osnaburg A rough coarse durable cotton fabric in plain weave.

packet A passenger vessel carrying mail and cargo on a regular schedule.

parceling or parslin Strips of burlap or canvas, two to three inches in width and treated with tar, laid round a rope bandage fashion as a protective covering.

pendant Pennant, any of various nautical flags tapering to a point or swallowtail and used for identification or signaling.

pinnace A small vessel propelled by sails and oars, usually schooner rigged, and employed as a tender to large vessels.

point One of the thirty-two equidistant spots of a compass card; the difference of 11 1/4 degrees between two such successive points.

point a rope To unlay, taper, and weave some of the outside yarns of the end of a rope, for neatness, to prevent wearing out, and for convenience in reeving through a block.

preventer A term applied to ropes, and so forth, when used as additional securities to aid other ropes in supporting spars, and so forth, during a strong gale.

puncheon A large cask of varying capacity; any of various units of liquid capacity.

purser A naval officer who has charge of the provisions, clothing, and so forth, on board a ship.

quarter boards Light bulwarks or raised extension of main bulwarks of a quarterdeck.

quarterdeck The upper deck abaft the mainmast.

quarter gunner A petty officer attached to each gun division to take care of the guns and gun gear, and at quarters, to supply the guns' crews and to be ready, during action, to furnish any reserved or spare article that may be required, such as breechings, ladles, worms, and so forth.

quartermaster A petty officer who assists the sailing master in the minor details of his various duties, attending the ship's helm, binnacle, and signals.

quarter rails Narrow-molded planks, generally of fir, reaching from the top of the stern to the gangway, and serving as a fence to the quarterdeck, to prevent the men from falling into the sea by the rolling of the vessel.

quoin A wedge-shaped wooden implement.

rammer A staff with a cylindrical head, used in loading to press home the charge of a gun.

ratline The small transverse ropes attached to the shrouds of a ship to form the steps of a rope ladder.

reef To reduce the area of a sail by rolling or folding a portion.

reeve To pass, as a rope, through any aperture; to fasten by passing through an aperture or around something.

round house A cabin or apartment on the stern of a quarterdeck.

rigging A general name for all ropes employed to support and work masts, yards, sails, and so forth. "Running rigging," the ropes that are hauled on in order to adjust the yards, sails, and so forth. "Standing rigging," rigging set up permanently, such as shrouds and stays.

sailing master, or master The officer in charge of navigating a vessel.

schooner A fore-and-aft rigged vessel having two masts with a smaller sail on the foremast and with the mainmast stepped nearly amidships.

sheet A rope fastened to the lower corner of a sail, to haul and keep it in place.

shifting plank Wooden bulkhead in a ship's hold, used to separate cargo.

ship A large vessel carrying eleven or twelve square sails on three masts, extended by yards, and also a number of fore-and-aft sails.

shroud One of the ropes leading, usually in pairs, from a sailing vessel's mastheads to give lateral support to the masts.

sloop A fore-and-aft rigged vessel with one mast and a single headsail jib. Also, a vessel of war next in size to a frigate.

splice To unite two ropes by interweaving the strands.

stanchion An upright support.

starboard The right side of a vessel when facing toward the bow. *See also* tack.

start To empty out liquids.

stauncheon See stanchion.

stay A strong rope, leading from the head of any mast, forward.

steer To direct or govern a ship by the motions of the rudder.

steerage That part of the ship below the quarterdeck and before the cabin bulkhead of a man-of-war. That portion of the berth-deck of a man-of-war just forward of the wardroom, and furnished with lockers, mess tables, and sometimes with berths.

steering sail See studding sail.

steward Assistant to the purser. He has charge of the storerooms, issues small stores, serves out rations, and assists in issuing clothing, and so forth.

stopper A short piece of rope, secured to a bolt, or to any point near a running rope, and used to check the motion of the latter by its friction when wound about it. Deck stoppers are short pieces of rope, having a large knot in one end, and a rope lanyard of smaller dimensions, and in the other end a large hook or shackle for hooking it into a bolt in the deck. The lanyard is wound about the cable and stopper, and the knot keeps it from slipping.

strap To attach a ring of rope or band of iron to a block.

streak Strake, one breadth of plank.

studding sail A sail set outside the square sails in good weather and when the wind is fair.

swivel A small gun fixed on a pivot.

tack The direction of a ship with respect to the trim of her sails. A vessel is on the "starboard tack" when the wind blows against the starboard side. A vessel is on the "larboard tack" when the wind blows against the larboard side. To change the direction of a vessel from one tack to another when close-hauled by bringing the head into the wind and causing it to fall off with the wind on the other bow, by using the helm and sails.

tackles Combinations of ropes and blocks used as a mechanical power for moving or hoisting heavy weights.

taffrail The rail about a vessel's stern.

tender A small vessel used for giving assistance to a large ship or a flagship, as carrying stores or dispatches, transferring men, and so forth.

thimble In sail making, an iron ring, the outer surface of which is concave so it can be held in position by a rope when spliced around it. It thus serves as a lining for the rope and protects it from the chafe of a hook or other thimble.

thrum To insert short pieces of rope yarn or spun yarn in a piece of canvas to make a rough surface or a mat that can be wrapped about rigging to prevent chafing.

tierce A cask of the capacity of forty-two wine gallons. A cask used in packing salt provisions, containing 336 pounds.

top A platform of semicircular form resting on the trestletrees of the lower mast of a square-rigged vessel. It gives spread to the topmast rigging, which is set up to the rim of the top. It also serves as a place for sharpshooters during an engagement.

topgallant The name applied to the mast, sail, yard, and the ropes belonging to each, which are next above the topmast and topsail.

topsail The sail next above the lowermost sail on a mast in a square-rigged ship. The sail set above and sometimes on the gaff in a fore-and-aft rigged ship.

truck A circular piece of wood placed on the head of a mast or flag-staff, in which the sheave for the signal halyards is placed.

veer To pay out a rope. To wear ship.

venture See adventure.

waistmen Landsmen and worn-out seamen stationed in the ship's waist.

watch A portion of time during which a part of a ship's company is on duty. The part of a ship's company required to be on duty during a particular watch.

water boards Large boards used to keep out the waves or spray of the sea.

wear To put a ship on the other tack by turning the bow away from the wind.

weather side The side toward the wind.

windlass A machine moved by levers or bars used for raising the anchor.

windward Toward the wind. The weather side.

worm A spiral of wire with a sharp point, attached to a staff, for withdrawing a cartridge from a gun.

DEFINITIONS ADAPTED FROM

Blanckley, Thomas Riley. *A Naval Expositor: Shewing and Explaining the Words and Terms of Art Belonging to the Parts, Qualities, and Proportions of Building, Rigging, Furnishing, & Fitting a Ship for Sea.* London: E. Owen, 1750.

Brady, William N. *The Kedge-Anchor; or, Young Sailor's Assistant.* 18th ed. New York: D. Appleton, 1876. Reprint ed. New York: Library Editions, 1970.

Falconer, William. *New Universal Dictionary of the Marine.* Modernized and enlarged by William Burney. London, 1815. Reprint ed. New York: Library Editions, 1970.

Hamersly, L. R. *A Naval Encyclopedia.* Philadelphia: L. R. Hamersly, 1881.

Lavery, Brian. *The Arming and Fitting of English Ships of War, 1600–1815.* Annapolis, Md.: Naval Institute Press, 1987.

Lees, James. *The Masting and Rigging of English Ships of War, 1625–1860.* 2d rev. ed. Annapolis, Md.: Naval Institute Press, 1984.

McEwen, W. A., and A. H. Lewis. *Encyclopedia of Nautical Knowledge.* Cambridge, Md.: Cornell Maritime Press, 1953.

Steel, David. *Steel's Elements of Mastmaking, Sailmaking and Rigging: (From the 1794 edition).* Arranged, with an introduction by Claude S. Gill. New York: E. W. Sweetman [19--].

Webster's Third New International Dictionary of the English Language, Unabridged. Springfield, Mass.: G. & C. Merriam, 1971.

INDEX

A long dash is used where a person's given name is unknown.

Shaw, Daniel, 107–9, 107*n*, 114

Shaw, Nathaniel, Jr., 130*n*; employs
Christopher Prince to transport
flour, 205; presides over victory cel-
ebration, 154; as privateer owner,
141–43, 149, 151; purchases Christopher Prince's Continental Loan
certificates, 156, 156*n*

Sheffield, Robert, 177, 183

Simsbury Mines, Conn., 63, 63*n*, 80

smallpox, 29, 70, 72, 78, 78*n*, 79, 87–88, 91,
144, 145–46, 148, 153

Smith, John, Lt., Connecticut Navy,
121, 121*n*

Smith, Justin H., 28

Snider, Christian, 26

Sorel River, 39, 40, 42, 81, 85

Sorel, Canada, 28, 29, 29*n*, 40, 46, 48, 55,
62

South America, 211

South Dumplings, 135*n*

Spring, Dr. Gardner, 222–23, 225

Spy, Connecticut Navy schooner, 112

Stamp Tax, xxii, 25

Stewart, Polly, 195, 195*n*

Stonington, Conn., 135

Stutson, ———, Capt., 15

Superstitions, 158, 160

Surprise, HM frigate, 29*n*

Talbot, Silas, xxviii–xxix

Tea Tax, xxii

Tenyck, ———, Capt., 78*n*

Thames River, Conn., 189*n*

Thayer, ———, Capt., 180–81

Thomas, John, Maj. Gen., Continental
Army, 76–77, 76*n*, 79, 79*n*, 81

Thomaston, Me., xxv

Thompson, John, 202, 202*n*

Thompson, Mrs. (N.Y. boardinghouse
keeper), 94, 96, 97

Thompson, Nathaniel, 143, 143*n*

Thompson, Sanford, 181*n*

Thomson, ———, Capt., 185*n*, 234

Thornbrough, Edward, 32, 32*n*, 201

Three Rivers. *See* Trois Rivieres

Ticonderoga, N.Y., Fort, 27, 27*n*, 38, 82,
91, 92

Townshend Duties, xxii

Trois Rivieres [Three Rivers], Canada,
62, 77, 77*n*, 79

Trumbull, Fort, Groton, Conn., 189

United States Marine Hospital, New
York, N.Y., 222, 225

Vassall, Elizabeth, 26–27, 36–37

Vassall, John, 26–27, 34–37

Venus, Massachusetts privateer brigantine, 182–83, 184*n*, 234

Vermont, 27

Virginia Capes, 234

Ware [Wyer], Josiah, 122, 123; befriends
Christopher Prince, 114; character,
130; defends Christopher Prince,
124; deserts Connecticut Navy, 133*n*;
joins *Oliver Cromwell*, 119–20, 120,
120*n*; journeys to New London, 117–
18; promoted to seaman, 124–25,
126; works alongside Christopher
Prince, 127

Washington, Fort, New York, N.Y., 88

Washington, George: and Battle of
Long Island, 90, 108; camp of, 173;
employs fleet of armed schooners,
113; orders Continental Army inoculated, 88; and sinking of navigational obstructions in Hudson
River, 89, 102

Weathersfield, Conn., 131, 151

Welding [Whellen, Weldon], Richard,
182–83, 184*n*, 234

ABOUT THE EDITOR

Michael J. Crawford was born and reared in the suburbs of St. Louis, Missouri, where he earned his bachelor's and master's of arts degrees in history at Washington University. He pursued doctoral studies at Boston University, which awarded him the Ph.D. in American history in 1978. After teaching for two years in the history department of Texas Tech University, he spent a year as a National Historical Publications and Records Commission fellow at the Massachusetts Historical Society, in Boston, where he worked as an editor with the Adams Papers project. He joined the staff of the Early History Branch of the Naval Historical Center in Washington, D.C., in 1982. He currently is head of the branch and editor of the two series *Naval Documents of the American Revolution* and *The Naval War of 1812: A Documentary History*. Dr. Crawford has published works on the early history of the American navies as well as on early American religion, including *Seasons of Grace: Colonial New England's Revival Tradition in Its British Context* (1991).